A Parents' and Teachers' Guide to Bilingualism

PEFC

PEFC/16-33-111
CATG-PEFC-052
www.pefc.org

PARENTS' and TEACHERS' GUIDES
Series Editor: Professor Colin Baker, *University of Wales, Bangor, Wales, Great Britain*

Second Language Students in Mainstream Classrooms
  Coreen Sears
Dyslexia: A Parents' and Teachers' Guide
  Trevor Payne and Elizabeth Turner
The Care and Education of a Deaf Child: A Book for Parents
  Pamela Knight and Ruth Swanwick
Guía para padres y maestros de niños bilingües
  Alma Flor Ada and Colin Baker
Making Sense in Sign: A Lifeline for a Deaf Child
  Jenny Froude
Language Strategies for Bilingual Families
  Suzanne Barron-Hauwaert
Bilingualism in International Schools: A Model for Enriching Language Education
  Maurice Carder

Other Books of Interest
Bilingual Children's Language and Literacy Development
  Roger Barnard and Ted Glynn (eds)
Bilingual Education: An Introductory Reader
  Ofelia García and Colin Baker (eds)
The Care and Education of Young Bilinguals: An Introduction to Professionals
  Colin Baker
Childhood Bilingualism: Research on Infancy through School Age
  Peggy McCardle and Erika Hoff (eds)
Developing in Two Languages: Korean Children in America
  Sarah J. Shin
Foundations of Bilingual Education and Bilingualism (4th edition)
  Colin Baker
Language Acquisition: The Age Factor (2nd edition)
  David Singleton and Lisa Ryan
Language and Identity in a Dual Immersion School
  Kim Potowski
Language and Literacy in Bilingual Children
  D. Kimbrough Oller and Rebecca E. Eilers (eds)
Raising Bilingual-Biliterate Children in Monolingual Cultures
  Stephen J. Caldas
Teacher Collaboration and Talk in Multilingual Classrooms
  Angela Creese
Three is a Crowd? Acquiring Portuguese in a Trilingual Environment
  Madalena Cruz-Ferreira
Understanding Deaf Culture: In Search of Deafhood
  Paddy Ladd
Words and Worlds: World Languages Review
  F. Martí, P. Ortega, I. Idiazabal, A. Barreña, P. Juaristi, C. Junyent, B. Uranga and E. Amorrortu

For more details of these or any other of our publications, please contact:
Multilingual Matters, Frankfurt Lodge, Clevedon Hall,
Victoria Road, Clevedon, BS21 7HH, England
http://www.multilingual-matters.com

PARENTS' AND TEACHERS' GUIDES 9
Series Editor: Colin Baker

A Parents' and Teachers' Guide to Bilingualism
Third edition

Colin Baker

MULTILINGUAL MATTERS LTD
Clevedon • Buffalo • Toronto

Library of Congress Cataloging in Publication Data
Baker, Colin
A Parents' and Teachers' Guide to Bilingualism/Colin Baker. 3rd edn.
Parents' and Teachers' Guides: 9
Includes bibliographical references and index.
1. Bilingualism. I. Title.
P115.B346 2007
306.44' 6083–dc22   2007006874

British Library Cataloguing in Publication Data
A catalogue entry for this book is available from the British Library.

ISBN-13: 978-1-84769-001-2 (hbk)
ISBN-13: 978-1-84769-000-5 (pbk)

Multilingual Matters Ltd
UK: Frankfurt Lodge, Clevedon Hall, Victoria Road, Clevedon BS21 7HH.
USA: UTP, 2250 Military Road, Tonawanda, NY 14150, USA.
Canada: UTP, 5201 Dufferin Street, North York, Ontario M3H 5T8, Canada.

The policy of Multilingual Matters/Channel View Publications is to use papers that are natural,
renewable and recyclable products, made from wood grown in sustainable forests. In the
manufacturing process of our books, and to further support our policy, preference is given to
printers that have FSC and PEFC Chain of Custody certification. The FSC and/or PEFC logos
will appear on those books where full certification has been granted to the printer concerned.

Typeset by Archetype-IT Ltd (http://www.archetype-it.com).
Printed and bound in Great Britain by MPG Books Ltd.

Contents

Section A: Family Questions

Section B: Language Development Questions

Section C: Questions About Problems

Section D: Reading and Writing Questions

Section E: Education Questions

Basic Education Questions

Acknowledgements

The idea for the first edition of this book was not mine. It came as a 'one liner' during a telephone conversation. 'Have you thought of writing a book to help parents?' No, I hadn't. I didn't really give the matter more thought.

One event changed all. An operation was required with a few weeks convalescence at home. I decided that recovery would be enhanced if something was accomplished. The parent book could be started. A highly skilled surgeon, Mike Jamison, ensured those weeks were totally trouble free.

The questions were provisionally agreed with the guardian angel of the project, Marjukka Grover. She grafted more questions onto the initial skeleton. After the draft was completed, Marjukka nursed the project through its successive stages. No author could have been more kindly treated or more sagaciously advised. Marjukka spent considerable time advising me on the draft, and made many comments that added to the width of the book. For the second and third editions, Marjukka spent much time giving very detailed feedback and exceptionally helpful advice. Her experience, expertise and enthusiasm were as crucial for completing each edition.

A thousand thanks to my favorite Finn.

Marjukka Groverin panos kaksikielisyyden innostuneena puolestapuhujana ja kaksikielisyyttä edistävien julkaisujen – jäsenkirjeiden, aikakauslehtien ja kirjojen – tuottajana on kansainvälisesti erittäin merkittävä. Kaksikielisten ihmisten ja monikielisten yhteisöjen erikoispirteet ovat saamassa osakseen tarvitsemaansa ymmärtämystä ja positiivista huomiota tutkijoiden, opettajien, erilaisten asiantuntijoiden, ja mikä tärkeintä, lasten vanhempien taholta, juuri hänen ponnistelujensa ansiosta.

Marjukan henkilökohtainen esimerkki kahden suomea ja englantia puhuvan pojan kasvattajana on ollut osoituksena syvästä ja voimakkaasta sitoutumisesta kaksikielisyyden periaatteisiin.

Marjukan kannanotto kaksikielisyyteen oli tärkeä tekijä Multilingual Matters kustan-tamon syntyvaiheessa, samoin MLM-julkaisujen puhjetessa kukkaan. Myös tämä kirja saa paljolti kiittää olemassaolostaan hänen innostustaan, kannatustaan ja tukeaan.

Tämä kirja on omistettu Sinulle ja Sinun elämäntehtävällesi, Marjukka!

My thanks go to all those who helped in different ways with the three editions: Professor Tony Cline, Anne Sanderson, Dr Charlotte Hoffmann, Dr Jean Lyon, Dr Geraint Wyn Jones, Dr Sylvia Prys Jones, Professor Ofelia García (New York), Professor Iolo Wyn Williams. *Diolch o galon.* To all who read the drafts and gave me help and support, I am most grateful. However, the responsibility for anything in this book that is not fair or just is totally mine.

This book would never have been written if I didn't live in a bilingual nuclear and extended family. In the home, my wife Anwen and three delight-ful offspring (Sara, Rhodri and Arwel) provide the experience, the stimulus for thinking, and a range of humorous incidents that form one basis for this book. All four are fully bilingual. They respond to my unending questions about their experience of bilingualism and bilingual education with honesty, openness and humor. They lovingly provide a homely, 'feet on the ground' dimension that balances the academic study of bilingualism. As time has advanced, each has understood better the reasons for mealtime interrogations about their personal bilingualism. Since 2005, the birth of Ioan Tomos allows me to take a different perspective on childhood bilingual development from the wonderful vantage point of a *Taid* (grandfather).

Ken Hall of Multilingual Matters has always been a pillar of strength and support – across many books. It is a great encouragement for an author to have someone of his expertise and experience to advise so readily. He has a rare combination of being highly methodical, totally dependable and utterly serene. Sami Grover gave me very detailed feedback on my draft version of this edition, and made many excellent suggestions. Following in the family tradition, he also proved to be a wise copy editor.

Finally, my thanks to Mike Grover for the telephone call, for the invitation to upgrade to a third edition, and especially for the very amenable and par-ticipatory style that has created a partnership born out of a shared vision of retaining mother and father tongues throughout the world by family language reproduction.

An Introduction
to the Third Edition

Since the first edition in 1995, new research and scholarly writings have moved the study of childhood bilingualism forward in many different ways. The third edition has been informed by such developments.

A critical and enhancing approach to the second edition developed from 2001 onwards. With further experiences at home, lecturing, writing and in contributing to the *Bilingual Family Newsletter**, ideas and perceptions were extended and enriched. Hence there has been elaboration and refinements in particular answers plus new material and extra questions and answers. The new material includes:

- Moving between countries, cultural adaptation
- Identity issues
- One parent–one language families
- Helping with homework
- Pre-schools and nurseries
- Multiliteracies
- Dyslexia
- Language scaffolding in classroom learning
- Dual Language Peace schools
- Multilingualism and trilingualism; trilingual families
- Adoption
- Identity issues
- WWW links, articles and books for further reading

Typical quotes from parents and children have also been added to the text. While these are not extensive, as family situations are often very individual and difficult to generalize from, where a telling point has been made, such quotes add another voice.

The hope is that the third edition will have retained the strengths of the previous editions, eradicated perceived weaknesses, and added new text to provide a comprehensive introduction to this increasingly important international topic.

Introduction

The different situations addressed in the book

The style of this book is to pose **frequently asked questions** that parents, teachers and others most often ask about raising bilingual children. These have been collected cumulatively across 30 years of interaction with parents, questions from the audience when giving talks to parents, training sessions with health visitors and midwives (the Twf Project in Wales), many queries and suggestions across email and topics raised in the *Bilingual Family Newsletter*.

Straightforward **answers** follow, written in direct, plain language. The book deals with family questions, educational questions, language issues and partic-ularly focuses on problems that arise. Such questions reflect **central issues** that people regularly meet in deciding about bilingualism in the home. Important questions about advantages and disadvantages, schemes and strategies of language development are posed. The answers to the questions will raise awareness of what **challenges** may be faced as bilingual family life develops and what decisions may have to be made.

The book is for parents and teachers who are bilinguals themselves, for monolingual parents and teachers, and for other professionals such as doctors, speech therapists, practicing psychologists, counselors and teachers who want to know more.

The language of bilingualism

This book is about **bilingual and multilingual children, bilingual parents and bilingual education**. Unfortunately, much fog surrounds these words. There is no agreed, common definition or understanding of these terms. Bilingualism is a simple term that hides a complex phenomenon. Does the term 'bilingual' cover those who are able to speak a language but don't? Those who understand what others say in one of their languages but rarely or never use that language? Does the term 'bilingual' cover those who are proficient in one language but are only just beginning to learn a second language (see Glossary)? Does the term 'bilingual' cover those who can speak a language without literacy, or only those who speak, read and write in both languages?

Such questions highlight that there are different dimensions of language. We can examine people's proficiency in two or more languages in their **listening (understanding), speaking, reading and writing** skills. In between those who are fluent in two languages and those who are learning a second language there are many variations. Where second language learning stops and bilingualism begins is pointlessly debated. Any cut-off point will be arbitrary and contentious. There are some people who do become approximately equally fluent in both their languages (sometimes called balanced bilinguals – see Glossary). These tend to be the few rather than the many. Most people are more competent in one language than another. Bilinguals sometimes find it easier to use one of their languages in one set of circumstances, another language in a different set of circumstances. Languages often have different uses in different places, with different people.

Calling someone a **bilingual** or a **multilingual** (see Glossary) is therefore an **umbrella term**. Underneath the umbrella rest many different skill levels in two languages. Being bilingual is not just about **proficiency** in two languages. It is also about **use** of language. Someone may be quite competent in two languages, yet rarely or never use one of those languages. Such a person has bilingual ability but does not act or behave bilingually. A different case is a person who regularly uses both their languages, even though one language is still developing. Such a person may be hesitant in speaking, finding it difficult to speak with correct grammar (see Glossary) or unable to use a wide vocabulary. In practice, that person may be bilingual, although ability in one language is lacking (but improving). Such a distinction between ability in a language and use of a language again shows why the simple label 'bilingual' hides a complex variety beneath its simplicity. Since this book is also about multilingual children, the complexity increases.

Types of family bilingualism

Bilingual families and parents raising bilingual children are constantly referred to in this book. However, the language abilities of mother and father, the use of language in the extended family, and the nature of the local language community or region create a **wide variety of bilingual families**.

Bilingual and multilingual families include many **different combinations** of answers to the following questions:

(1)   What language(s) does the mother speak to the child?
(2)   What language(s) does the father speak to the child?

(3)   What language(s) do brothers/sisters speak to each other?

(4)   What language(s) do the extended family (grandparents, aunts, uncles, etc.) speak to the child?

(5)   What is the impact of society and the dominant culture on the family? What pressures are there on identity? For example, are the language(s) of the home:
      (a) majority languages
      (b) a majority and a minority language
      (c) minority languages/dialect
      (d) one minority language?

(6)   Is a different language to the home being acquired outside the home (e.g. in the street, in school)?

(7)   Are the language(s) of the home spoken and supported in the local community/social networks (see Glossary) of friends/region? and/or . . .

(8)   What are the attitudes of the family to the languages they use and those others languages with which they are in contact?

(9)   Are the language(s) of the home spoken in a different region/abroad?

(10) Is the family geographically stable or mobile with changing language needs?

A variety of **language strategies** are used by parents to produce bilingual and multilingual children. The **main strategies** are as follows (with many other alternatives possible, e.g. changing patterns over time, variations due to siblings, carers, the extended family, societal influences, use of three or more languages):

Strategy 1:   Each parent speaks a different language to the child. This is often called the **'one person–one language'** (OPOL) approach. While the parents each speak their own language to the child from birth, they will tend to speak just one language to each other. However, it is not only the family that influences language acquisition. Community influences are also important (e.g. pre-school, extended family, mass media). One variation can produce multilingualism. If each parent speaks a different language to the child from birth, the child may gain a third language outside the home. This often results in trilingualism. (Example: mother speaks German; father speaks Spanish; the community language is English.)

Strategy 2:   The parents speak one language to the child who acquires a second language (see Glossary) outside the home. This often occurs in language minority (see Glossary) situations. Also, one parent may be using their second language.

Strategy 3:   Both parents speak both languages to the child. Language mixing is acceptable in the home and the neighborhood. The child will typically code-switch (language switch) with other bilinguals but not with monolinguals. (Example: mother and father speak Maltese and English; the community language is Maltese and English.)

Strategy 4: The parents may delay the introduction of the second language. Where the neighborhood, community and school language is a much higher status and dominant language, parents may delay exposure to that dominant language. For example, parents may exclusively speak their minority language in the home until the child is two or three years of age, then add a majority language such as English. The tactic is to ensure a strong foundation in a heritage language (see Glossary) before the dominant language outside the home becomes pervasive.

Strategies 1 and 2 tend to be associated particularly with 'elite' and middle-class families. Types 3 and 4 are sometimes found among relatively economically disadvantaged heritage language groups, immigrants and working-class families.

It is also important to remember that there are **agencies** other than the family that can play a major role in early childhood bilingualism. Before the age of three, the language experience with neighbors, networks of friends, crèche, mass media and the nursery school may be a particularly important part of becoming bilingual.

This book attempts to cover a wide variety of **bilingual family** situations (including other situations not listed above). Specific multilingual issues are addressed. Some answers to questions cover all types of situation. There is a generalization irrespective of the type of bilingual family. There are other questions specifically posed for specific circumstances. For example, **minority language parents** may live in a region where the minority language has a long and valued past. Such indigenous minority languages often coexist with a majority language such as English, French, German, Spanish, Arabic or Italian. The attitudes and motivations with regard to language and culture of such families will differ widely. This book covers the issues raised by parents in different contexts.

The book is also written for parents in **mixed language marriages** (and inter-cultural marriages). Mixed language marriages are on an increase as international borders open, transnational employment increases and communications between countries become easier. For example, if the mother speaks French, German or Swedish as her first language and is married to a monolingual English-speaking father, there are many answers in this book for such a mixed language situation. If both parents have a **different language from the majority language of the host country**, this book also applies. Advice covers those families with **two internationally prestigious languages** such as French and English, and when there is a **combination of a majority and a minority language**.

Other families travel to neighboring or distant countries for employment, advancement or because of the **international nature of their employment** (e.g. those working for the European Union, the Council of Europe, the United Nations and transnational companies). Such mobile, 'international' families are on the increase. There is guidance in this book for such situations.

Another situation covered in this book is that faced by **refugees, guest workers, migrants and recent or established immigrants** into a country. (The term **in-migrants** is used as a more neutral term to encompass immigrants, migrants, guest workers and refugees – see Glossary.) For example, there are various language minority groups residing in Germany, the different Asian, Turkish and Greek language groups in England, and many in-migrants in the Scandinavian countries. In such cases, the home language (heritage language) is a minority language and the 'new' or 'host' country operates in a majority language. One example is the minority language speakers in Canada, England and the United States who are surrounded by mass media and education in the dominant English language. This book also provides advice for such situations.

Different bilingual situations

These different bilingual situations lead to an important distinction. There is a dimension ranging from **additive bilingualism** (see Glossary) to **subtractive bilingualism** (see Glossary). When children use a majority language and have the possibility of becoming bilingual in another majority or a minority language, this is usually regarded as an **additive** bilingual situation. The first language (see Glossary), a prestigious majority language, is not under threat. It won't be replaced by the second language, be it a majority or a minority second language. Through the home and/or the school, a child adds a new language and culture without loss.

A different situation is where a **minority language child** is expected to learn a second majority language in the home or, more often, at school. The idea is that the second (majority) language should become dominant, even replace the minority language. This is termed **subtractive bilingualism**. For example, Asian families in England sometimes find that the school depreciates the home language and strongly promotes the dominant language of school and society – English. In the United States, children who acquire Spanish at home as their first language attend schools that often insist on the English language becoming dominant in their lives.

Politicians, administrators, educationists often seek to replace the minority language with the majority language. Their arguments for majority language supremacy range around: finding employment, equality of opportunity, the importance of a common denominator language such as English in integrating society, the melting pot idea (see Glossary) that in-migrants should become part of the majority by losing their minority language and culture and becoming, for example, English-speaking. The drive is to assimilate language minorities into mainstream life. Differences are to be replaced by similarities. Language variety is to be replaced by language uniformity. This can result in **subtractive** bilingual situations. The aim is to replace the home language by the majority language. The learning of a second language may be at the expense of the first language, unless parents take care. The term 'bilingual children' is sometimes a euphemism for children whose home language is being replaced by the majority language of the region.

This book deals with both types of situation – the **additive** bilingual situation and the **subtractive**. It provides advice for both majority language and minority language parents, whether they are in their home country or have traveled to a host country. The book addresses parents living in a community that supports their home language or depreciates it. There is information for those in a region that has a large or small number (or no speakers) of the languages of the home.

The content of the book

The intention of this book is to provide a **readable introduction** that is of practical value to parents. No attempt is made to provide an introduction to the terminology academics use to discuss bilingualism. Technical jargon and academic theories have been translated into everyday language wherever possible. Readers wishing to progress to books with a more academic bias are invited to study the list given at the end of this book.

Since **education** affects the bilingual development of the child, a separate section discusses the role of the school in fostering and sometimes hindering bilingual development. Different and varied circumstances are covered by such questions. The book covers a variety of school and classroom contexts: where the language of schooling is different from the language of the home, where parents have a choice of maintaining their minority language in the school, where the only available schools are majority language schools that foster monolingualism, where parents frequently move from country to country as part of their employment, and where children move from one school to another.

No technical discussion is given about the variety of bilingual education that exists worldwide. The author's book *Foundations of Bilingual Education and Bilingualism* (2006) provides such an introduction, as does the colorful *Encyclopedia of Bilingualism and Bilingual Education* (1998), both published by Multilingual Matters.

At the end of this book, a **glossary** is given. This provides a quick and easy understanding of key terms used. For example, the term in-migrant is used instead of immigrant. The reason will be clear from the glossary ('in-migrant' is more inclusive and has less negative connotations in English). The glossary also includes technical terms, deliberately not used in this book but which are common in academic writings on bilingualism. For example, United States parents will encounter specific US terms used to describe bilingual children and bilingual education. Where these are not explained in a particular question, their meaning is given in the glossary.

Some **readers** will read through the book question by question. For those, the book has been arranged in a logical and developmental order. Foundations laid early on will increase understanding of later issues. However, many readers will dip into it. Some questions will be read, others returned to at a later date, yet others regarded as not important. The book has been designed with such readers in mind. Each question and answer can be read in isolation. Each answer attempts to give sufficient important information to help the inquirer and this means that there is a little duplication of content to achieve self-sufficiency in each case.

Answers will lead to other questions, other answers. Hence, there is some cross-referencing in the book. Also, an **index** at the back of the book will help readers to find other related topics to build on answers. The use of emboldening certain words is used to enable readers to quickly scan the text for important and relevant topics. Such highlighting will make it quicker to find the information needed.

Wherever possible, answers to the questions are based on up-to-date international **research**. In the last two decades there has been an ever-increasing supply of research on bilingualism and bilingual education. The results of this research inform this book and can be followed up by reading various references given at the end of the final section. An overview of recent research and scholarly writings is found in my *Foundations of Bilingual Education and Bilingualism* (2006) published by Multilingual Matters. At the end of this book, information is given about **extended reading**, about the *Bilingual Family Newsletter*, and about establishing a **network** with like-minded parents who wish to raise their children bilingually.

The author

Some readers will want to know about the background and qualifications of the **author** in writing this book. The perceived validity of the answers needs judging against the degree of experience and expertise that an author brings to the task. **First**, the author specializes academically in bilingualism and bilingual education. He has published 14 **books** alongside over 100 other publications on the subject. The books include: *Aspects of Bilingualism in Wales* (1985), *Key Issues in Bilingualism and Bilingual Education* (1988), *Attitudes and Language* (1992) and *Foundations of Bilingual Education and Bilingualism* (1996). With Professor Ofelia García of the City College of New York, he has edited two books of readings: *Policy and Practice in Bilingual Education: A Reader Extending the Foundations* (1995) and *Bilingual Education: An Introductory Reader* (2007). With Dr Sylvia Prys Jones, the author wrote an *Encyclopedia of Bilingualism and Bilingual Education* (1998). Therefore, this book is informed by a knowledge of international research, and three decades of academic writing and research on bilingualism and bilingual education. The book also contains insights gained through lecturing in this area for over two decades to undergraduate and postgraduate students, teachers and parents. The author was elected a Fellow of the British Psychological Society in 1994 for his work on bilingualism.

Second, the author and his wife, Anwen, have successfully raised **three bilingual children**. During many years of varied experience, discussions between parents (and with our children) have constantly occurred. Problems have been met, as no journey to bilingualism is trouble free. Our three children, Sara, Rhodri and Arwel are fully and functionally bilingual in English and Welsh. Anwen (the mother) has always spoken Welsh to the children, while I have usually spoken English. The children normally speak Welsh to each other. Each has experienced bilingual education from kindergarten (age three or four) into secondary education. However, their routes to bilingualism have been varied, different and not trouble free.

Third, the author works in a School of Education in a **University that specializes in bilingualism and bilingual education**. Hence, there is a constant dialogue with colleagues about bilingualism, plus engagement in research on bilinguals and in bilingual schools.

There is a **fourth** experience that influenced the writing of this book. When giving formal talks and in informal conversations, the author has frequently discussed bilingual family issues with **other parents**. In the indigenous minority language situation in Wales, among Asian, Turkish and Greek language minority parents in England, with several Spanish–English families in the United States, and with parents raising their children in two and sometimes three European languages, experiences have been shared and ideas swapped. This book has been informed by observing, listening and talking to parents in different bilingual situations.

The style of the book

Readers need to be aware that the **style and approach** are deliberately different from an academic textbook. To make the book more reader-friendly and less off-putting, the chosen style is not academic. Continuous referencing to research and other forms of evidence is given in another of my books. For those readers (and reviewers) who seek the evidence-base of this book, my *Foundations of Bilingual Education and Bilingualism* (2006) published by Multilingual Matters provides a comprehensive study of bilingualism and bilingual education. Where a particular published article provides more detailed information than the *Foundations* book, this is usually listed at the end of the appropriate question in this book.

When writing the textbook *Foundations of Bilingual Education and Bilingualism* (fourth edition, 2006), every effort was made to represent a variety of viewpoints so that readers could make up their own minds on difficult issues. Often options are presented in such an academic book without a firm conclusion about 'best bets' or 'successful recipes'.

This book has a different approach. While alternatives are often given, an attempt has been made, using whatever expertise and experience exists, to give advice. Parents and teachers often don't want prevarication. They usually seek informed help and direction. Such advice in this book will reveal personal values and experiences, alongside information from international research and academic writing.

Not everyone will agree with the **advice**, nor should they. Specific circumstances, particular attitudes, cultural lifestyles, varying convictions and motivations will lead parents to disagree with some viewpoints. No advice can cover all circumstances. Real situations are very complex, such that no single recipe will be possible.

In writing this book, I have been aware that there will be disagreements, sometimes differing advice and residual uncertainty. No book for parents can provide perfect recipes, give totally authoritative and successful advice for all circumstances, or hope to convince every reader.

I do not wish readers to follow the advice slavishly as if the book presents the commandments of bilingualism. My hope is that the book stimulates thinking, opens up new ideas, helps parents discuss issues, and work out what is, for them in their specific circumstances, the optimal strategy. Such a book aims to inform and 'enable' the journey through childhood bilingualism, stimulate deeper thought and reflection, provide a variety of ideas, and to encourage.

Bon voyage.

Family Questions

What are the advantages of my child becoming bilingual?

A1

Bringing up children to be bilingual is an important decision. It will **affect the rest of their lives and the lives of their parents**. For children, being bilingual or monolingual may affect their identity, social arrangements, schooling, employment, marriage, area of residence, travel and thinking. Becoming bilingual is more than owning two languages. Bilingualism has educational, social, economic and cultural consequences.

There are many advantages and very few disadvantages in becoming bilingual. These are summarized in a table below. Some of these advantages are discussed in this answer. Other advantages that require detailed explanation are considered in separate questions in this section. Potential disadvantages are discussed in Section C.

Where parents have differing first languages (see Glossary), the advantage of children becoming bilingual is that they will be able to **communicate** in each parent's preferred language. Other bilingual children communicate with their parents in one language and with their friends (and in the community) in a different language.

For many mothers and fathers, it is important for them to be able to speak to the child in their first language. This may enable a subtle, finer texture of relationship with the parent. Many parents can only communicate with full intimacy, naturally and expressively in their first (or preferred or dominant) language. A child who speaks to one parent in one language and the other parent in another language may be enabling a maximally **close relationship** with the parents. At the same time, both parents are passing to that child part of their past, part of their heritage.

A bilingual child can **bridge between generations**. When grandparents, uncles and aunts and other relatives in another region speak one language that

1

The Advantages of Being Bilingual

Some of the potential advantages of bilingualism in a child are:

Communication Advantages

1. Wider communication (extended family, community, international links, employment).
2. Literacy in two languages.

Cultural Advantages

3. Broader enculturation, a deeper multiculturalism, and two 'language worlds' of experience.
4. Greater tolerance and appreciation of diversity.

Cognitive Advantages

5. Thinking benefits (e.g. creativity, sensitivity to communication).

Character Advantages

6. Raised self-esteem.
7. Security in identity.

Curriculum Advantages

8. Increased curriculum achievement.
9. Easier to learn a third language.

Cash Advantages

10. Economic and employment benefits.

is different from the child's language, the monolingual child may be unable to communicate with such relations. The bilingual child has the chance of bridging that generation gap, building relationships in the extended family, and feel a sense of belonging and rootedness.

A bilingual has the chance of **communicating** with a wider variety of people than a monolingual. When traveling in a country, in neighboring countries and in international travel, bilingual children have the distinct advantage that their languages provide bridges to new relationships. While a monolingual is able to communicate to a variety of people in one language, that monolingualism sometimes becomes a barrier to building relationships with people of other

Adapted, with permission, from *Negotiating Identities: Education for Empowerment in a Diverse Society*, by Jim Cummins (CABE, 1996)

nationalities and ethnic groups. Being a bilingual enables a person to bridge between cultures.

Another communication advantage of bilinguals is when they are literate in two languages (biliterate). They can then access two literatures, opening up different traditions, ideas, ways of thinking, feeling and acting. When there is **biliteracy**, reading novels and magazines, the writing and reading activities of home and education, the pleasures of writing to friends and the requirements of literacy in employment are all 'doubled' for bilinguals. A celebrated New York expert of bilingualism, Professor Ana Zentella, has a lovely Spanish phrase: *'la persona que habla dos idiomas vale por dos'* [someone who speaks two languages is worth two people].

One of the advantages of a bilingual child and adult is having **two or more worlds of experience**. With each language goes different systems of behavior, wise folk sayings, valued stories, histories, traditions, ways of meeting and greeting, rituals of birth, marriage and death, ways of conversing (compare Italians, Arabs and English people when they are speaking), different literatures, music, forms of entertainment, religious traditions, ways of understanding and interpreting the world, ideas and beliefs, ways of thinking and drinking, crying and loving, eating and caring, ways of joking and mourning. With two languages goes a wider cultural experience, and, very possibly, greater tolerance of cultural difference and less racism (see Glossary).

The monolingual also experiences a variety of **cultures** – from different neighbors and communities, who use the same language but have different ways of life. The monolingual can also travel to neighboring countries and experience other cultures. To participate and become involved in the core of a culture requires knowing the language of that culture. The bilingual has an improved chance of actively penetrating the two language cultures.

Within any language, there is a kaleidoscope of cultures. Monolinguals may be able to experience the periphery of the kaleidoscope of a different culture. To experience fully the inner colors and excitement of the kaleidoscope of culture of a language requires a knowledge of that language.

One major difference between animals and humans is language. Through language, a child is cared for, cherished, cultivated and cultured. One barrier between nations and ethnic groups tends to be language, and it is sometimes a barrier to communication and to creating friendly relationships. Bilinguals in the home, in the community and in society can lower such barriers; they can be **bridges** within the nuclear and extended family, within the community and across societies. Those who speak one language symbolize that essential difference between animals and people. Those who speak two languages symbolize the essential humanity of building bridges between peoples of different color, creed, culture and language.

Apart from social, cultural, economic, personal relationship and communication advantages, research has shown that bilinguals have the chance of particular advantages in **thinking**. Bilingual children have two or more words for each object and idea (e.g. 'kitchen' in English and '*cuisine*' in French). This means that the link between a word and its concept is usually looser. Sometimes corresponding words in different languages have different connotations. For example, 'kitchen' in English has traditionally been a place of hard work (as in the phrase 'tied to the kitchen sink'). The French concept of '*cuisine*' is a place for creativity, a place where the family congregate, not only to eat, but also to socialize.

When slightly different associations are attached to each word, the bilingual may be able to **think more fluently, flexibly** and creatively. Being able to move between two languages may lead to more awareness of language and more sensitivity in communication. When meeting those who do not speak their language particularly well, bilinguals may be more patient listeners than monolinguals. This is considered in detail later in the book.

There are potential **economic advantages** (indeed increasing economic advantages) of being bilingual. A person with two languages may have a wider portfolio of jobs available in the future. As economic trade barriers fall, as international relationships become closer, as partnerships across nations become more widespread, ever more jobs are likely to require a person to be bilingual or multilingual. Bilinguals and multilinguals are increasingly needed in the international retail sector, tourism, international transport, public relations, banking and accountancy, information technology, secretarial work, marketing and sales, the law, teaching and overseas aid work. Where a **customer interface** needs to be bilingual or multilingual, then bilinguals and multilinguals are in demand. Sometimes a bilingual's languages bring value-addedness to a job. Other times, such multiple language proficiency is essential.

Jobs in multinational companies, jobs selling and exporting, and employment prospects generated by the European Union make the future of employment more versatile for bilinguals than monolinguals. In Wales and Catalonia for example, in particular geographical areas knowledge of the minority language is required to obtain teaching and administrative posts, and is of prime value in business and commerce. Bilingualism does not guarantee a meal ticket or future affluence. However, as the global village rises and trade barriers fall, bilinguals and multilinguals may be in a relatively strong position in the race for employment.

Are some families better placed than others to produce bilingual children?

Some parents choose bilingualism for their children. For many other parents, bilingualism is automatic. In bilingual and multilingual communities, monolingualism is unusual, even peculiar. In such communities, children and adults need two or more languages to operate daily and successfully. In locations where bilingualism is the norm, families are well placed to raise bilingual children.

Irrespective of the type of community in which the family is placed, for a child to become fully bilingual there needs to be plenty of **stimulating language experience** (listening and speaking, and reading and writing) in both languages. Some families enable this to happen better than others. In such families, there is a natural and straightforward dual language pattern enabling both languages to flower. For example, when one parent speaks one language, the other parent a different language, and when the father and mother are both at home interacting with the child for considerable periods of time, the child may have plenty of exposure to both languages. Another example is where the child is learning one language at home, the other language in a playgroup, school or community.*

There are other situations that are less likely to promote bilingualism. For example, if the father is away from the home for long periods and he is the source of minority language experience for the child, uneven growth in language may occur. When the child is in nursery school all day, and only hears the home language for a short time in the evening and at weekends, parents will find creating bilingualism a challenge requiring effort and enterprise.

In families where bilingualism seems more of a challenge than cloudless sunshine, **language planning** (see Glossary) is important. How can the language menu of the family be arranged to create the conditions for the long-term growth of bilingualism? This does not mean equal amounts of stimulation in each language. It is impossible to achieve a perfect balance in exposure to both languages. The minority or weaker language may need stimulating more in the home to counteract the dominance of the majority or stronger language outside the home.

Where bilingualism is more difficult to achieve in particular family situations, a well thought out **plan of action** is needed. It is important for parents to talk about their child's language development not only before, or as soon as the child is born, but also for constant discussion and monitoring to occur. Bilingualism will flourish even in difficult circumstances when there is a plan of how, when and where a child will be exposed to both languages to ensure both languages develop well.

When a child has insufficient experience in listening and speaking a language, a **strategy** is needed. The strategy needs to include a consideration of the quantity of exposure to each language and the quality. A child who hears one language for half an hour a day is unlikely to grow competent in that language. When a child is deliberately exposed to an ever increasing variety of language in different contexts (e.g. books, listening to cassette tapes, visits to the zoo and park), a realistic chance of bilingualism exists.

The **quality of language** interaction is important. In some homes, there is a paucity of **communication between parents and children**. There is also the other extreme. Some parents bombard their children with a never ending stream of language. The child receives but is not encouraged to give. Interesting questions to the child, asking the child to relate a story rather than always to be the listener, nursery rhymes and songs said together, language games (e.g. 'I Spy', simulated telephone conversations), using role play (e.g. playing doctors and nurses, puppets, cops and robbers) are just some examples of ensuring that language development is active, alive and appreciated by the attentive child.

The 'bottom line' question is whether there are circumstances where bilingual development is nearly impossible? The answer is that bilingualism is possible in many different situations, if thought and care, pleasure and purpose are injected. It requires motivation and a positive attitude from parents, often considerable perseverance to achieve a distant goal, and a willingness not to expect too much too soon. Children's **bilingual skills constantly change**. They become stronger in one language or the other, as geographical and socioeconomic movement of families, changes in friends and school, and relationships within families all develop. There will be periods of darkness. For example, a teenage child may stop using their minority language at home. At other times, there will be top-of-the-mountain experiences. For instance, when a child translates or interprets (see Glossary) to help a monolingual listener, there is that sparkle of pride in the eye of the child and the parents.

Some of the **factors** that are likely to affect the ability of a family to produce bilingual children include: geographical stability and mobility, changing relationships within the nuclear and extended family, the father's and mother's employment conditions, the language situation and attitudes of the local community, being a recent or established in-migrant, changing priorities in the family (how important is language development compared with other developmental issues in the family), the attitudes and motivations of the child itself, the influence of brothers and sisters, friends and 'significant others' outside in the community, and the effects of the child's school.

In some situations, producing bilingual children is easy and natural. In other situations it is a struggle. However, if it is a high enough priority in the **family's personal balance sheet**, the advice of this book, constant discussion and careful family language planning are likely to make the journey possible and the destination reachable.

Is the mother more important than the father in the child's language development?

There is a danger in this question. It unfairly assumes that it is the mother's place to stay at home and raise bilingual children. That is neither fair nor reasonable. It is discriminatory both to the role of females in a relationship, and unfair to fathers whose role in child language development can have many different profiles, including being a full-time parent. There is no reason that a father cannot be as successful in raising bilingual children as a mother.

In those families where the father goes out to work and the mother raises the children, it is not surprising that the term '**mother tongue**' (see Glossary) is used. In such a situation, the amount of time a mother spends with the child will strongly affect the nature of the child's language development. Many mothers whose first language is different from the language of the community or region still prefer to talk to their child in their **first language**. To speak in a different language, even if it is the language of the father, the local community or the majority language of the nation, can feel artificial, impersonal, distant, even distasteful.

Some mothers choose not to use their heritage language (see Glossary) with the child. To them it feels sound and sensible, effective and educative to use the local language, the language of the father or the language of the school. Parents who are **in-migrants** sometimes strive to integrate into the host nation. For such families, this means language change.

Research has shown that much of mothers' language interaction with their children is about basic housekeeping functions (e.g. feeding, bathing, dressing, discipline). Leisure time has grown in recent decades, allowing the father's role in language development to become more important. Fathers have opportunities to play with their children, allowing considerable language stimulation. As many fathers interact with their children in child-centered ways, their contribution to a child's language development can be underemphasized. Thus fathers need to be aware of the important role they play in child language development. Some fathers stay at home to raise the children while the mother goes out to work.

In some families (e.g. where one parent speaks one language, the other parent a different language), both parents promote bilingualism. In this situation, fathers and mothers need to be conscious of their important role in the child's language development. **Fathers** as well as mothers can be encouraged to take pride in their conversations with the child, including at the babbling and cooing stage. Even before birth, the baby can pick up the sounds of the second language from the father as well as the mother. As the baby grows to a young child, the father plays an important role in the quantity of language interaction. Fathers as well as mothers need to vary the contexts in which language is used to give that child a wider language experience.

Fathers also influence the attitudes of their children to languages. Whether the father is positive or negative about bilingualism will considerably affect the child. If the father is sceptical about bilingualism, or doesn't like the mother using her

Parents who each use a different language with a child from birth typically produce fluent bilinguals. (Photo © Liisa & Fraser Watt).

Developing bilingualism in a young child helps build relationships across generations, with grandparents helping to pass on their heritage language. (Photo © Liisa & Fraser Watt).

Bilinguals have advantages in communication across communities, countries and cultures. (Photo © Jonna Gilbert).

The message in English, Japanese, Finnish and Spanish proclaims that bilingualism gives thinking advantages, and is a blessing and not a burden. (Photo by Don Williams, Bangor).

Marriage can make a bridge between different languages and cultures. A multilingual and intercultural Greek-Cypriot and British/Finnish wedding in Spain creates a colourful occasion. (Photo © Liisa & Fraser Watt).

North Americans and Japanese celebrate the diversity of language and culture with a shared meal. (Photo © Joseph Shaules).

Saturday Schools help pass on a heritage language from one generation to another.
(Photo © Kirsti Gibbs).

A trilingual sign in Jerusalem in
Hebrew, Arabic and English points to
a multilingual city landscape.
(Photo © Colin Baker).

'own' language, the child will soon pick up these negative vibrations and language behavior will be affected. On the other hand, if a father encourages his children's bilingualism, applauds them speaking to their mother in her 'own' language, the effect on the child's language confidence and attitudes will be substantial.

An important decision between parents concerns **what language to use with each other when the child is present**. Usually that language is naturally the one always used in the partnership. Yet for the child's sake, consideration needs giving to achieving an appropriate **balance** within the family between the two languages. If, for example, the child hears one language for 90% of the time, and a second language for only 10% from the father, then the husband and wife may consciously choose to use the lesser heard language in front of the child.

One important example of the value of the father (and/or mother) using a **minority language** is when the children are in their teenage years. If a parent speaks the majority language inaccurately with a 'foreign' accent (see Glossary), the teenager may be embarrassed. By speaking a minority language, the parent may retain more authority and credibility, and be more valued by the teenager. Continuity in minority language experience from early childhood through the teenage years is important if that minority language is to survive through to early adulthood.

Therefore, the answer to the question is that **both parents** are very important in the child's language development. That includes the father being the full-time carer. Both parents need to be aware of the importance of the language that the child hears and uses with each parent. There is a need to **engineer the language environment** in the home. Just as the dietary balance of meals is increasingly of interest and debate in families, so it is important that the diet of language in the home is also open to discussion. Both mothers and fathers are important chefs in the language kitchen.

What happens if parents don't agree that their children should become bilingual?

For some parents, raising bilingual children is **natural**, normal and not discussed. In many countries of the world, bilingual, trilingual and multilingual children are often the norm rather than the exception. In such areas, there is nothing peculiar or exceptional about bilingual children. Bilingualism is accepted and expected.

In other families, **debates** about the languages in which a child should grow take place before birth, after birth, during childhood and adolescence. The most positive thing is that children's bilingualism is discussed and debated. Just as many parents discuss the manners, mass media experience, hair styles, diets and clothes of their children, so language is an important area for a family to consider openly.

A child's languages can enter into discussions about the pattern of relationships that exist in the family, about relationships with grandparents and uncles and aunts, about schooling, about interaction with the community, about future employment and job prospects and, importantly, about a child's self-concept, self-esteem and self-enhancement. Discussion about raising a child bilingually or monolingually is not just about language. It is very much about the whole child. It is about the sense of security and status that a child will have, a child's self-identity and identity with a community and language group.

When there is **disagreement**, consider language as just one part of a child's whole development. Discussion about bilingualism in the child is not just about two languages. It's about personality, potential and the pleasure of a secure and stimulating period of childhood. Bilingualism in the child cannot be considered in total isolation. Bilingualism is one major part of the jigsaw of the child's total development. The fit of the bilingualism part of the jigsaw into the total picture of the child's development requires dialogue between parents.

If there is disagreement in the family, consider writing down the pluses and minuses on a '**balance sheet**'. Rather than argue about one or two points and let emotions sway, consider the widest variety of factors mentioned in this book. There needs to be a long-term view of the development of the child. In the final balance sheet, who counts most? Consider the interests of the child and not just the short-term preferences of the parents. One danger is that one parent may insist on a personal strongly felt language opinion, without adequate consideration of what is in the best interests of the child.

With care and consideration, a parent may feel it possible to sacrifice an opinion in the **best interests of the child**. For instance, if the father worries that he cannot understand what the mother is saying to the child in her heritage language, is a child's bilingualism to be sacrificed because of the father's concern? With diplomacy, love and meeting problems as challenges to be overcome, solutions can be achieved and understanding gained. A father in this situation may find it possible to forgo understanding the conversations between mother and child to help the child become fluently bilingual. The challenge may be for the father to change rather than the child. Can the father at least gain a passive understanding of the minority language rather than a child lose out on bilingualism?

In short, disagreements need tactfully resolving. Open and frank, positive and empathic discussion is the route to resolution. The most important destination to discuss is the long-term interests of the child.

A5   If we raise our child to be bilingual, will it affect our marriage?

If raising the child to be bilingual or multilingual doesn't affect the marriage, there is something odd about the marriage! However, the way the question is posed hints that it will have a negative effect. For example, if a child is able to say things about the mother to the father in a language the mother does not understand, the child may be undermining the husband–wife relationship. Another example is when parents have to consider what language to speak to each other in front of the child; whether to switch languages when grandparents, relations, friends and others come into the home. When a minority language is used at home, and majority language monolinguals come into the home, do parents **switch** their languages when speaking to their children?

Bilingualism in the family opens up extra areas for discussion and decisions. Just as there are policy decisions within the family on the distribution of money across various headings, so also there needs to be discussion about the **distribution of language in family situations**. Such discussions are not once and for all. Just as family income changes over the years leading to changes in spending, so language situations change over time, leading to constant decisions about the **language economy**. Are the child's two languages in profit? Is there a growing debit account in one language? Can this be rectified? When new and different people enter the family situation, how can this be used to raise the profit of languages?

In raising children, their physical, social and intellectual development are full of **mountains and valleys**, periods of pleasure and occasions of worry and pain. In bilingual language development, there are also going to be mountains and valleys, peaks and troughs. There are the **joys** of hearing a child speak two languages to different people, of being able to break down barriers and build bridges with their two languages, of having two worlds of experience. There are also the **anxieties** and self-doubts about whether a child's two languages will develop to proficient bilingualism, of apparent interference (see Glossary) between the two languages, a silent period with understanding but not speaking, and of people being excluded when a child is using one of their languages.

The answer is, therefore, that a child's bilingual development will affect a marriage and it should do. There will be highs and lows, **moments of glory and moments of grief**. This is no different from physical, social or intellectual development. Just as the vast majority of children turn out to be physically mature, socially effective and intellectually well-developed adults, so children's dual language development also tends to have more glories than griefs. Just as parents care for a child's social, emotional, physical and intellectual development, so two languages need to be cared for.

What happens if grandparents and the extended family disapprove of bilingualism?

A6

There are situations when **grandparents** and the **extended family** have a vested interest in the bilingualism of children. Where the grandparents live in another country, for example, a monolingual child may be unable to communicate with grandparents, uncles and aunts, cousins and distant relatives. When a family is in-migrant, guest-worker or refugee, bilingualism in the child may help secure close family relationships with those left behind.

Disapproval of bilingualism may be found among monolingual grandparents and monolingual extended family members. For example, if an English speaker marries a French speaker, grandparents who are rooted in a tradition of monolingualism and monoculturalism may express a distaste for grandchildren who are bilingual. For such grandparents, their strong monolingual culture is seemingly being usurped and replaced by a diluted bilingual and bicultural experience (see Glossary).

There is also the historical legacy of bilingualism being identified with less intelligence, language underdevelopment, problems of personal identity and school underperformance. None of these attributions has been found fair or correct by research. Nevertheless, **prejudices** about bilingualism still abound, particularly among Western monolinguals.

* See page 199

Such disapproval, if based on prejudice, needs meeting with more up-to-date and **better informed evidence**. Information found in this book and other books* may be used to counteract misjudgements by grandparents, uncles and aunts and others. Where bilinguals are characterized negatively, there needs to be a clear assertion that bilingualism tends to have advantages and raises individual potential.

A different type of disapproval occurs when grandparents or others feel personally **excluded**. Therefore, parents of bilingual children need to be **social as well as language engineers**. There is a need to explain to children and grandparents alike how communication can best be facilitated. It is possible to explain even to young children that grandma and grandad may not understand them talking English and therefore they need to use Spanish. Children, as young as two or three, become amazingly adept at switching to the appropriate language and have everything to gain from communication with grandparents in the latter's preferred language.

Grandparents and others also need an **explanation**. Grandparents can be helped to understand the advantages of the child being bilingual, of the naturalness of the child switching between two languages, and that no loss of love or care is implied when a language is spoken that is not understood by grandparents. Where disapproval exists, diplomacy is needed. Bilingual parents and bilingual children are often relatively well equipped (language-wise and socially) to act diplomatically in cases of disapproval. The very act of having to deal diplomatically with languages only adds positively to a bilingual's life experiences and enhances their portfolio of skills and accomplishments.

If grandparents live in the same house, street or community, there is a wealth of language experience that can benefit the child. Grandparents, and other members of the extended family, provide an opportunity to learn or practice one language. For example, if parents speak one language to the child and the grand-parents don't speak that language, the grandparents (and other extended family members) can be used to introduce and extend a second language (see Glossary). Their objection can be 'turned on its head' to foster bilingualism. Grandparents become the second language model for the child. Not only is the child taught a second language, but the wise and pithy sayings, nursery rhymes, songs, folk stories and traditions of that language can be passed on to the new generation.

What is the 'one person–one language' (OPOL) approach? Is it effective?

Much of the academic literature on bilingual children is about the successes of the one person–one language approach (OPOL – also this can mean 'one parent–one language'). This strategy has a history that goes back to early civilization when languages were in contact and marriages were formed across language groups. The term is over 100 years old and derived from a French book by Maurice Grammont (1902) who used the term *'une personne-une langue'*.

Basically, one parent speaks one language to the child; the other parent speaks a different language. Both parents keep as much as is practically possible to such language separation. Its advantages appear to include: learning two languages from birth; reducing fears of language mixing in children; and each parent being a good role model of language for the child.

Many authors and researchers regard such an approach, if reasonably con-sistent and continuous, as effective. There are well-researched case studies of 'two elite languages' that demonstrate that this approach produces children for whom **bilingualism is their first language**. Such children not only learn to speak **two first languages** but also retain, at least, an understanding of both of their languages for life.

There are a series of **constraints** about OPOL that need mentioning.

(1)   OPOL children will not normally have two equal or balanced first languages. The input in the family will never be equal in two languages. For example, when parents talk to each other, one language is used, and will usually be the dominant family language. The child will not usually say the same thing to each parent by repeating the message in each language. One language may to be used as the 'common denomina-tor', especially as children get older. When siblings arrive, the balance of family languages will be affected by the language used between siblings. Extended families, neighbors, friends, visitors also affect the language experience of the child. Parents are just one source of language. Within OPOL there are many language experience variations.

(2)   Case histories find that, in some OPOL families, the child, teenager or young adult retains both languages but one becomes more passive (understood rather than spoken).

(3)   The child is not a piece of clay that can be moulded to exactly the shape desired by OPOL parents. Apart from shaping by the extended family and friends, there are other powerful influences on the child's own choice of language use. The child's (and especially the teenager's) peer group, the school curriculum and culture, school teachers and mass media are examples of modifiers on the child's two or more languages. Such people and institutions affect the child's attitudes, preferences for identity and sources of self-esteem. Such factors (attitude, identities, self-esteem) each affect language proficiency and use. Outside OPOL, there are many other sources of impact on a child's bilingualism.

(4)   Constant monitoring, language balance seeking and nervousness about success can be emotionally draining for OPOL parents. This is further discussed in Section C1.

There is a very helpful book that comprehensively considers the OPOL approach and contains much detailed and valuable advice: Suzanne Barron-Hauwaert's *Language Strategies for Bilingual Families: The One-Parent – One-Language Approach* published by Multilingual Matters in 2004 (http://www.multilingual-matters. com/).

A8   I'm a one-parent family. How can I raise my child bilingually?

Almost all books and case studies of bilingual children assume a two-parent family. By accident and not by intention, this tends to lead to the assumption that a one-parent family has much less chance, or no chance of raising a child bilingually. A seemingly sympathetic view may be that a one-parent family has enough problems without taking on board the additional 'problem' of raising a bilingual child.

One-parent families are usually good at meeting challenges. Having often overcome or accommodated a variety of financial, social, moral and interpersonal obstacles, a one-parent family may take on the idea of raising a child bilingually without flinching.

It is possible to raise a child bilingually inside a one-parent family. This is simply because a child's bilingualism may be acquired outside the mother–child or father–child relationship. What languages do the brothers and sisters speak? What language do the uncles and aunts, neighbors and friends speak to the child? Does the child go to a nursery school or a school where a different language is spoken from that at home? What is the dominant language of the community? If a child has sufficient experience of a different language from that of the home, such a child may become bilingual with unsuspected ease. If, for example, the mother speaks one language continuously to the child, the child may receive sufficient experience of a second language (see Glossary) in a nursery school, in the street and in school to ensure dual language development.

A less likely and a more difficult option, but not an impossible one, is for the parent to use two languages on different occasions. If the parent uses two languages during the day to the same very young child, a potential issue is separation within the child of those two languages. If a single parent feels it important to use two languages with the child, then there need to be clear **boundaries** of separation between the two languages (e.g. using a different language on different days), at least when the child is very young (e.g. two and three years of age).

Neither of us speaks a second language. How can we help our child become bilingual?

A9

If you are keen on your child becoming bilingual, there are many other routes than within the family. Some children pick up a second language by attending a nursery school, play group or with a childminder, carer, babysitter or au pair. If a child has a continuity of second language experience outside the home, the child can become bilingual. There are many successful histories of children speaking one language at home, and through regular attendance at nursery school, quickly becoming fluent in a second language. If that experience is consolidated in formal schooling, a competent bilingual may result.

Children can also be successful in acquiring a **conversational second language** in the street. Playing with friends over successive years in the evening, during holidays and at weekends, provides the opportunity to acquire a second language painlessly and effortlessly. Other children attend Saturday schools or Sunday schools sponsored by embassies, religious organizations and ethnic groups. For example, children have learned Arabic, Turkish, Greek, Hebrew, Spanish, Italian, various Asian languages, French and German through evening, Saturday and Sunday language classes. Such 'conversational competence' in a second language may not be enough to cope in all language situations (e.g. the classroom). How a child can best learn a second language through school is left until later in this book when education questions are considered (see Section E).

The dangerous conclusion would be that the first language should be learned in the home and the second language can be acquired outside the home. This is a false and dangerous position because parents' attitudes, encouragement and interest are vital in a child's second language development. **Praising** the child when they hear the child speaking the second language may do wonders for the child's language ego. **Visiting** the nursery school or childminder and showing interest in the language development of the child in that context may both encourage the teacher or carer. It will also signal to the child the parents' interest and awareness.

There is a danger in allowing interest to become concern, and enthusiasm to boil over into anxiety. A smile, a 'well done', a pat on the back and kindly praise do wonders for a child's motivation. If the parent thinks that second language development is important, the child will soon regard it as important as well. If the parent thinks that second language learning is of high status, the child will grow in status by identifying with the parents' wishes.

Second language support may also be provided by parents in the form of CDs, DVDs, videos, books, posters, satellite TV, the Internet and comics. One limitation of bilingualism learned in the street is that the level of language development is specific to that environment. The relatively simple conversational skills required to communicate in the street and playground need to blossom further. The language level of the classroom and office is more advanced.

The child ideally needs to grow from listening and speaking a second language to **literacy** in that language. Reading and writing the second language enables that language to develop more fully and broaden. Parents can encourage literacy in the second language in two ways. First, they can provide stimulating material in the second language (e.g. books and magazines). Second, they can listen to the child read in the second language even if they are 'encouragers' rather than 'correctors'. Research has shown that even if a parent doesn't understand what a child is reading, the child engaging in reading practice (plus the visible encouragement and interest of the parent) facilitates development in reading. While parents in such a situation may not be able to give language help, **the language of support and encouragement** is definitely needed.

My children get little practice in speaking one of their languages outside the family. What should I do?

When one language is not used in the community, the only constant source of language practice may be inside the home. In this situation, parents need to consider how to establish a **richness of language experience** for their children in that particular language. In order for the language of the child to extend beyond food, bedtime and family chores, it is important to arrange language experiences in a variety of contexts.

New vocabulary needs developing alongside a wider and deeper understanding of the shared meanings of words. Appropriate use of language in **different situations**, holding a sustained conversation, pronunciation, an awareness and a love of language, accuracy of grammatical structure are all enhanced when language frontiers are continuously pushed back. Visits to beaches, banks and bookshops, swimming pool and sports events, carnivals and cafes mean that new experiences stimulate language growth. Meeting different people who can speak the home language (on trips abroad or within the region), allows the experience of different styles of speaking and pronunciation to be absorbed by the child. CDs, DVDs, satellite TV, parents creating their own recordings of family stories and old traditions, video tapes, songs, photo albums, festivals, WWW, books and comics from the home country will give opportunities for extending the child's language experience. Listening to nursery rhymes, songs, jokes and wise sayings in the home language will allow the child's language canvas to be painted with a wider variety of colors.

The examples given above emphasize that richness of language experience must not become 'homework'. Language practice means **pleasurable participation** and not deadly drills; inspiration rather than perspiration; a motivating challenge rather than an imposition.

It may be important for the child to realize early on that the nuclear family's language island connects with language territory and language communities elsewhere. The child needs the experience of speaking the home language to relatives and people in a native country. **Vacations** abroad are often very successful in this endeavor. Parents who take their bilingual child to visit family and friends in another region or country tend to find that even a short two-week stay has dramatic effects on a weaker language. When the child is immersed in that language, a passive language (see Glossary) often becomes active. Listening turns into speaking; doubt turns into conviction; anxiety turns into confidence.

When watching television, should my child be encouraged to listen to one language or both languages?

When there is insufficient exposure to one language, the use of DVDs, videos and television programs may be a helpful supplement to a child's language diet. Minority language parents often buy language minority resources to encourage their children to grow in that language. They feel it important that the minority language and not just the majority language is identified with high status mass media images. Another example is when French speakers in English-speaking areas buy in French language recordings or obtain French television channels by satellite. Not only does a child receive language experience by such enjoyable and captivating means, the language itself may be raised in status in the child's eyes by being attached to this important modern image.

There are limits to parental power concerning television choice. Children at a very early age become adept at tuning to the channel of their (and not their parent's) choice. Watching a favorite cartoon becomes more important than the attempted language engineering of the parent. This occasionally works to the advantage of bilingualism. Watching Mickey Mouse or Bugs Bunny is important, watching it in German, French, Japanese or English can become relatively unimportant to the child. I spotted my own children watching German language television – particularly sports and children's programs – even though they have not been taught that language. So, in many family situations, the child votes for their television language experience with their finger on the remote control rather than via the guiding hand of the parent.

Since languages are typically not mixed on television, there seems an advantage for children to watch television in either of their languages. Watching one program in German and the next in French seems to be valuable since these are separate language experiences.

However, the value of television in children's language development should not be exaggerated. While it may help to a limited extent in extending the language versatility of the child, television is essentially a **passive medium**. A child does not practice or use their language with a television set – or only in rare situations. The child is the recipient of language rather than the producer of language. A child's listening vocabulary may be extended, but television does not usually produce direct opportunities to extend speaking perform-ance. At the same time, television has some input in a child's literacy. Titles and subtitles, lists of football teams, teletext, subtitles with the news may give the child language experience that is small but valuable.

Another danger with television is that it often extends a child's stronger language rather than their weaker one. The tendency of children is to watch television in majority languages – particularly English. Lesser-used languages in the mass media have relatively few hours of television prime time. Therefore, the danger is that the television diet does not provide the appropriate language vitamins to encourage fluent bilingualism.

My children can speak two languages. How can I help them belong to two cultures?

In one sense, merely speaking a language to a child conveys **culture** to that child. Embedded in the meanings of words and phrases is always a culture. Through language, a child learns a **whole way of life**, ways of perceiving and organizing experience, ways of anticipating the world, forms of social relation-ship, rules and conventions about behavior, moral values and ideals, the culture of technology and science as well as poetry, music and history. Culture is repro-duced in the child through the fertilization and growth of language.

However, it is possible to speak a language fluently yet not really understand, fully experience or fully participate in the culture that goes with a particular language. This is like saying about a person 'they speak Italian but don't act Italian'. It is paradoxically possible to be bilingual yet relatively monocultural. How can we lead a child to **identify** themselves with a particular language culture? How can we help them belong to a particular language group?

Many adults and children who are bilingual do not belong to two language cultures as a monolingual belongs to a one language culture. A person who speaks English and French, for example, may partly share and identify with English language culture, and partly identify with French language culture and sub-cultures. Being **bicultural** (see Glossary) is different from being two monoculturals glued together. A bilingual tends to be bicultural in a unique sense. There is a complex but integrated combination of both cultures inside one person. It is like the overlapping of two circles rather than two circles side by side.

With considerable differences from person to person, and considerable changes over a time within a person, an individual may feel more French or more English but neither to the exclusion of the other. In this **hyphenated variety**, there is a separation of cultures and integration, distinct French and English varieties yet also a unique combination. To be Anglo-French is to be neither English nor French.*

* See page 78ff

As bilingual children get older, they decide mostly for themselves to enhance one or both their cultures. **Parents** can only act as **gardeners**, showing their children the variety of cultures within each language. Gardeners can aid growth but not cause it. The language seeds sown need watering, tending and fertilizing. Some language flowers need extra care and protection, other flowers will grow quickly and effortlessly. Sometimes reseeding is necessary.

Through meeting speakers of their two languages, visiting a variety of cultural events – from markets to sports matches, from religious meetings to rural festivals – parents can introduce their children to the cultures that surround each language. Where first-hand experience is not possible, television and video allow second-hand experience. Introduction to the broadest range of sub-cultures that goes with each language will potentially broaden the **horizons of the child**, open up more and new opportunities, and give a world view where there are fewer barriers and more bridges.

How important is it that the child's two languages are practiced and supported outside the home?

Where families are **in-migrants, guest-workers or refugees**, there may be little support for the home language in the community or in formal schooling. When such parents feel **isolated**, there is sometimes the tendency to feel like giving up the heritage language and speaking the regional majority language to the child. The pressure in the community tends to be to speak in the language of the region rather than a foreign language (see Glossary).

The answer is that bilingualism inside the child can be effectively **sustained** through the language of the home being different from the language of the community. However, this will be a challenge. If the child learns the regional language via the school and the street, there is sufficient support for that language outside the home for the child to become fully bilingual.

The problem is not usually with learning the majority language of the region, but in maintaining the language of the home. Determined parents should not be deterred by their language being an island in the home.*

* See page 22

What kind of community support is valuable for bilingualism?

In an 'isolated language' situation, the danger is that the home language will wither and fade as the child increasingly grows stronger in the majority language through experiences outside the home and with the mass media.

When a child is being brought up bilingually at home, any possibility of similar parents and toddlers **getting together** needs encouragement. Sometimes this is impossible due to geographical distance. Yet with mother and toddler groups, small nursery groups or compulsory schooling, groups of same-language speakers can each help a language minority family feel less isolated and less of a minority. This includes two different types of situation.

First, there is the **example** of local mothers, fathers and children meeting and using their common minority language. In some mother and toddler groups for example, the language of playing and conversation will be the minority language only. In a **second** situation, bilingual parents with bilingual children of different combinations of languages may meet to exchange ideas, hunt out answers to problems, swap information and literature, and importantly, encourage each other. If you feel that you are an isolated language island, try to find other similar islands near you and develop links with them. If those different islands speak the same language, there can be an exchange of materials as well as inter-action in the home language. If the islands use different languages, there is still the opportunity to reduce isolation and feel part of the community of islands. Sharing needs to replace isolation.

A particularly good example of community support is found with the Waltham Forest Bilingual Group formed by a group of parents in north-east London (UK). This is a voluntary parent support group with a variety of languages, mainly European and Asian, where parents enjoy a mixture of (1) exchange of experiences and ideas about raising children in two or more languages (mainly during a monthly drop session at a local children's centre), (2) talks from experts with question and answer sessions and workshops run by members of the group, (3) a library of books and videos about multilingual families that members can borrow, and (4) activities, for example at weekends, where parents and children enjoy communal picnics or trips to local attractions. (http://www.wfbilingual.org.uk/).

There is another side to this question. Research and writing on raising children bilingually tends to assume that it best occurs via the family. The underlying belief tends to be that it is a nuclear family (especially mothers) raising children bilingually from birth that is most effective. That is not so. **Extended families** (e.g. in India, many parts of Asia and Africa) have, for many decades, very successfully raised bilingual and multilingual children, with grandparents, relatives, older siblings giving a rich language learning environment. **Schools** are also sites where language learning can occur effectively (e.g. preschools, immersion education, dual language education). This is discussed fully in Section E of this book. **Communities** or local **networks** (see Glossary) themselves may organize language learning for children (e.g. Saturday schools, religious organizations). There are many roads leading to bilingualism. The nuclear family is just one of those routes.

My neighbors think we should integrate more which means using a different language from the home. Should we keep separate or integrate? A15

Such neighbors are usually monolinguals. The monolingual view of the world tends to be that languages keep nations and people apart. Having a common language is the only way to integrate. The problem is that integration tends in reality to be **assimilation** (see Glossary). Monolingual neighbors really want you to become the same as them.

Neighbors who are bilingual themselves are usually more happy with the idea of language variety. Bilinguals seem more adept at accepting people as they are, and not feeling challenged or excluded when they hear different languages being spoken. Bilinguals tend to be more accepting of language diversity.

When neighbors believe that integration means monolingualism, kind and gentle education of such neighbors may be desirable. If neighbors believe that local assimilation demands monolingualism in their language, the price of friendship needs weighing against the wealth gained from **language preservation**.

One issue raised by this question is whether children should be kept away from neighbors so that they do not develop superior performance in one language rather than another. The answer is that one language does not usually develop at the cost of another. Languages do not develop like a balance: the more one side rises, the lower the other descends. **Languages grow interdependently** and with no long-term cost to each other. Therefore, it is sensible and natural that children should have language practice with people around them who matter, and who are important in a local network (see Glossary) of relationships. To stop a child talking to neighbors for fear of language pollution is unreasonable.

Language is about **communication**. Who better to communicate with, and build relationships with, than local neighbors? However, this does not mean that there should be a free language economy in the locality. When an 'isolated' language is used in the home, parents will have to engineer situations and visits for children to use their minority 'island' language. There is a cost to bilingualism in such situations – financial as well as time-wise. There are also great benefits for children.

Can I learn a second language alongside my child?

This is not as unusual as it sounds. There are many examples of a parent learning a language from the other parent alongside their children. For example, a father may pick up a minority language spoken by the mother while listening to the mother speaking to the child. The father will be able to understand many minority language conversations in the family. At the same time, he may continue to speak in the majority language. In this example, the father may find it artificial and unnatural to speak to the child in anything except his first language.

In other cases, a parent will attend a language learning class as soon as a child is born, keeping a few months ahead of the child. One aim is to establish some kind of language uniformity inside the house so that all the occupants are speaking the same language to each other, or at least, understand each other speaking. In a minority language situation, particularly where that minority language is not strong in the local community, there is value in this. The child will later become bilingual outside the home.

One danger is where language uniformity exists in the home that parallels the same language uniformity in the community. For example, **in-migrant** parents decide to lose their heritage language and speak the language of the host country instead. In such cases, the chance of bilingualism will be lost and monolingualism may result. Another danger in this 'in-migrant' situation is that the parent speaks an incorrect form of the majority language to the child. If the parent learning the second language is a poor **language model**, the child may be placed at a disadvantage. The errors made by the parent may become part of the child's normal language (error fossilization). Children may also come to despise and show dissatisfaction towards a parent who they later realize speaks a second (majority) language 'incorrectly'.

We have just moved to a different country. Should we speak the host country's language in the home to help our children?

First, if one or both parents can speak (as a second or third language) the host country's language, it still tends to feel unnatural and stilted to speak that language to the children. In this sense, the **artificiality** of changing the language spoken by the parents will not help but hinder the settling down period.

Second, if children already have **confidence** in a language, suddenly to switch languages at the same time as switching country, home and friends can be psychologically disruptive for the child. Some continuity and reassurance for the child will be gained by continuing to speak the language of the home.

Third, speaking the host language to children already **competent** in a language, means that the level of conversation will change. The language will have to be simple and the conversation sometimes tedious. Importantly, the children's intellectual and conceptual growth may be hindered by their being spoken to in a new language.

Nevertheless, many parents want their children to become fluent quickly in the host country's language. Therefore, they automatically want to provide the environment where quick acquisition of that language occurs. If the children are very young, they will usually pick up the **host country's language** in the street, shops and particularly in nursery or kindergarten. Generally, young children pick up a new language with some degree of ease. Since the vocabulary and complexity of language structure required in children's conversation is much less than adults, and since young children acquire language almost accidentally and painlessly, children are often more adept at adjusting to a new language than most adults.

The specific advice is that children (when infants and quite young) do not need parents to speak the host country's language in the home. They will usually pick up that language easily outside the home. It is usually better for the heritage language (see Glossary) to be taught in the home, giving the child the chance of bilingualism, biculturalism and a sense of continuity.

In later childhood and teenage years, children may be expected to operate in the host country's language in school. Even if simple conversational proficiency is acquired relatively easily by such children, the level of language competence and confidence needed to work in the school curriculum is much harder to attain. A child learning algebra, gravity, world climatic variations, the history of the Renaissance, plus religious doctrine will often find that the **gap** between simple conversational skills and the language required in the curriculum is many kilometers apart.

When children are in their middle childhood and teenage years, advice from 'experts' differs. When competence in school work becomes important to the child, and where there is no choice in the language of the curriculum, parents may feel it their duty to provide **extra support** in the host country's language for their child. On such occasions, a family may decide to switch the language of the home to the school language after discussion and agreement with the child, so that the child gains maximally from education. Other 'experts' argue for the **continuity** of language and culture in the home. Therefore, no language switch is needed or necessary. This argument is rooted in keeping family traditions alive, maintaining heritage language culture and retaining a sense of the past in the present.

There are occasions when bilingualism cannot be the highest priority within the family. Bilingualism may need sacrificing for the greater good of the child. On such occasions, following discussion with the child, supporting the language the child requires in education and employment may be a higher priority than preserving the heritage language. Fortunately, in most cases, bilingualism can be maintained. Ultimately, bilingualism has to be a pleasure and not a pain, a means of enhancing the quality of life and not an end in itself. A belief in bilingualism is based on a belief about what is best for children.

 ## What should our language strategy be with an adopted child?

Choices about bilingualism will be different according to the age of the adopted child (e.g. whether that child already speaks one or more languages) and whether the parents speak the language of that older child.

If an adopted child is very young (e.g., up to the age of two), it seems quite appropriate for parents with different first languages to use both those languages with the child in ways explained in this book. When a child is very young, there will be some, but not an extensive recognition of a different language being spoken, particularly if the parents present those two languages in a sympathetic, caring and loving way.

However, what needs to be addressed with **very young children** is whether their 'native' or 'heritage' language (see Glossary) should also be introduced, by whatever means are available. An introduction of the child's heritage language (or not) will be based on parental values, such as whether they want the child to become, for example, an American or have dual American–German identity. A decision will also be made on whether language support in German can be offered.

It is important for every child to reach a high level of **self-esteem**, to be secure in their self-identity and this, for some parents, will mean celebrating the child's ethnic roots as well as their adopted country. As time goes on, the child will probably express a preference for retaining or rejecting dual (multiple) **identity**. For some parents, such continuity of identity from birth is a cultural rather than a linguistic matter. That is, such parents will wish to celebrate the heritage culture of the adopted child without always being able to provide the linguistic input for heritage language continuity.

If the child's 'native' language is encouraged by the parents, it may not become a fully functioning language, as often there are not the people, or the community contacts, to use that language frequently. Nevertheless, a child who has passive understanding of a heritage language may in the future be able to activate it, if he or she so chooses.

Before language considerations, there are usually more basic considerations in adoption, such as the child feeling a sense of belonging to the adopted family, feeling love and support from parents and others, and growing up to have a strong sense of self-identity and high self-esteem, a belief in oneself and a sense of success in friendships and work. Strategies to retain the child's heritage language may certainly help those basic and fundamental aims. Perhaps on less frequent occasions, there will be times when hard enforcement of the child's heritage language, and an unwanted exaggeration of the child's origins, may work against the child's own wishes. Therefore, it is important for parents to keep an open mind, to be sympathetic and sensitive to the child's development. No two children ever develop linguistically, culturally or in relationships in exactly the same way, and the child's own preferences can play an influential role.

Next, there is the case of adoption of an **older child**, for example, over the age of two or three. With such a child, a first language will already have become well established (e.g. a Finnish family adopting a seven-year-old girl from Russia). The question becomes: Should the parents effect a rapid but smooth transition from Russian to Finnish? Or should they attempt to maintain the child's first language, Russian?

Again, the important starting point is probably not language, but engendering a sense of family belonging, support, affection and love. Children are both resilient and fragile; they are optimistic and very adaptable while being sensitive and tender creatures. It is probable that supporting the child's first language is important. Some reasons why such support is valuable now follow.

When an older child is adopted, the child's **self-esteem** and self-concept will be enhanced when the parents explicitly show they value the child's home language. In this (real life) case of the Russian child being adopted in Finland, an acknowledgement of the child's first language is an acknowledgement of the child itself, his or her identity and origins. If parents explicitly value Russian, then they are valuing the child, showing their love and affection. To ignore the first language may send an implicit message that the child's origins, first language and culture, and the early years of their life are unimportant, irrelevant and valueless.

How do parents, who have adopted a child and do not speak that child's first language, come to value the adopted child's first language, and support bilingualism or trilingualism in the child?' There is no easy or guaranteed method, but here are some ideas worth considering:

(1)   Before the adopted child arrives, the parents could make an attempt to learn some of the child's first language. Using a few phrases with the child in that language sends a message beyond the words themselves. Using some Russian, in this example, sends the message to the child that 'we value your language, your culture, and therefore you'. While the parent is not going to be a good language model for the child, simple

communication in the child's first language is about care and support, and starting a loving relationship.

(2)   At the same time, the adopted child needs to learn the language of the country, particularly the language of formal education. Parents will naturally reward and encourage the development of the second language in the child, and will often be delighted at how quickly young children pick up a new language at home, particularly if there are lots of gestures, actions and all kinds of non-verbal communication to accompany the early stages of learning a second language.

It is even better if parents reward and encourage bilingualism and not just the learning of the second language. For example, the parents may comment not only on increasing facility in Finnish, but congratulate the child on being able to speak Finnish and Russian. Taking pride in one's bilingualism can be an important component in developing and retaining high self-esteem.

(3)   Try to keep the first language of the child going if at all possible. This will usually develop a securer **self-identity** and help to avoid a demolition of the child's initial identity. Many children and adults find multiple identities an asset and a strength. In this example, celebrating a Finnish and a Russian identity can be a sense of addition rather than diminution.

This leaves the question: How can the first language be retained? The adopting parents may often find it difficult to retain the child's heritage language. It may be difficult even to preserve the child's level of language competence, let alone effect progress. Also, the child's own wishes and wants need to be taken into account.

At the time of adoption and afterwards, parents can, first, consider buying books, videos, and use of the Internet to give the child the opportunity to use, albeit passively, their first language. Such media will not only provide a limited form of language practice, but will also symbolize that their 'native' language is accepted and valued by the parents.

A second ploy is to try and find a person, family or group of people who speak that child's home language. This is more beneficial than the media in many cases as it provides the child with a chance of active speaking rather than just passive listening.

A third way of keeping the language alive is satellite television. An increasing number of countries and an increasing number of languages are going onto satellite, giving the potential, if the child so wishes, of accessing their 'native' language.

(4)   An important choice by parents is of a sympathetic **school** for their adopted child.* Some schools are more attuned to language diversity, to language development for first and second language speakers, to celebrating the different languages that children bring to school, rather than being on a monolingual campaign. When the adopted child is of primary and

secondary school age, the choice of a language-sensitive school will affect the child's achievement and progress in school, and their self-esteem.

To conclude. What adopting parents can do is to provide their children with a wider set of choices with respect to languages and cultures. To give an adopted child the chance of retaining their language, of a bicultural or multicultural heritage, is to give freedom and power to the child. The parent who insists on ignoring and burying the child's linguistic and cultural origins can so easily be restricting and constraining the child.

Parent-centered parents often find monolingualism the most efficient for their needs. Child-centered parents may, in contrast, find bilingualism and biculturalism most appropriate to serve the child's short-term and long-term interests.

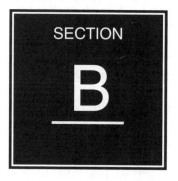

Language Development Questions

B1

What are the most important factors in raising a bilingual child?

Children are **born ready to become bilinguals and multilinguals**. Too many are restricted to becoming monolinguals. No caring parent or teacher denies children the chance to develop physically, socially, educationally or emotionally. Yet we deny many children the chance to develop bilingually and multilingually.

Language is much about **communication and identity**. We need language to communicate information, to build relationships, to play games and tell stories, to make new friends and work in groups. Some bilingual parents worry endlessly about **correctness** of grammar (see Glossary), accuracy of vocabulary, not mixing two languages, and skilled interpreting (see Glossary) and translating. Instead, the most important factor in raising a bilingual child is to make their language development a pleasure, a positive and enjoyable experience. Children need to value their two languages, two cultures and in a modest way, become aware of the advantages of being bilingual, biliterate and bicultural.

Parents are likely to work against themselves if they make the development of proficiency in two languages a **crusade**, a source of conflict, a series of mini crises, and a competition against monolingual standards. A language castle is simultaneously built and attacked. The child has learned that bilingualism is associated with pressure, anxiety and constant correction.

It is important that children's attitude towards their two languages (and their motivation to extend their two languages) is **encouraged continuously**. Show delight at small steps forward in bilingual development. The occasional pat on the back, a quiet 'well done', a wink or a smile works wonders for a child's **language ego**. For example, when a child has correctly switched languages in front of grandma so she understands, or automatically translated something for a friend to help relationships in a group, gently show your delight. We all need encouragement to carry on learning and refining our skills. Encouragement and aptly directed praise will provide the positive ambience, the caring ethos and a helpful family atmosphere to surround the development of bilingualism.

When the child speaks a minority language, encouraging use of that **minority language** may need to be more rather than less. When there is discouragement in the street, little reinforcement on the screen and in the school playground for minority language usage, parents are often pivotal in fostering favorability of attitude among the children to that minority language. It is important to amplify that minority language rather than the majority language, especially in the early years. The winds of influence usually blow in the direction of the majority language: mass media, employment, communication with bureaucracy, for example. Therefore, the balance of language experience needs tilting in favor of the minority language. While ensuring the child becomes fully fluent in the majority language, some **sheltering** from a pervasive majority language may be important.

A most important factor in raising a bilingual child is **the language that surrounds language**. The gardener cannot make the language seeds grow. All the gardener can do is to provide certain conditions: a rich soil, light, water and careful tending. Language growth in children requires the minimum of pruning – these are tender, young plants. Correcting language continuously, getting the child to repeat sentences is the kind of pruning that can have a negative effect on language growth. The role of the language gardener is to provide a stimulating soil – a variety of pleasurable environments for language growth.

Language growth can be slow. There will be many anxious days when tender young shoots do not develop smoothly, and later they are in danger of breaking among the strong winds of peer pressure. The parent as language gardener can help maximize those conditions that are open to influence, but parents cannot control the growth of language.

Do some children find it easier than others to become bilingual?

B2

Children develop at **different speeds** in their bilingual language development. Just as some children learn to crawl, walk or say their first words earlier than others, so the speed of language development varies between children. This is even more so in the development of two languages.

The speed of language acquisition is only partly due to the child's **ability**. Indeed, some children who turn out to be very able in academic terms are slow in their language development. There is generally little relationship between how quickly someone learns to speak one or two languages and eventual school success. Early language developers are not likely to be more successful in adult life – however success is defined.

A child's **interest** in language is also important and is partly separate from ability and language aptitude (see Glossary) for language learning. When a child is encouraged and stimulated in language development, an interest in reading, for example, will be increased. Parents who listen with attention to what the child is saying, answer the child in a child-centered way, make language fun by rhymes and songs, will aid language development. A child's motivation to engage in conversation will affect their speed of development.

Given adequate encouragement, practice and a stimulating environment for language growth, young **children** find the acquisition of two languages relatively straightforward, painless and effortless. Many children tend to reflect parents' attitudes, behavior, expectations and beliefs. A positive parent tends to breed a successful child. Parents who expect failure tend to breed less success. This is particularly true of a child's bilingual development.

There are **hurdles but few insurmountable barriers** to children reaching whatever bilingual language destination is possible. However, routes to dual language proficiency are sometimes long. This is one reason for undue concern by destination-seeking parents. Early acquisition of two languages for some parents seems like slow motoring. For other parents, the journey in later childhood and the teenage years seems troublesome, even like backpedaling.

Such **concerns** seem usual and prevalent among parents of bilingual children. However, if safety in numbers doesn't satisfy, consider comparing your bilingual child against other bilinguals and not against the fastest moving monolingual who sets the pace. Some bilinguals show similar language performance to monolinguals in one of their languages. Some, but not all, develop considerable competence in a second language. **Rarely** are bilinguals **equally fluent** in all situations in both their languages.

Not all bilingual children will reach the same **language destination**. Family, community and educational circumstances sometimes mean the journey halts at passive bilingualism (that is, understanding but not speaking a second language). Partial or passive bilingualism is not a finishing line. Given a need to become an active bilingual (e.g. by visiting the country where the hitherto 'passive' language is dominant), the journey can be continued to more complete bilingualism.

If the analogy will stand, language development is like distance running. Some people complete the course with speed, others go at a slower pace but still successfully manage to complete the language distance. Parents as spectators sometimes become agitated by the slow speed of the bilingual course. Parents

There is no simple reason why some children are quicker than others in dual language development. For each individual child, there is a **complex equation affecting the rate of bilingual development**. Into the equation go factors such as the child's personality, ability and aptitude for language learning and social development, and the quality and quantity of interaction with parents and peers, neighbors and extended family, the variety of language inputs and a stimulating environment for language development, the perceived attitudes of significant other people around the family and the child's own attitudes about bilingualism.

Effective language learners are often willing to make guesses and make mistakes, enjoy social communication, are relatively more extrovert and uninhibited, and monitor themselves by seeing how their language efforts have been received. The child's own priorities, the family language balance sheet, and the place of languages in the child's community life are also important.

want adult-like language performance while the child is in the early and middle stages of development.

Is it easier to become bilingual as a young child?

B3

The answer is both yes and no. The answer is 'yes' in that **young children** pick up language so easily. Language is acquired unwittingly, subconsciously, without the effort of secondary school language classes, without the pressure of 101 other important matters to consider. Young children learn languages as **naturally** as they learn to run and jump, paint and play. They are not worried by their language mistakes, nor about not finding the exact words. They are only interested in getting their message across and receiving needed information.

Language among young children is caught rather than taught. The process is not learning but **acquisition** when children are young. Language acquisition is a by-product of playing and interacting with people. There is plenty of time to acquire the language. The pressure and competing opportunities that exist among older children are not present. Competence in language from the 'one word' baby stage to the fun of the five-year-old is a pleasure without pain.

When children are very young, they pick up accurate **pronunciation** quickly. Children easily learn the distinct sounds of two or more languages and local dialects. Compare such young children pronouncing their languages with adults learning a second language. Such adults often struggle with pronunciation. For them, rolling the 'r', tonguing a 'th', guttural sounds and nasal sounds are more difficult, seemingly impossible to perfect. Even when adults become perfectly fluent in a second language (see Glossary), usually their pronunciation still carries the ring of the first language. Compare mainland Europeans, Africans, Arabs and Asians who have learned to speak English fluently. Rarely do they pronounce English like a North American or British person. The sounds and pronunciation of their first language affect the way English is intoned. Young children are more likely to pick up appropriate pronunciation of their two languages compared with those who learn a second language later.

The second part of the answer is 'no'. Very young bilingual children tend to learn a language relatively slowly. Because **older children and adults** have better developed thinking, information handling, analytical and memorization capacities, they can learn languages faster than very young children. So, if efficiency is defined by the amount of time it takes to learn a second language, teenagers and adults tend to be superior to young children.

The **speed** with which adults become bilingual through learning a second language will vary according to: the amount of time for lessons and practice, attitude and motivation, aptitude and ability for language learning, and persistence in using the second language when there are incorrect utterances. As a generalization, most adults learn a second language faster than most children. However, there is sometimes resistance to learning a new language, particularly during the teens. This can be part of a general resistance to a variety of things, no perceived need to learn a language, even a narrow monoculturalism.

The answer given so far mustn't be seen as suggesting that either earlier or later bilingualism is preferable. It is possible for both young children, teenagers and adults to become fluently bilingual. Many routes can produce an equally successful outcome. The routes on the language course may be different, the timing to complete may be varied. Success is possible among both young and old.

 How early do bilingual children recognize that they have two languages?

The answer depends on what is meant by 'recognize'. However, if we take this to mean when a child knows to switch from one language to another, then recent case studies (published in academic journals) are striking.

(1)   One study of a Hebrew/English-speaking child at one year seven months showed that he spoke one language to one parent, another language to the other parent, with clear separation. Thus children under two years of age seem to recognize one language from another.

(2)   A similar study of a Spanish and English bilingual child revealed that the child could switch from one language to another with accuracy at the age

of one year and eight months. This not only includes which language to use with each parent, it also includes accuracy in different **contexts** and environments (e.g. nursery, home). The **context** seems in itself to trigger appropriate language choice. For example, switching between English and Spanish was not random but governed by the presence of others or being in a crèche). This illustrates a danger of the 'one language–one parent' model in that it can restrict discussion to the home, as if the parents are the only language influence. In contrast, siblings, extended families, carers, crèche, pre-schooling, friends of the family and many varying contexts have an additional language effect.

(3)   A case study of a German and French bilingual indicated that at two years and three months, the child showed dissatisfaction when either of the parents addressed the child in anything other than the usual language.

(4)   A replicated study of a Dutch and English bilingual aged three showed that the child would always choose the appropriate language when speaking with a monolingual person. However, with people she knew to be fluent bilinguals, she was much more ready to **use both languages** (i.e. code-switching – see Glossary) both within and across her contributions to the conversation. Research suggests that many bilingual children tend not to mix languages when addressing monolinguals, but are aware enough of bilinguals to move between both languages when addressing them.

Is it better for my child to learn a language early to secure better storage in the brain?

B5

One recent area of research on bilinguals is how their **two languages are stored and used in the brain**. For example, if someone learns two languages from birth, with bilingualism as their first language, are the two languages stored differently in the brain from someone who learns a second language at school or in adult life?

One much publicized piece of research by Mechelli and colleagues (2004) suggested that learning a second language increases the density of the brain's gray matter. When comparing 25 monolinguals, 25 early bilinguals and 33 late bilinguals, brain gray matter density was greater in bilinguals than monolinguals, with early bilinguals having an increased density over late bilinguals. The authors concluded that 'the structure of the brain is altered by the experience of acquiring a second language' (p. 757). However, the implications of such early findings for everyday thinking and language performance are not clear.

Kim *et al.* (1997) showed a difference between early bilinguals (e.g. both languages learnt before three years of age) and late bilinguals. Their finding was that in early bilinguals, the two languages are found in distinct but adjacent sites in the brain. This suggests that similar or identical regions of the brain serve both languages. In comparison, among late bilinguals, the native and second languages are stored more separately.

This research received much attention in the press, and has not been well replicated. Also, a note of caution is needed. There is a danger of believing that brain images represent language and thought. They do not. Such brain images convey the location of languages but do not reveal the complex operation of the mind in using languages.

References for further reading

Kim, K., Relkin, N., Lee, K-M. & Hirsch, J. 1997, Distinct cortical areas associated with native and second languages. *Nature*, Vol. 388, pp. 171–174.

Mechelli, A. *et al.*, 2004, Neurolinguistics: Structural plasticity in the bilingual brain. *Nature*, Vol. 431, p. 757.

Will my child become equally fluent in two languages?

B6

The answer is 'no' with only a few exceptions. One idealistic and unrealistic notion of some parents is that children become perfectly bilingual. The hopes of many parents are that their child will be two monolinguals inside the one bilingual person. For example, the expectation is that the child's French or German will be equivalent to that of French and German monolinguals. This idea of balanced bilinguals (see Glossary), perfectly balanced in both their languages, is one myth that surrounds bilingualism. This myth is part of a monolingual view of languages, where monolinguals are seen as fully fluent in one language, and therefore bilinguals must become fully fluent in two languages.

The reality that surrounds most bilinguals is different. For a bilingual, **each language tends to have different purposes, different functions and different uses**. Bilinguals tend to use their two languages in different places at different times with different people. For example, a person speaks English at work or when playing a particular sport. That person uses the other language at home, in church or chapel, mosque or temple and with neighbors and friends in the community. The two languages are mostly different tools for different jobs.

Many bilinguals are 'stronger' in one language than the other. Take an example. If one language is used much of the time, and the person has been educated in that language, it may have a width of vocabulary and complexity of structure not found in the other language. However, this other language may be the one that is naturally used in the nuclear and extended family. That family language is developed to meet the needs of home life and is thoroughly sufficient for that situation.

Such **varying strength in two languages** is unlikely to be stable and consistent over time. As children and adults move house, move school, move employment, go for long or short trips abroad, have new friends and extend their personal culture, so the balance and strength of the languages change. Children who were passive bilinguals (able to understand but not speak a second language), often quickly become speakers, readers and writers in that hitherto weaker language when moving to a region which demands use of that language. The only certainty about a bilingual's future dual language use is uncertainty.

Even children brought up by the **one parent–one language** method rarely show equal proficiency in both languages. And that unequal balance between the two languages rarely stays constant. For example, as brothers and sisters arrive and develop, the balance between the two languages may change. As the child gathers a group of friends inside and outside school, proficiency in the two languages may change and fluctuate. As the child moves through school and into college or employment, the balance between those languages may change again.

It is important **not to compare bilinguals with monolinguals** in their language development. Bilinguals should be compared with bilinguals. Bilinguals are not two monolinguals inside one person. They own a unique combination of two languages that are both separate and integrated within the thinking system. While two languages are visible in production (e.g. speaking), in the thinking quarters of the brain, one feeds the other. One language helps the other to grow. In this sense, there is integration between the two languages. Ideas and concepts learned in one language can be easily transferred into the other language. Mathematical multiplication and division learned in one language do not have to be relearned in the second language.

Since bilinguals use their different languages in different circumstances and with different people, it is unnatural to expect them to have the same linguistic repertoire as two monolinguals. For example, children's religious vocabulary may be strong in one language and not in the other as they attend church or chapel, mosque or temple in one language only. The child may be strong in scientific vocabulary in one language only, having been taught solely in that language. However, there will be transfer in thinking from one language to the other (e.g. in religious ideas and scientific concepts).

Another **danger** is to compare bilinguals with monolingual 'native country' speakers. Take, for example, the case of a child who has learned German in a country outside Germany. In the country of residence, German is rarely heard by the child. It is false to expect the child to speak German like a native German child. Width of vocabulary, complexity of language structure and pronunciation, for example, may be different. However, communication with other Germans is very probable. The language competence the child has in German enables both the gaining of information and the gaining of friendships – two key aspects of communication. From that base, when the child visits Germany, there will be adaptation to the German spoken in Germany, and a growth in 'native' language skills.

The bilingual is a different language creation from the monolingual. For many bilinguals, **bilingualism is their language**. For those who acquire two languages from birth, bilingualism is their first language (see Glossary). They are not two monolinguals.

Parents of bilingual children should not therefore expect their children to become as language competent as two monolinguals. Rather, bilinguals have the advantage and flexibility of being able to move between two languages and two or more cultures in a way that monolinguals cannot. There is no deficit or disadvantage implied when there is an imbalance between the languages. Such an imbalance only reflects the reality of the circumstances in which bilinguals live, and their ability to be decathletes rather than specialists in one event only. However, the difficulty arises in school and employment markets where bilinguals are sometimes compared with monolinguals. This can work both for, and admittedly, sometimes against bilinguals.

Is it better to develop two languages together or one language later than the other?

Developing two languages at the same time or learning one language later than another are **both successful routes to bilingualism**. As expressed in this section already,* there are many cases of older children and adults successfully learning a second language. Through language learning classes, immersion in a new community and, occasionally, a change in the language pattern of the home, older children and adults can be quicker and more efficient in learning a second language than very young children. There are examples of adults learning Hebrew and Welsh when they were aged 60, 70 and 80. Success in becoming bilingual is possible whatever the age.

However, if the home conditions allow, there is much value in developing children's bilingualism **earlier rather than later**. Because of the ease with which young children acquire language, the uncluttered nature of early childhood and the tendency to acquire pronunciation better when very young, early bilingualism needs encouragement wherever possible. Such early bilingualism gives immediate cognitive and social advantages, and possible longer-term economic, interpersonal and cultural advantages. If the family situation allows bilingualism early in the child's life, the best current advice is to start as soon as possible.

Teenagers and adults learn to swim by attending swimming instruction lessons. They learn the breast stroke, front crawl, back stroke and butterfly through practice, watching examples and through thinking about their physical movements in the water. Young children seem to learn swimming much more easily and naturally. They may be slower in perfecting their swimming strokes, but there is the joy of seeing the young child move through the water and enjoy all the fun of the pool. The same occurs with language. When learning the four language strokes (listening, speaking, reading and writing), both children and adults can become good language swimmers. If a bilingual language pool is available for the very young child, it seems sensible to give the child a chance to swim in two or more languages as early as possible.

There are situations where learning one language thoroughly first and then the other language later is possibly preferable. This occurs in minority language '**subtractive**' (see Glossary) situations. Where the majority language dominates in the community and country, it may be preferable to concentrate on full development in the minority language first. Once a child is in the street, school, supermarket, swimming pool, and socializing at discos and parties, the majority language usually develops at great speed.

The **danger for minority language parents** who introduce the majority language early on is that the child increasingly uses the majority language. The majority language is perceived by even young children as of higher status, more prestigious and having more uses and purposes. Therefore, developing a deep-rooted minority language and culture is important. A child who learns the majority language later (e.g. at age five when attending school), learns quickly. There is a transfer of language learning skills, awareness of majority language status, and an availability of experience in the majority language. Hence, learning the majority language later rather than earlier is rarely a problem.

How do I know my child's language development in each language is normal and acceptable?

B8

Children vary considerably in the speed of their language development. Early developers in language are not necessarily those who will be the great linguists of the future. In the same way, those children whose language development seems slow early on, may be those who catch up very quickly later. Einstein did not speak until the age of three.

There is great variety in the range and type of experiences that a child receives in both of their languages. For example, in some families French and English may receive roughly equal input. In other families, the balance may be more towards, for example, 80% English and 20% French. It is unrealistic to expect these two families to show similar development in their children in French.

When a child's language is definitely not developing normally, it is important to seek professional advice. Speech therapists, audiologists, clinical psychologists, educational psychologists, counselors and doctors may be contacted for advice and treatment. It is important that such professionals have some training regarding bilingualism, and preferably experience of bilingual children. In

Sections C and E of this book, there is a discussion of language disorders and bilingualism.

Set out below is an average **pattern of development for bilingual children**. Children in families where both languages are approximately equally developed will be close to these norms. However, it must be stressed that many children differ from these general averages and will show perfectly normal language development later in childhood. It is only when children approach formal schooling (and require sufficient language development in one of their languages to be able to understand the curriculum), that most developmental language concerns should begin. A separate question* later in the book deals with language delayed children.

* See page 88

Age	Language
0–1 year	Babbling, cooing, laughing (dada, mama, gaga)
Around 1 year old	First understandable words
1–2 years	Two-word combinations, moving slowly to three- and four-word combinations. Three-element sentences (e.g. 'Daddy come now'; 'That my book'; 'Teddy gone bye-byes')
3 to 4 years	Simple but increasingly longer sentences. Grammar and sentence structuring starts to develop. Conversations show turn taking
4 years onwards	Increasingly complex sentences, structure and ordered conversation. Use of pronouns and auxiliary verbs

If a personal experience is allowed, one of our children was very slow in learning to speak. One grandparent immediately ascribed this to his bilingualism. A lack of clarity of the speech in those early years was also obvious. Since no problems of hearing were found, no action was necessary. Three years on, both languages were well developed, with appropriate vocabularies, complexity in sentence structure, and later, school/university achievement, that made those early years no predictor at all.

Will learning a second language interfere with development in the first language?

The answer is no, definitely not. There may sometimes be some minor knots on the wood that are easily planed off over time. For example, mixing words from the two languages often temporarily occurs among children. Generally, becoming bilingual has positive effects on language development, including on the first language (see Glossary). For example, when learning two languages,

the child may become more sensitive and aware of language itself. There may be more sensitivity in communication and more awareness of the needs of listeners. Having two (or more) words for each object, idea or concept will **expand** rather than contract **the mind**.

Above is a picture of bilinguals that is **incorrect**. This picture is of someone with two **language balloons** in their head. In the picture, this incorrect idea of two languages is that they are stored within two separate language areas in the brain. The apparent assumption is that there is just enough room for one language inside the head. If one language is poured into that balloon, the mind will work maximally efficiently. If two languages are poured into the thinking quarters, the result will be two half-filled language balloons. Such underfilled language balloons in the bilingual will create an inefficient brain.

This 'two balloon' concept is wrong. First, there is more than enough room inside the thinking quarters for two or more languages. It seems impossible to set limits on the amount of learning, understanding and knowledge that a person can hold within their thinking quarters. Second, the picture is wrong because there is **transfer** between the two languages.

Take the example of a child taught how to use a computer in one language. This does not have to be retaught in the second language. They immediately transfer as an idea and an understanding into another language (so long as the child has the vocabulary to reproduce it in that second language). Thus, the two language balloons merge inside the thinking quarters. There is common thinking that can be serviced and supplied by both languages.

The incorrect balloon picture can be replaced by the picture of a dual **iceberg**. Two icebergs are separated above the waterline. A bilingual's two languages are

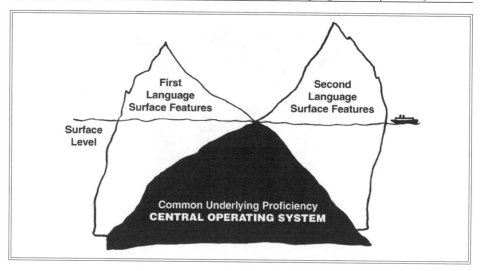

separate when speaking (and on the 'exterior', separate when reading and writing). Below the surface of the water, they are fused. A bilingual's two languages are joined together beneath the surface in the operating area of the brain.

So, rather than a second language interfering with the development of the first language, it is more likely to provide thinking advantages, social and cultural advantages, even economic advantages in the long term.

 ### Are there benefits if my child has a less well-developed second language?

For many parents, however caring and careful, the chance of their children having two well-developed languages is not high. The reality is that the child will have more experience of one language rather than the other. In many if not most families that wish to raise bilingual children, the ideal of two well-developed languages becomes a reality of one strong language and one weaker language. Parents sometimes feel failure and frustration when this occurs despite their best efforts. Books, articles and advice often fail to recognize this scenario as very frequently found in bilingual families.

There is no failure in this. Often it is due to a context (e.g. where only one parent speaks the second language and there is almost no community support, visits or vacations to develop the weaker language). Sometimes it is due to a child taking against the second language, even before the teenage years (e.g. when the child receives abuse or teasing for being 'different' from peers).

Take heart and think positive. A less well-developed language is still a success. The child or teenager will still have a foundation, a passive knowledge of that language, a readiness to develop and use that language in the future.

Early second language learning that fades does not die. Relearning from the beginning will not be needed. Much can be quickly reactivated.

We cannot predict the future of a child or teenager. When students, they may want to travel and find the second language suggests new destinations and opens up new experiences. In the twenties and thirties, they may find employment where that second language is a real advantage. Or they may want to celebrate being part of an extended family and heritage that operates through the second language. In these circumstances, the second language will be reactivated and will develop quickly into a much valued asset.

The gift of a second language can be stored. Later, when the time, people and place is right, the gift is employed, expanded and esteemed. Developing a weaker second language in the family is not failure. It is an investment that can be banked for the future.

Three Australian researchers (Yelland *et al.*, 1993) have shown that when a child has a fairly limited experience of a second language, there are still advantages over monolinguals in thinking and in learning to read.

The children in the research were aged four to six. One group were English monolinguals; the other group had only one hour of Italian language instruction each week. After just six months of such lessons, the 'marginal bilingual' children were much more aware of the notion of words (metalinguistic awareness – see Glossary) than their monolingual counterparts. This advantage carried through to when the children started to learn to read. The 'marginal bilinguals' showed quicker word recognition skills than the monolinguals. The authors argue that children do not need to have equal competence in two languages to gain thinking and reading acquisition benefits.

When the child becomes aware of two languages simultaneously representing the same objects and ideas, there are knock-on benefits in learning to read. When first learning to read, children have to learn that their existing oral language has a different symbol system in the written language. Such children have to work out how a new symbol system (e.g. written letters) relates with their existing oral language.

Bilinguals have an **awareness** of two language systems that seems to make this task easier. They are aware that one symbol system (e.g. spoken Italian) relates to another symbol system (e.g. spoken English). This makes movement from an oral to a written form more expeditious, and seems to give bilingual children a head start when learning to read.

Reference for further reading

Yelland, G.W., Pollard, J. & Mercuri, A. 1993, The metalinguistic benefits of limited contact with a second language. *Applied Psycholinguistics*, Vol. 14, pp. 423–444.

What effect will bilingualism have on my child's intelligence?

One totally discredited view about bilingualism is that children's intelligence will suffer if they are bilingual. Some of the earliest research into bilingualism examined whether bilingual children were ahead or behind monolingual children on **IQ tests**. From the 1920s through to the 1960s, the tendency was to find monolingual children ahead of bilinguals on IQ tests. The conclusion was that bilingual children were mentally confused. Having two languages in the brain it was said, disrupted efficient thinking. It was argued that having one well-developed language was superior to having two half-developed languages.

Early research was badly designed. First, such research often gave bilinguals an IQ test in their weaker language – usually English. Had bilinguals been tested in Welsh or Spanish or Hebrew, a different result may have been found. The **testing** of bilinguals was thus **unfair**. Second, like was not compared with like. Bilinguals tended to come from, for example, impoverished New York or rural Welsh backgrounds. The monolinguals tended to come from more middle-class, urban families. Working-class bilinguals were often compared with middle-class monolinguals. So the results were more likely to be due to social class differences than language differences. The **comparison** of monolinguals and bilinguals was unfair.

The most recent research suggests that bilinguals are, at the least, equal to monolinguals on IQ tests. When bilinguals have **two well-developed languages** (in the research literature called balanced bilinguals – see Glossary), bilinguals tend to show a slight superiority in IQ scores compared with monolinguals. This is the received psychological wisdom of the moment and is the good news for raising bilingual children. Take for example, a child who can operate in either language in the curriculum in school. That child is likely to be ahead on IQ tests compared with similar (same gender, social class and age) monolinguals. Far from making people mentally confused, bilingualism is now associated with a mild degree of **intellectual superiority**.

One note of **caution** needs to be sounded. IQ tests do not measure intelligence. IQ tests measure a small sample of the broadest concept of intelligence. IQ tests are simply paper and pencil tests where only 'right and wrong' answers are allowed. Is all intelligence summed up in such simple right and wrong, pencil and paper tests? Isn't there a wider variety of intelligences that are important in everyday functioning and everyday life? For example, Howard Gardner's famous list of multiple intelligences includes: logical-mathematical, verbal-linguistic, visual-spatial, musical-rhythmical, bodily-kinesthetic, naturalist, interpersonal, intrapersonal and existentialist. Recently, there has been much interest in emotional intelligence. Thus, there are many forms of intelligence.

The current state of psychological wisdom about bilingual children is that, where two languages are relatively well developed, bilinguals have **thinking**

advantages over monolinguals. Take an example. A child is asked a simple question: How many uses can you think of for a brick? Some children give two or three answers only. They can think of building walls, building a house and perhaps that is all. Another child scribbles away, pouring out ideas one after the other: blocking up a rabbit hole, breaking a window, using as a bird bath, as a plumb line, as an abstract sculpture in an art exhibition.

Research across different continents of the world shows that bilinguals tend to be more fluent, flexible, original and elaborate in their answers to this type of open-ended question. The person who can think of a few answers tends to be termed a convergent thinker. They converge onto a few acceptable conventional answers. People who think of lots of different uses for unusual objects (e.g. a brick, tin can, cardboard box) are called **divergers**. Divergers like a variety of answers to a question and are imaginative and fluent in their thinking.

While many monolinguals are divergers, there is a tendency for bilinguals to be ahead of monolinguals on such tests of creativity and divergent thinking (see Glossary). Having two or more words for each object and idea may mean there is more **elasticity in thinking**. A child may have different associations for the word 'brick' in each language. For example, a Welsh/English bilingual has the word 'school' and its Welsh equivalent '*ysgol*'. '*Ysgol*' also means ladder. The idea of school is thus extended to an image of schooling being a ladder. There is a sequential climb through school learning with the aim of getting to the top rung.

There are other dimensions in thinking where bilinguals with two well-developed languages may have temporary and occasionally permanent advantages over monolinguals: increased **sensitivity to communication**, a slightly speedier movement through the stages of **cognitive development**, and being less fixed on the sound of words and more centered on the meaning of words. For example, imagine young children are asked: which is more like the word 'cap', 'cat' or 'hat'? There is a tendency for bilinguals to center more on similarity of meaning (i.e. the word 'hat') than similarity of sound (i.e. the word 'cat'). Such ability to move away from the sound of words and to fix on the **meaning of words** tends to be a (temporary) advantage for bilinguals around the ages four to six. This advantage may mean an initial head start in learning to read and learning to think about language.

Recent research indicates that relatively balanced bilinguals (see Glossary) show superior skills in tasks that require **selective attention** to information (e.g. when there is competing or misleading information). Such selective attention relates to (1) bilinguals' enhanced **analyzing** of their language, and (2) their greater **control** of attention in internal language processing. The research evidence in this area (called metalinguistic awareness – see Glossary) shows that bilinguals have a definite advantage in cognitive processing. This advantage may be due to bilinguals needing to differentiate between their two languages.

Top Floor   Balanced Bilinguals

At this level, children have age-appropriate
competence in both languages and there are
likely to be positive cognitive advantages

SECOND THRESHOLD

Middle Floor   Less Balanced Bilinguals

At this level, children have age-appropriate
competence in one but not two languages.
There are unlikely to be positive or
negative cognitive consequences

FIRST THRESHOLD

Lower Floor   Limited Bilinguals

At this level, children have low levels of
competence in both languages, with likely
negative cognitive effects

**FIRST
LANGUAGE**

**SECOND
LANGUAGE**

Since both languages remain active during language processing (rather than a switch mechanism occurring), there is inhibition of the one language when in conversation so as to avoid intrusions. This, in itself, seems to lead to thinking advantages.

When a child is functioning in two languages well below age expectations, and in situations (e.g. the classroom) where more complex language forms are demanded, thinking disadvantages may be present. When one language is well developed and the other language is catching up, bilinguals and monolinguals may be no different in their cognitive development. Where a bilingual has two reasonably well-developed languages, there can be some temporary and a few permanent thinking advantages for the bilingual. This is illustrated in the picture of the three-floor house.

Up the sides of the house are placed two language ladders, indicating that a bilingual child will usually be moving upward and is not stationary on a floor. On the **bottom floor** of the house will be those whose current competence in both their languages is insufficiently developed, especially compared with their school age group. When there is a low level of competence in both languages, there may be detrimental cognitive effects. For example, a child who is unable to cope in the classroom in either language may suffer when processing instructional information.

At the **middle level**, the second floor of the house, will be those with age-appropriate competence in one of their languages but not in both. For example, children who can operate in the classroom in one of their languages, but not in their second language, may reside in this second level. At this level, partly bilingual children will be little different in thinking from monolingual children. They are unlikely to have any significant positive or negative cognitive differences compared with a monolingual.

At the top of the house, **the third floor**, reside children who have two well-developed languages. At this level, children will have age-appropriate competence in two or more languages. For example, they can cope with curriculum material in either of their languages. It is at this level that the positive cognitive advantages of bilingualism may appear. When a child has age-appropriate ability in both their languages, they may have thinking advantages over monolinguals.

Research provides good news for the raising of children bilingually as far as thinking is concerned. There are advantages for those children whose two or more languages are relatively well developed.

I want my children to be successful. Should I concentrate on developing their first/majority language skills?

B12

All parents want their children to be **successful**. Some parents want their children to be musicians, entrepreneurs, athletes, airhosts/hostesses or fashion models. Other parents hope their children will become devoutly religious, scientifically expert or socially skilled. Many parents want their children to excel academically at school and show examination and test success. So the answer to the question partly depends in what way you want your child to be successful.

The positive answer is that bilingualism is favorably connected with many of these aims and goals. **Bilingualism** is **valuable** for musicians, entrepreneurs, sports people, airline personnel and many other areas of 'success'. In the twenty-first century, it is likely that employment will increasingly demand language skills. So in the long term, children raised bilingually may receive an extra boost to their employment prospects, economic success and chances of affluence.

For those parents who want their children to be **skilled interpersonally and socially**, bilinguals are often the ones who are sensitive and sympathetic in communication. Bilinguals can break down barriers and build bridges, and are often more open-minded about racial and ethnic group differences. Academic success is not usually impeded by a child being bilingual. On the contrary, it may lead to greater success.*

* See page 161

However, there are parents in minority language situations where **minority language bilingualism** coexists with poverty, unemployment, deprivation, subservience and less political power. In the ghettos of inner cities, bilinguals are often the ones with less security, less status and less chance of success in life. Therefore, it is natural for minority language parents to focus on the importance of fluency in the majority language to increase the chances of success.

In such a minority language situation, there is little to gain by moving from bilingualism to majority language monolingualism. To deny one's heritage and to lose one's home language may create a loss of identity, even rootlessness (*anomie* – see Glossary), a lack of clear purpose and disruption in the family. It is possible to preserve the minority language and still become fully fluent in the majority language. The idea of the balance, the majority language going down as the minority language rises, is incorrect. Rather, gaining **competence in the minority language** may allow the later development of the majority language to proceed with more ease.

Suddenly to submerge someone who can speak a minority language in the majority language may not only cause psychological dislocation, it also denies the language abilities the child already owns. Such language abilities **transfer** easily into the majority language. The majority language can be successfully learned alongside the minority language.

Supporters of bilingualism do not usually deny the importance, economically, politically and socially, of a high level of **competence in the majority language**. To compete for jobs, economic advance and political power, fluency in the majority language is often required and demanded. To deprive someone of majority language competence is to deprive them of chances of success in later life. However, ensuring a high degree of competence in the majority language need not be at the cost of minority language skills. Bilingualism is usually a case of addition and not subtraction; multiplication and not division.

B13 Should my child keep the two languages separate in different situations and with different people (e.g. visitors)?

One idea in raising very young children bilingually is that of **language boundaries**. Experts on bilingualism have traditionally placed stress on the importance of keeping the context of very young children's languages more or less compartmentalized. Complete compartmentalization is almost impossible and unrealistic (e.g. when brothers and sisters arrive).

An example of language boundaries is when one parent speaks one language and the other parent speaks a different language to the child (see Section A7, p. 13ff on OPOL). For the child, there is a clear division when listening to those two languages. Language separation makes it easy for children to recognize when they should speak which language to which parent.

The value of **some degree of very early language separation** becomes apparent when we consider a lack of partition. Imagine a parent who speaks both Spanish and English to their child (see Strategy 3 in the Introduction).* This parent changes languages inside a 'sentence' and across 'sentences'. One outcome may be that the child will emulate the parent, mixing the languages inside a 'sentence'. Very early on in a child's production (speaking), this can be natural and is to be tolerated. The older the child grows, the more important separation becomes, socially and culturally. If a parent jumbles two languages, the child may consider that there is one overall language system. Therefore, mixing languages may become normal and natural to that child. Parents of bilingual children usually want to avoid such mixing early on (unless switching languages is used for a particular effect). However, there are many families who mix languages and the children learn to separate their languages, although sometimes a little later. As one parent remarks,

* See page xviii

> Both my husband and I chop and change quite freely between English and Italian when speaking directly to each other, as do many other bilingual couples we know . . . our children understand English and Italian perfectly. They don't consistently speak one or other language to either myself or their father . . . Our children show no signs of being confused. (*Bilingual Family Newsletter* (1997), Vol. 14, No. 2, p. 6)

Family life is rarely sufficiently simple to make **language compartmentalization** easy, particularly if a balance between languages is attempted. In the one language–one parent situation, there is the issue of which language parents speak to each other. Which language does a family speak when together (e.g. mealtimes, with visitors)? Such a decision may tilt the balance towards one language rather than the other in the family. The guiding principle is for parents to try to achieve an **approximate balance** in the quality and quantity of the two languages as experienced by the child. This cannot be achieved mathematically, with equal percentages of time or stimulation. However, the balance needs careful thought and consideration. When brothers and sisters are part of the nuclear family, language interaction between siblings cannot be programmed so easily.

Parental discussion of language balance needs to include the dominance and status of the languages in the community, in school as well as in family life. For

How is language separation achievable? What strategies can be employed?

(1)   'One language–one parent'. Each parent speaks a different language to the child who responds in that language.
(2)   Minority language only inside the home. Outside the home, the child will experience the majority language.
(3)   Speak the second language on certain days of the week – for example on weekends or alternate days. This has been achieved by bilingual families but the residual question is about its naturalness or artificiality.
(4)   A different language from the home is used at school or in another institution (e.g. when children use Hebrew in the synagogue or Arabic in the mosque, or go to Saturday schools and Sunday schools for language experience).

example, when one language is of lower prestige, that language may be given much more prominence in the home. A case in point is a father who speaks a majority language to the child, the mother speaking a minority language. The father needs to consider speaking the minority language in the home to raise its status in the eyes of the child.

Where both parents speak one language to their children, the question is what language to speak to their children when 'other language' **visitors** are present. Some parents carry on in the home language even if the visitor does not understand. This keeps continuity for the child. Other parents switch to the visitor's language so as to include the visitor. Others translate for guests. The choice is often as much about 'good manners' as it is about language.

If no change is made, visitors, out of courtesy, need an explanation of the 'language rules of the home'. So as not to exclude visitors, someone may interpret for the visitor when needed. If all members of the family temporarily switch to the visitor's language, it is possible to signal to the child that this is an occasion where social etiquette requires a switch in family language. Young children are quick at catching on which language to speak to whom in which situation.

A mid-way solution is to switch to the visitors' language when talking to them directly. When the family are talking to each other, they use their normal language pattern.

There is no simple answer about what to do when normal language patterns are disrupted. Issues about language development become entwined with etiquette and manners, personal relationships, tolerance and habit. Answers will naturally vary from culture to culture, family to family. However, some guidelines are possible. It is desirable for parents to **discuss** in prospect or retrospect the general situations that occur most often. It is advantageous to plan ahead the language that will be used with strangers and with each other. An understanding in the family will give language strength to that family and present a common and stable situation for the visitor. Yet, and in paradox to this, it is important to be natural and well mannered, making language life enjoyable and not a burden.

It is part of a bilingual's natural and usual repertoire to switch languages purposefully.* There are many occasions when bilinguals valuably switch their languages in conversation: to emphasize ideas, convey important messages, relay past conversations, occasionally to exclude people from conversations. So language **switching** is a valuable part of a bilingual's language accomplishments that has function and purpose.

* See page 57

Should my child use two languages with the same person?

B14

In the very early stages of bilingual development, it tends to be helpful if the child consistently speaks **one language with a particular person**. For the very young child, it may be confusing when anything different from 'one language per person' is apparent. Imagine the situation where a child speaks French to the father who answers in English. The child attempts a reply in English and then the father switches to French. The child may become insecure and muddled. The younger child requires some security and stability when speaking and listening.*

* See page 55

A typical situation is the child moving away from the language routines that have been established. For example, in the one parent–one language situation, the father may find the child starts to speak to him in the child's stronger language hitherto reserved for the mother. To maintain the language routines, the parent can use polite and gracious 'reorienting' tactics such as:

> 'I'm sorry. What did you say?'
> 'What did you say you wanted?'
> 'Please say that in our language'.
> 'Tell me again, please'.
> 'I didn't quite understand. Can you repeat it in [French]'.

If such **tactics** are consistently applied, the child soon learns that language boundaries are fixed and enduring. Young children (e.g. age two and three) then become amazingly adroit at knowing when to switch languages. Partly for this reason, in a language situation bilinguals seem to have an increased degree of social sensitivity compared with monolinguals.

Such language adjustment carries with it the danger of one language becoming stronger. If experience and stimulation of the other language diminishes, then that language may not develop as fully. Parents thus have to steer a **compromise** between (1) a 'free market language economy' where chance events partly dictate the flow of the two languages and (2) a structured and rule-bound language strategy.

In reality, many bilingual families cannot keep to a separation of languages by parent. If the mother speaks French to the child and the father English, the child will both listen and participate in conversations between parents that have to use French or English or switching. When siblings and visitors arrive, then the language pattern can be colorful, even complex. Children cope surprisingly well in moving between languages, in knowing what language to use, when, where and with whom. They swiftly pick up cues and clues about what language is appropriate on different occasions and subconsciously choose the suitable language.

Will my child's attitudes affect the learning of a second language?

A parent can provide a stimulating language environment, but that is not enough. A parent can take a child on lots of trips, provide plentiful resources and materials in the home for language practice and variation. A parent can ensure that a child meets other speakers of the minority language. All this is valuable and will give the child a good chance of becoming bilingual. Yet, if children's **attitude, motivation and interest** in their languages are not inspired, the parent may find that hopes about bilingual development are not fulfilled.

Consider this question with an analogy. Some parents buy lots of books for their children. Such parents often believe that, by providing a vast library of books, their children will develop literacy. While creating the right physical reading environment is important, it is clearly not enough. Children need to be encouraged to read. Another cluster of parents tends to think of (and teach) reading as a skill. Religiously, every evening there is half an hour's practice for the child to learn to read. That is excellent, but not enough. Such parents may find that when such children are able to read by themselves, they are no longer interested in books. Reading has been taught as a skill and not as a pleasurable activity of value in itself. Encouraging a positive attitude to reading, making books an enjoyable experience for children and encouraging them when learning to read is important in the long-term development of reading habits.

The same idea holds with bilingual language development. Providing a stimulating and varied environment for vocabulary and linguistic structures to evolve, ensuring that a child's linguistic skills become well developed is important but it is not enough. It is also important for the child to have a **positive self-concept about their two languages**.

As soon as bilingual children enter school, or earlier, they may become aware they are different (e.g. in a monolingual school). Rather than bilingualism being celebrated, such children may be teased or taunted about their accent (see

Glossary) or 'other language and culture'. Being different can be embarrassing, and language attitudes may change. Children in such circumstances may stop speaking the non-school language and ask their parents to only speak to them in that language. To reverse a decline in attitude, the teacher's help may need to be enlisted, raising a positive profile about 'other languages' in her classroom (see Section E).

Parents are only one source of language encouragement for the child. For example, the perceived status of a minority language in society will affect the child's language self-concept. To a rebellious teenager, parental approval can have the opposite effect to that intended. Before and during these pivotal teenage years, parents can engineer an appropriate language environment for the child. Examples of parental language engineering include: wisely chosen secondary schooling, taking children to enjoyable events where the minority language is used and inviting friends who speak the minority language to the house.

The **language self-esteem** of children can be raised by admiring and not just observing their skills in two languages. The occasional gentle word of praise, the smile, the 'pat on the back' for their bilingualism will encourage a favorable attitude towards two languages. A positive attitude to bilingualism is a long-term preserver of bilingualism in a child.

Is it sensible to raise my child in three languages?

In different parts of the world, there are children who learn two or more local languages and learn a national language as well. In parts of India and Scandinavia, Africa and Asia, there are many children who become trilingual and multilingual. In some parts of the globe, **multilingualism** is a fairly usual and natural occurrence. However, such multilingualism tends to be at the oral rather than the literary level.

There is little research on trilingualism and multilingualism in the family to provide clear advice. However, in Canada there has been research on children becoming trilingual in English, French and Hebrew (and in English, French and an indigenous North American Indian language). In mainland Europe, there are many children who become fluent in three languages (e.g. Swedish, Finnish, English; German, French, English). The **Scandinavians** seem particularly experienced and successful in producing trilingual children. Many Scandinavian children learn two languages in school (e.g. English, German) as well as being fluent in their home language. Language learning has relatively high status in Scandinavian countries. In parts of Africa, Asia and India, trilingualism is also relatively frequent and accepted. Multilingualism is possible and valuable.

One documented route to trilingualism is **parents** speaking two different languages to their children at home. The children then take their **education** through a third language. The majority language of the community will influence the relative strength of the three languages. Proficiency in the three languages will change over time. Stable trilingualism is less likely than stable bilingualism. Establishing trilingualism early on is slightly easier than successfully maintaining trilingualism over the teenage years. A school that is positive towards multilingualism and multiculturalism is needed to ensure children's attitude to their language agility is favorable.

One well-researched example is by Suzanne Quay. She researched a child raised (1) in German by the father (and German was used between mother and father) and (2) in English by the mother when addressing the child. Since both parents were fluent in Japanese (which was the language of the local community where their son attended daycare), (3) he also acquired Japanese. There was a change in language exposure over the first two years, for example due to visits abroad and changes in the father's work schedule (see below). Such changes are quite common for early trilinguals.

Age of child	*% English heard*	*% German heard*	*% Japanese heard*
Birth to 11 months	70	30	0
11 months to 1 year (attending daycare)	50	20	30
1 to 1.5 months	43	23	34
1.5 to 1.6	45	10	45

The table shows that this child was less exposed to German than English. At 15 months, the child appeared not to understand much German. Yet after two weeks in Germany at 15 months, the mother reports that he 'shocked us with how much he understood in German when spoken to by the extended family'. This is also a common experience for families: understanding (and speaking) a second or third language quickly grows once there is sufficient exposure and incentive. However, Quay also shows that the child was a developing trilingual rather than an active trilingual. This child preferred to speak Japanese to his parents as he had more vocabulary in Japanese, and his parents understood and accepted his Japanese utterances. He tended to be a **passive trilingual**, understanding English and German, but speaking Japanese.

Another family case study is by Jean-Marc DeWaele, following a girl raised in Dutch by her mother, French by her father, with English acquired in the London neighborhood. The mother and father used Dutch when speaking together, making Dutch the dominant language of the family. English quickly became her 'default language' when meeting new children in London. From five months to two and a half years, Livia learnt Urdu from a child-minder, thus becoming quadralingual at an early age. Awareness of her languages came before her second birthday, for example, in suggesting that the mother duck in her bath was Dutch-speaking. The **value of multilingualism** was also understood at a very early age: 'If she doesn't get the cookie she ordered in one language, she code-switches to the other, just to make sure we understand her request'. However, by five years of age, status and **acceptance** by peers had become important. Her father reports that she 'does not want me to speak French to her at school and addresses me . . . in English, or whispers French in my ear'. She wanted to avoid standing out from her peers.

Some parents of trilingual children find it valuable when one (or both) of the parents is also learning a new language. While this parent may not be a perfect language model for the child in the new language, nevertheless it sends out an important message to the child, that multilingualism is valued greatly in the family. While there is always a danger of such a parent teaching errors to the child and the child modeling incorrect forms, the child will become aware that acquiring a new language is part of valued life-long learning and part of family life.

One proviso about trilingualism is that at least one language needs developing fully. It is important in a child's cognitive development that at least one language develops at age-appropriate levels. For example, children need sufficient language competence to operate in the increasingly abstract nature of the school curriculum. A slight danger is a low level of development in all three languages. This would impede the child's cognitive development and requires extra **vigilance**, extra commitment and thoughtfulness within the family.

References for further reading

Dewaele, J.-M. 2000, Three years old and three first languages. *Bilingual Family Newsletter,* Vol. 17, No. 2, pp. 4–5.

Quay, S. 2001, Managing linguistic boundaries in early trilingual development. In J. Cenoz & F. Genesee (eds), *Trends in Bilingual Acquisition.* Amsterdam/Philadelphia: John Benjamins.

Do bilinguals learn a third language easier than monolinguals learn a second language? **B17**

For a review of existing research on **trilingualism**, it is possible to conclude that bilingualism does not hinder the acquisition of an additional language. Instead, in most cases bilingualism favors the acquisition of a third language. Bilinguals tend to be better at learning a new language than are monolinguals. They tend to progress faster.

The reasons for bilinguals being better language learners than monolinguals, as a generalization, are not yet clear from the research. The thinking advantages of bilinguals, such as having a wider linguistic repertoire, enhanced learning strategies, cognitive flexibility and metalinguistic awareness, may help explain this positive effect of bilingualism.

It may also be about **confidence**. Bilinguals may feel relatively more positive and sure they can acquire a new language as they have learnt and use two languages already. Monolinguals may be relatively less certain that they can take on a new language. This is suggested by Australian research (Clyne *et al.*, 2004) that found trilinguals to be more effective and persistent language learners, whose bilingualism is a language apprenticeship for further language learning.

An expert in this area, Professor Jasone Cenoz, also has the following good news:

> children exposed to three languages do not usually mix languages more than other children. When speaking one language they sometimes borrow words from the other languages they know but this does not mean they are confused about the languages they know, they just use their other languages as a strategy to go on speaking.

References for further reading

Cenoz, J. 2003, Are bilingual better language learners? *The Bilingual Family Newsletter*, Vol. 20, No. 1, pp. 3 & 6.

Clyne, M., Hunt, C.R. & Isaakidis, T. 2004, Learning a community language as a third language. *International Journal of Multilingualism*, Vol. 1, No. 1, pp. 33–52.

 ## Do girls and boys differ in their progress towards bilingualism and biliteracy?

Children differ widely in their rate of progress in acquiring two languages. Girls differ widely among themselves, as do boys. Such **differences** may be related to personality, the quality and quantity of language interaction with parents and other people, contexts, environments and the atmosphere in which language flourishes, and the pressures on, and motivations of the child. However, as a broad generalization with many exceptions, girls tend to show slightly faster bilingual development than boys. This may be partly due to parent expectations which differ for girls and boys. For example, many parents expect girls to become fluent readers earlier than boys. The gender difference may be due to the type of language interaction that occurs between parents and girls and boys, gender stereotypes, and the expectations and behaviors of teachers.

There is no reason to believe that girls are better equipped to become bilinguals than boys. There is no reason why girls should be treated differently from boys (or vice versa) with regard to the childhood development of bilingualism.

The attitudes of the two genders to minority languages, particularly in the **teenage** years, may become a problem. In Wales, for example, there is evidence to show that boys tend to develop less favorable attitudes to the minority language compared with girls. Girls tend to retain their bilingualism and boys veer slightly more to English monolingualism in the teens and twenties. This partly reflects the behavior that gives status and peer approval, as well as mass media influences, and continuing parental and 'heritage culture' influence. There are many exceptions to this gender pattern. Also, teenage trends are not permanent.

Are first-borns different to later-borns in developing bilingualism?

B19

There is research from the 1950s onwards to show that the pattern of relationships between brothers and sisters has an **effect** on child development. Only-children, first-borns and younger siblings tend to show slightly different personality and motivation characteristics, different levels of achievement in school and in later life. How siblings affect the language environment of the home, particularly in bilingual families, is almost an unexplored research territory.

When the second child arrives, the language pattern of the household tends to be relatively well established. With the second birth, decisions about **language interaction** in the home have already been **established**. The language the first-born child speaks to each parent will have been standardized, with the likelihood that younger children will follow a similar pattern.

What is new is the language interaction between older and younger siblings. If the mother is the full-time carer, her language may be replicated in the interaction between siblings (particularly when the children are young, and if she speaks a majority language). For example, if the mother speaks Spanish to her children, the children may speak Spanish to each other. What is novel is that the language balance may change within the home with each new arrival. The **balance** of languages heard and spoken may be different for the younger than the older child. The younger child may learn much language through listening and talking to older children. The older child provides a **language model** for younger siblings and younger children tend to follow the lead of their elder siblings. Older siblings have more power and become influential language models. Thus, younger siblings are sometimes slightly slower in their bilingual language development partly because they are excluded from the more advanced language interaction between mother and older siblings, and partly through copying older siblings. Older siblings also may tend to answer for their younger brothers and sisters!

The language that siblings use with each other tends to remain constant, even over a lifetime. Hence, early established patterns tend to be long-lasting and affect the balance of language experience of the siblings. However, parents cannot easily control the language siblings use with each other, especially after the first few years of life.

What tends to be an advantage for younger siblings is that **parents** have accumulated valuable **experience** in the language life of the home. Parents have acquired craft and competence in raising bilingual children. The anxiety that accompanies the development of the eldest is less. Decisions will have already been made about which languages to use in which circumstances with which people. Alternatively, there is a latently agreed and accepted **pattern of language interaction** within the family (and with 'outsiders') already established by the arrival of second and later children who then fit into a well-established language routine. Thus, there will sometimes be less nervousness and anxiety about the bilingual development of later-born children.

Later-borns sometimes show **different language histories** over time compared with first-borns. As family circumstances change, as patterns of friendship vary, geographical and social and vocational mobility occur, so the varying opportunities for bilingual development may also change over time. For example, first-borns invite friends home who may be majority language speakers. The language of play will switch to the majority language. Younger siblings may thus experience relatively more exposure to the majority language.

Another example is when parents emigrate early in the life of the second-born. The language of the host country may come to play a more dominant place in the life of the later-born than the first-born. In this case, the eldest may become a more active bilingual and the younger children more passive bilinguals (see Glossary). However, the reverse can also occur. Published case histories of bilingual families rarely show exactly parallel bilingual development between siblings. Language variety is found within bilingual families and not just in the wider world.

My child mixes their two languages. Is this normal?

There is probably no child raised as a bilingual from birth who does not mix words from their two (or more) languages. Bilingual adults tends to do this regularly, but almost only when with other bilinguals. For adults, switching or mixing is seen as fully utilizing linguistic resources; for a child it is sometimes seen as linguistic incompetence. That is unfair on the child.*

* See page 57ff

Instead, we need to see suitably switching between two languages as effective child communication. A child is using all the language resources available to convey meaning. These are clever children showing both cognitive competence, linguistic adeptness and social aptitude. If they lack a word in one language, they use the word in the other language, often knowing that the listener understands. For example, they are using their stronger language to help communication in a weaker language. It is not that such children are cognitively confused, talking inappropriately or are unable to separate their two (or more) languages. They are being pragmatic and purposeful in conveying meaning. They may even be copying their parents who mix a little and know it is appropriate when with other bilinguals.

What tends to occur is that the grammar (see Glossary) of one language dominates and directly influences the way words are used in a 'sentence'. Even in very young children, their use of words from 'another language' is rule bound in terms of one grammar. The grammar of one language provides the rules for inclusion of words from another language. By observing which grammar leads, a parent can gain an understanding of the relative dominance between a child's two (or more) languages.

This suggests that instead of using terms like 'interference' (see Glossary) or 'mixing' which can be negative, we use a word such as 'insertion' to imply a positive use of language and thinking abilities.

In some communities, it is acceptable and normal to code-switch. For various Puerto-Rican communities in New York, Spanglish is a symbol of pride in a dual language heritage. Mixing Spanish and English is a badge that they identify with two cultures, two language worlds.

Does switching between languages have any value or purpose? B21

When both or all participants in a conversation understand both languages, switching has a purpose. It's almost as if a third language is introduced. Code-switching may occur in large blocks of speech, between sentences or within sentences.

Some authors have made a distinction between language mixing and code-switching. Language mixing has been used to refer to early bilingual infants who sometimes seem (on the surface) to use either language indiscriminately. Code-switching was then used to refer to bilinguals who had separated their two languages. Many authors now feel that a distinction between mixing and code-switching is not sensible or real.

This discussion relates to another debate about whether a young bilingual child develops two separate linguistic systems, or just one integrated system (the unitary language hypothesis), or no initial system followed by language differentiation. Research does not support the old idea that children initially use their two languages as a single or 'unitary language system'. It is generally agreed now that the languages of the bilingual child develop both autonomously and interdependently, and this is partly a function of transfer between types of language combination (e.g. French-English compared with Mandarin-English). There is also growing research that bilingual children (as young as

Major Uses of Code-switching

(1) **Emphasize** a particular point in a conversation.

(2) If people do not know a word or a phrase in a language, they may **substitute** a word in another language.

(3) **Express more adequately** an idea. In discussing computers, mathematics or science, children may switch from their home language to the language used in school to increase expression and enhance understanding.

(4) **Repeat** a phrase or a command. For example, a mother may repeat a demand (e.g. go to bed. *Dos i'r gwely*) to accent and underline a demand. Repetition may also be used to clarify a point. Some teachers in classrooms explain a concept in one language, and then will explain it again in another language believing that repetition adds reinforcement or depth of understanding.

(5) Communicate **friendship**. For example, moving from the common majority language to the minority language both listener and speaker understand well, may communicate friendship, common identity. The use of the listener's stronger language in part of the conversation may indicate deference, wanting to belong or be accepted.

(6) In **relating a conversation** held previously, the person may report the conversation in the language or languages used. For example, two people may be speaking Spanish together. When one reports a conversation with an English monolingual, that conversation is reported authentically – in English as it occurred.

(7) A way of **interjecting** into a conversation. A person attempting to break into a conversation may use a different language to that occurring. Alternatively, interrupting a conversation may be signaled by changing language.

(8) **Ease tension and inject humor** into a conversation. If in a committee or conversation, discussions are becoming tense, the use of a second language may signal a change in mood.

(9) Indicate **social distance**. For example, when two people meet, they may use the common majority language (e.g. Swahili or English in Kenya). As the conversation unravels, roles, status and tribal identity are revealed, a change to a regional language may indicate that boundaries are being broken down, with expressions of solidarity and growing rapport indicated by the switch.

(10) **Exclude** people from a conversation. One example of this occurred in a London theater. A very tall and wide professor was sitting in front of two ladies who had been talking English. Before the curtain rose, they switched to Welsh and protested to each other that their view was blocked by this large male. The amused professor said nothing. At the end of the play he simply turned round to the two ladies and, in Welsh, expressed his hope that they had enjoyed the play.

(11) To indicate a change of relationship and a **change of attitude**. For example, at the end of the business conversation in a world language, farewells may change to the native language.

two years old) notice two different languages depending on who is talking, where and when. Very early on, young children know which language to speak to whom in what situation.

Monolinguals who hear bilinguals code-switch may believe that it shows a deficit, or a lack of competence in both languages. Bilinguals themselves may be anxious or apologetic about their code-switching and attribute it to sloppy language habits. Few bilinguals keep their two languages completely separate. Few bilinguals speak both their languages with native speaker fluency. One language may influence the other, and sometimes the bilingual's dominant language influences his or her less dominant language. However, code-switching is a valuable and purposeful communication strategy. It does not happen at random. There is usually considerable reason and logic in changing languages.

Children tend to code-switch only when they are talking to people who understand both languages. Also, children soon become aware if code-switching is acceptable or not with different people. That is, bilinguals quickly learn to recognize those social situations and those people with whom they can and cannot code-switch. One parent of trilingual children (English, Italian, Urdu) wrote the following:

> When my children need to speak in only one language . . . they have no trouble speaking it correctly. When they are in the company of friends who speak two languages . . . they mix these two languages only. (Shera Lyn Parpia Khan writing in the *Bilingual Family Newsletter*, 1999, Vol. 16, No. 1, p. 5)

The table on page 58 provides some examples of the major uses of switching between languages. To make a point, stress an argument, report something somebody else said more authentically, highlight warmth of friendship, and sometimes exclude people from a private conversation, code-switching isn't interference or mixing-up languages. It is a third subtle language that bilinguals use to a clever effect.

Familiarity, projected status and the ethos of the context as well as the perceived linguistic skills of the listeners affect the nature and process of code-switching. This suggests that code-switching is not just linguistic; it indicates important social and power relationships.

When will my bilingual child be able to interpret and translate from one language to another? **B22**

Children around the ages of three and four begin to be able (if their two languages are both relatively well developed) to **translate** simple words and sentences from one language to another. Children sometimes do this automatically, much to the amusement, enjoyment and delight of their parents. For example, if one parent is unable to speak a language, the child may quickly advise the parent what has been said in another language. Situations include the doctor's surgery, with sales representatives on the doorstep, at parents' meetings in school, with government officials and in shops.

There is a very **positive side** to children translating and interpreting (see Glossary). It gives children a position of privilege and power. In conveying a message from one person to another, children can add their own slant, take part in a decision, gain praise from a parent, acquire status and self-esteem, be of increased value to the family, even work a message to their own advantage. Children may become close to their parents when they have a 'translator' value. There is reciprocal dependency. The act of being an interpreter is an act of empathy, an act of bridge building. Such an act may lead to increased maturity, sensitivity, shrewdness and self-reliance.

However, translation can become a **burden** for children. Being the middle person between one adult and another often means translating language that is at a higher level than is customary. For example, if the bilingual child or teenager accompanies the mother to a doctor and the mother cannot understand the language of the doctor, translating the medical language may place a strain on the child. A child may be placed under emotional stress by being privy to private information. If there is constant pressure to translate when parents do not understand the language, the pleasure and fun of childhood may partly be lost in providing a language bridge between parents and outside society.

A child is also placed under **pressure** in translating when parents expect that child to perform on the spot, showing off their ease of movement from one language to another. For children, language is something that is natural, ordinary and subconscious. Performing language tricks in two languages seems strange to many children. Translating as a game is artificial, patronizing and embarrassing.

There is thus a thin line between encouraging a child's bilingualism and celebrating their ability in two languages, and their performing language tricks to a captive audience. The **child's self-esteem** and attitude to their languages is all important in such a situation. Ensuring a favorable attitude and a delight in their bilingualism is the guiding principle.

How much will experience of majority language mass media affect the development of bilingualism in my child?

One key question often raised by minority language parents is about the effect of the mass media on their children. The **concerns** are twofold. First, such parents are concerned about the language diet provided by television, video, the Internet, personal computers, radios, CDs and DVDs. Since many children consume large amounts of television, the passive reception of the majority language may affect both skills in the minority language and productive use (speaking and writing) in both the minority and majority language.

Some **minority languages** (and most languages other than English) have tended to respond to a diet of Anglo-American children's television by producing television programs in the minority language or dubbing cartoons and children's films. This is much to be applauded. Also, it is important that the minority language **culture** is spread through the mass media. The danger is that dubbed films and minority language cartoons still contain majority language or particularly Anglo-American culture. The cultural elements in television broadcasts and videos are as important as the language content in conveying the status of a language community to the child.

Parents who want their children to acquire a non-local language will need to obtain as much variety of mass media material as possible for their children. A diet of minority or 'foreign' language mass media input is important, not only to enhance language competence, but also in the implied **prestige** value of the language.

At the same time, we need to be aware that the mass media provides **receptive language** only. Rarely does the child speak a language when watching television or listening to a record. Records, cassettes and compact disks that invite children to join in are more valuable in providing language practice.

As children move through middle childhood, and particularly when they enter their teens, there is often pressure towards mass media in the dominant, majority language. The peer group listens to high-status Anglo-American pop music, films and television programs. The **influential images** in the pre-teen and teens are too rarely from the minority language and too often via the English language. During these years, children's bilingualism may be at risk due to their conformity to peer-group norms which stress majority culture.

The **prestige of a language**, or its negative image, is quickly picked up outside the home. When children join street groups, clubs and teams, at a tender age (e.g. seven years onwards) they perceive the pecking order of languages. This is reinforced and extended by the media. Parents thus need to monitor and sometimes be creative in language arrangements to ensure the language diet is not becoming stale in one language and a feast in the other.

Research shows that children who **maintain their minority language** are the ones who, in their teenage years in particular, participate in out-of-school events in their minority language. Research from Wales suggests that it is not majority language mass media in and by itself that is a threat to the minority language in teenage children. Rather it is movement away from the minority language, to less participation in out-of-school events in the minority language, that causes language decline in teenagers. The culture of the teenager becomes a most important element in the language life of that teenager.

Can music and drama help my child's bilingual development?

For a language to live within the child, there needs to be **active participation** in that language. That language needs to be valuable and useful to that child, enjoyable and pleasurable in a variety of events. Music and drama are just two of a whole variety of activities through which children can enjoy using their language. In such events, language is a means and not only an end in itself. In music and drama, language growth occurs almost unnoticed by the child in an enjoyable way.

For example, imagine young children in a nursery school **dancing** vigorously in an action song, shouting the words while moving enthusiastically around the floor. The child is subconsciously learning the language, connecting words with actions, being exhilarated and educated – all at the same time. Children **singing** nursery rhymes or acting out a folk tale are not only learning language, enjoying the drama and having fun, they are also picking up part of the culture allied to that language. The language is becoming anchored.

When language is learned through activities that are intrinsically motivating to the child (e.g. shopping, cooking, singing, acting, as well as authentic and lively desk work), then language is loved by the child.

In the **teenage** years, it is important that children have stimulating activities – activities that are intrinsically motivating for teenagers – to maintain their languages. This is particularly so in the 'weaker' or minority language. If rock music and parties, laughing and loving is in the minority language, bilingualism may advance in these difficult years. Unless teenagers are given the opportunity to participate in their minority language, all the good work achieved in the home in producing early bilingualism may wither and fade.

Will computers and information technology affect my child's bilingualism?

With the growth of microcomputers, electronic mail and library databases, computers in schools and information communication technology, the majority language (particularly English) has been promoted. Vast amounts of software are only available in the English language. When children access a computer, they are likely to work through the medium of English. It also means that this high status electronic equipment is aligned with the high-status English language. The prestige of English tends to be exalted at the expense of the minority language that seems more old fashioned, more traditional and more historical.

We cannot bury our heads in the sand and imagine that the Internet and personal computers are not going to be an important part of future existence. The information society is going to demand that almost all children gain some knowledge of the value and use of computers in the home, in school, in business and in society. The English language dominance of computers means that parents have to take this into account in working out the **language equation of their family**. It may become even more important that certain activities take place in a language other than English (e.g. attending clubs and societies, living in particular neighborhoods so that the child can regularly practice their weaker language). The bilingual language software that runs a child's thinking system needs a multimedia experience that extends beyond captivating computers and the intriguing Internet.

How important are employment prospects to preserve my child's languages into adulthood?

B26

In the life of a language, **two** very **important factors** are: (1) A language needs to be **reproduced within the family**. Bilingualism exists because of its place in the life of the mother and father, in the community, and the relationship of language with culture and heritage. (2) A language also must have **social and economic utility** for its owner. Language life within the individual and within society is considerably strengthened when that language has economic value. Take the case of a child who speaks a minority language through which they are taught in school. If there are no jobs in that language, its value will be considerably reduced, even undermined. When languages have **utilitarian value** in the employment and promotion market, then language learning and bilingualism will have extra drive and vigor.

Like everyone else, bilinguals need access to the employment market and to affluence. Bilinguals will first and foremost wish to avoid poverty, deprivation and disadvantage. The quality of home, community and cultural language life is partly based on finance. Language and the family economy are not separate.

In present and future employment markets, some bilinguals will have an **advantage** as they can move between markets among different language groups. Bilinguals can act with more flexibility and mobility as bridges and brokers, sales staff and shop sellers. Where a customer interface is needed, bilinguals and multilinguals can be especially valuable. Those who can speak French and English, German and English, German and French, Japanese and French, and lots of other combinations may be well placed in future international jobs markets. The European Union is attempting to give status to the different languages of Europe. This includes full recognition of major international languages such as German, French, Italian, Spanish and English, recognition of indigenous 'first' languages such as Irish, and support for the 'lesser used languages' of Europe such as Luxembourgish, Occitan and Frisian.

What of the plight of those whose one language is a **minority language**? It is important for those to be fluent in a majority language. As Spanish-speaking Americans will testify, access to power and employment usually demands full English fluency. Minority language speakers need to be bilingual to maximize their chances of economic success.

Wherever possible, **employment** in and through the minority language needs to be encouraged for that minority language to survive. For a minority language to be seen to have utility and value in society, there need to be employment prospects which demand and value the minority language. For example, in the county of Gwynedd in North Wales, becoming a teacher, civil servant or local business person, demands fluency in both Welsh and English. In Catalonia, fluency in Spanish and Catalan is often demanded for economic advancement. In the Basque Country, having both Basque and Spanish is helpful in security and status of employment.

For a parent to be persuaded to raise children bilingually, the employment advantages of bilingualism can be most attractive. For teachers, enabling children to be best fitted for an employment market that places a premium on bilinguals gives a strong *raison d'être* for language learning and bilingual teaching.

Helmut Schmidt, former Chancellor of the old Federal Republic of Germany once said: 'If you wish to buy from us, you can talk any language you like, for we shall try to understand you. If you want to sell to us, then you must speak our language'.

Where employment prospects demand or prefer bilinguals, there is a much greater incentive for bilinguals to retain their two languages well into adulthood. For a language to have no economic value, there may be less **incentive** to retain that language during adulthood. Language preservation then depends on social and cultural life.

 ## I need to change the language(s) I've used with my children. How will it affect them?

This question is typically asked when parents, through choice or necessity, **move from one country to another**. Parents will often contemplate using the language of that region inside the home so that the child quickly achieves plenty of experience and practice in that new language. This is particularly likely if parents intend to stay in that new country for a long period.

When a **family lifestyle changes** (e.g. when there is divorce, one parent dies, one or more grandparents join the nuclear family relatively permanently), established language patterns may need to change.

The first debate needs to be about whether it is vital to change languages or not. Will the child's **emotional and personality development** be affected by a sudden change in language? Will a child in a new country, who already feels dislocated and initially isolated, feel further upset by a change in the language of the home? Isn't language stability in the home an important rock on which the child can build new relationships and a new pattern of life?

When a decision is being made, it is important to **discuss the matter with the child** at a level the child can understand. A child deserves and needs an explanation. Wherever possible, the child should become part of the decision-making process.

Children are able to express in their own way their worries and concerns, their preferences and priorities. If the child is vehemently against change, it is probably wise to put off any change or introduce it very slowly. If the child is willing for change to occur, it is still vitally necessary to **monitor** that change, to discuss it with the child and to be extra supportive of the child.

Children tend to manage language change faster than adults. They often have the ability to make new relationships, and adjust quickly to new circumstances in a way that inflexible adults find difficult. Given support and care, children are amazingly resilient. However, it is important at the outset to discuss the needs and problems of the child with his or her carers, teachers and any others who support that child during the day. While total protection is impossible, a **supportive environment** is possible so that temporary psychological problems are minimized.

When children aged two, three and four are involved in this change situation, explanations may be more difficult for a child to understand. Certainly with very young children, a **transition period** will be important. Very young children may not notice this transition where one language is slowly decreased in usage and another language is increased. With loving support, care and sensitivity, such transition may be relatively smooth. A sudden overnight switch may not be understood by the young child and may lead to a sense of rejection, distrust and anxiety.

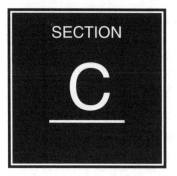

SECTION

C

Questions About Problems

C1 What are the disadvantages of my child becoming bilingual?

There are always worries and anxieties in a child's physical, social, personality and health development. There is no such a thing as a trouble-free child. Therefore, raising children to speak two languages is not going to be trouble free either and there are going to be times when parents will worry about the language development of their children.

Whenever there is a language, educational or social problem, many parents of bilingual children tend to think of bilingualism as a possible cause of the problem. If a child lacks success at school, the parent of the monolingual child may lay the blame with the child's motivation, personality, the standard of teaching or the school itself. The parent of the bilingual child may think of all these causes, but add on the child's bilingualism as another major potential cause.

If a child does have social, motivational, educational or personal problems, don't immediately focus on bilingualism or biculturalism as the first cause. Rarely will this be so. Try to hunt down a variety of possible causes and not just highlight language. Discuss the problems with friends, the child's teacher and the child. All too often, bilingualism is wrongly blamed for whatever problem occurs.

It would be false and misleading to suggest that there are never any disadvantages to bilingualism. **First**, there will be a disadvantage if a child's two languages are both **underdeveloped**. The most crucial definition of under-development is that a child is unable to cope in the curriculum in the school in either language. This very rarely occurs, but it is important to avoid. The more usual situation is that bilingualism gives the child marginal advantages over the monolingual child in the curriculum.*

* See page 161ff

Some children who have been raised as bilingual from birth will not necessarily speak both languages as children or teenagers. Professor Annick De

Houwer, an expert on childhood bilingualism from the University of Antwerp (Belgium) found that one in five children who grew up bilingually from birth do not speak one language. This 20% of children in her 2500 sample understood both languages, but only spoke one. This must be considered success and not failure. The 'passive' language can easily be activated into speaking given the right context and language immersion experiences (e.g. when visiting family on vacations).

A **second** potential problem parents experience is the **amount of effort** often required to raise bilingual children. Parents need to engineer thoughtfully and creatively their child's bilingual development. It is not like scattering a few seeds on the ground and expecting swift, strong and simple growth. The tender language shoots need to be nourished, the garden well fertilized in order for later blossoming to occur. As the seasons of language development change, the parent has constantly to tend the language garden.

Not all agree with this. Some will argue that the 'amount of effort' issue in raising bilingual children is over-management of children in a period of their lives that should be carefree, joyful and creative. Such critics suggest that carefully managing all aspects of a child's life is 'hyper-parenting'. Hyper-parenting means the precise and detailed management of children's lives to maximize their success along parent-defined outcomes. Alongside the fetus listening to music in the womb, swimming from birth, engaging with reading and number before walking, producing bilingual children in elite families is seen by critics as driven by the need for parent accomplishment. This seems hyper-critical. It fails to understand the sheer pleasure that children gain from music, swimming, reading and writing, and not least from being bilingual.

Third, raising children can be emotionally demanding. Teething, infant illnesses, crying, colic, non-eating, poor sleep patterns, 'bad' behavior, unlimited exploration of everywhere when crawling and walking, each and all can make parenthood hard work. Adding bilingualism to the list can, for some families, seem like adding another problem. For example, supporting a child's bilingualism may mean organizing plenty of opportunities to use the weaker language. That takes time and effort.

Another example of the demands of child bilingualism is a potential tension between loving and warm communication between parent and child, and the constant monitoring and even correcting of two languages. At one point the parent is encouraging and kind; at the same moment there is a need to instruct (e.g. reminding the child to speak German and not English). Parents may feel pulled emotionally in different directions, and feel they cannot get it right whatever they do.

An example is sometimes found among language minorities in the United States or United Kingdom. The first language may be, for example, Arabic or

Welsh, and with English as the second language. The parents and child are criticized by some in the community (e.g. English language monolinguals) for the child having imperfect English, *and* criticized by others (e.g. language minority members) for making the child too American or British. The parents are criticized from two opposing perspectives: for not being sufficiently loyal to a heritage culture, religion or identity, and for the child's English language not being sufficiently perfect. The result can be despairing parents.

Occasionally, bilingual child-rearing introduces arguments in a marriage. If the husband does not understand the communication between mother and child, is there a feeling of exclusion? Competing marriage and child-rearing demands on such a mother can be emotionally draining. Such mothers have to balance competing pressures and priorities. Managing the development of two languages is just one aspect of family life. Languages are just one aspect of child-rearing and cannot be easily divorced from other family decisions, pressures and even conflicts. There is also a danger if language(s) are seen as the work of the mother, even to the point of making the mother stay at home.

For some parents, the route children take to full bilingualism is relatively straightforward. For others, there are moments of concern, where challenges seem more like problems. The individual, cognitive, social, cultural, intellectual and economic advantages given to the child via bilingualism make the spadework and effort spent in sowing and cultivating all worthwhile.

A **fourth** problem area tends to be with the **identity** of the child. If the child speaks English and French fluently, are they French, English or Anglo-French? If a child speaks English and a minority language such as Welsh, are they Welsh, English, British, European, Anglo-Welsh or what?

For many parents and children, identity is not a problem. While speaking two languages, they are predominantly identified with one ethnic or cultural group. For example, many German/English bilinguals from Germany may see themselves as German first, possibly European, but not English. Being able to speak the English language is important to them. However, to be considered as 'English' would be an insult.

At the other end of the spectrum is the **in-migrant**. Sometimes, the first or second generation in-migrant desperately wants to identify with majority language people and culture. They may actively want to lose the identity of their home or heritage language (see Glossary). For example, in the United States, Spanish speakers from Mexico or Cuba or Puerto Rico, may want to assimilate and become monolingual English-speaking North Americans.

* See page 78

Between the two opposites presented above, there are potential cases of **identity crisis and conflict**.* There are some bilinguals who feel both English and French, Spanish and Basque, Mexican and North American. There are some people who feel quite happy being culturally hyphenated (e.g. Anglo-German, Chinese-Canadians, Italian-Americans). There will be others who feel uncomfortable moving between two identities. Bilinguals may ask: Am I Asian or am I British or am I Asian-British? Am I Swedish, am I Finnish or am I Swedish-Finnish? Am I Chinese from China, like the Chinese scattered throughout the world, or a Canadian? Am I Italian, North American or some integrated or uneasy **combination** of these?

Such identity conflicts are not inevitably the result of owning two languages. However, languages are clearly a contributor. Languages provide the potentiality of mingling in two or more cultures, of thinking and acting in two different ethnic groups, of identifying with each group or neither group. Language is a vehicle through which an **identity tension** may arise. It is important to be honest and not to suggest that everything in the garden is perfect. Self-identity, cultural identity and ethnic identity (see Glossary) can be a problem for some bilinguals.*

* See page 78ff

Fifth, a family does not live separately from the rest of the world. There are relatives, social friends, work colleagues, communities, societies and nations that all influence family lives. We are not autonomous individuals who make decisions about languages in the family in a vacuum. Others have a powerful influence on us. Such 'others' may be, for example, the extended family, religion, mass media and dominant language politics in a region. Even when parents feel it would be valuable to raise their children bilingually, the force of opinion outside the family (socially, economically, politically) may make that decision too nonconforming.

In conclusion, a danger can be having too high expectations of success. There is an **idealized** scenario that is sometimes impossible to achieve: both parents being fluently bilingual and with highly positive attitudes to bilingualism; friends, family and others are encouraging and have positive experiences themselves; the children richly experience both languages in the home, school and community; children becoming proficient in both languages for life and using each for varying purposes; parents celebrating bilingualism and their children feeling it to be a wonderful personal advantage.

Realities are rarely this simple. More usual is a scenario that includes some of the following: one parent is not fluent in a family language; both parents having worries about eventual success in producing bilingual children; one parent has more concerns than the other and sometimes feels marginalized in conversation; one parent feels the burden of raising bilinguals is placed on them and it is emotionally draining; those outside the home being critical; language experience across the two languages being imbalanced and changing across time; children having one stronger and one weaker language; children changing their attitudes to, and use of their two languages; periods of refusal by the child to speak a language; the future of languages across the lifetime not being predictable.

My child mixes the two languages. What should I do?

Consider yourself a **very typical** family. There are probably only a few bilingual families where the child does not mix the two languages, at the very least in the early stages. Moving between two languages is very normal in bilingual children and adults.

Language mixing is given other labels:

> **transference** (transfer between two languages);
> **code-mixing;**
> **code-switching***; and
> **interference** (see Glossary) between languages. This is now regarded as a disparaging and injurious term that is inaccurate in its view of how bilinguals use their languages.

Many people are concerned about the purity of a language – language standardization. Listening to a person mixing two languages is anathema to the purist. While the purity of a language is an important issue, from the child's point of view, any language mixing helps the message to be communicated and understood. While hybrid languages (e.g. constantly mixing Spanish and English) may be temporary (e.g. in early childhood), they can also occasionally be relatively stable and shared by a large group (e.g. the mixing of Spanish and English in certain parts of New York).

Mixing is **typical** and to be expected in the **early stages** of bilingual development. However, some parents do not like to hear children mixing two languages. Others are more tolerant, because in the company of other bilinguals, they switch languages themselves.

Parents can help in the process of language separation by various dos and don'ts. The most important is to avoid criticizing, or constantly pointing out

---

Whether or not a young bilingual mixes two languages may be affected by differing factors such as:

- the amount of separation a child experiences in listening to the two languages (different people and in different contexts);
- the balance of the two languages in the child's home and community life;
- the quantity of language experience in both languages;
- the quality of language experience;
- parents acceptance (or not) of mixing the two languages; and the experience of mixing in the community.

mistakes, revealing anxiety and concern. This is unlikely to have a positive effect on a child's language development. On the contrary, it is more likely to make the child inhibited in language, anxious about their bilingualism and may slow down language development. A constant focus on language correctness and form is unnatural for the child, who is more interested in facts and ideas, stories and activities. For the child, **language is a means to an end**, not an end in itself. Language is a vehicle to help move along the road of information exchange and social communication.

Parents can also ensure that **language boundaries** are mostly kept. A parent who speaks one sentence in French to a child, the next sentence in English, may latently be teaching the child that languages can be mixed. However, children tend to learn quickly with whom they can code-switch, and with whom they should use one language almost solely.

One form of language separation is the **one parent–one language strategy**. Each parent speaks a different language to the child **(see Section A7, p. 13)**. An alternative is if both parents only use one particular language, with the other language used in different contexts (e.g. in the school, for religion, in the mass media, in the community). When language is separated along divisions of different people, different contexts, even different times of the week or day, a child is learning that language compartmentalization exists. Mixing may still occur early on, but boundaries enable a smooth transition to a stage where children keep their languages relatively separate.

The good news for parents is that almost every bilingual children in every country acquires the language behavior and language norms of their community. Children soon mirror others use of two languages in their family and environment. Children learn the accepted and socially appropriate ways of speaking each language, including code-switching (see Glossary). Children become socialized into the patterns of speaking that they hear others use. That includes both separating two (or more) languages and using both when this is acceptable.

My child refuses to use one of his/her languages. What should I do?

For most bilinguals, there is language shift (see Glossary) and change. Languages do not stay static and equal. In the teens, there is often movement towards a prestigious majority language. Having worked so long and so hard to produce bilingual children and gained a measure of success, parents may find it hard to accept that their child prefers one language rather than another. A child may refuse to speak one language in the home, preferring to operate in the higher status language used in the peer group. This is quite customary among language minorities.

Even young children refuse to speak one language. Sometimes this is because they have a stronger language and are able to express themselves better in that language. If one language is relatively underdeveloped, then a child is just being pragmatic. For example, if a child has a lack of practice in one language, then they are using the currently more proficient language. Occasionally, the child is also signaling something about relationships. There are occasions when one language is associated with a much adored person (e.g. the mother), such that the child tends to stick to that language.

But there is usually no reason to stop surrounding the child with two or more languages. Just by hearing one language on a regular basis, even if the child is not speaking that language, understanding that language is being developed. That is, the child is still storing that language, and thus it can be activated in the future, given, for example a change of circumstances. Passive bilingualism (see Glossary) can easily change into active bilingualism.

In giving talks to different groups of parents, during the question and answer session, this is a regular concern. A child understanding but not speaking one of their two languages seems a more regular occurrence than case studies have recognized. Even the most loving parents may become tearful when their child does not respond in one of the parents' languages. The worst choice is to abandon one language. That does the child no short- or long-term favors at all. At its worst, it abandons the chance of bilingualism in the future. The best choice is for the parent to continue to use his or her preferred language, even if the child does not respond in that language. The child is still becoming bilingual, or at least very ready to be actively bilingual.

Often within the same question and answer session, there will be parents who will tell a story of how their passive bilingual went, for example, abroad to stay with the extended family or friends. Within as little as two to four days, they were using that second language (see Glossary) with ease. The child has stored all the vocabulary, sentence structuring and pronunciation in that language. All that was needed was a trigger to activate that potential.

However, not speaking one of the two languages is not necessarily only about lack of practice. There can be personality, motivation and attitude dimensions to this. The locally felt status and prestige of a language plays a major part in acceptance or rejection of a language. Young children quickly pick up the pecking order of languages in the family and the community. Even a young child may decide not to use a language because they recognize it has negative associations. In the school playground, young children can be disparaging about minority or immigrant languages. When one language is associated with relative material poverty, particular ethnicity or religion, then there are occasions when young children reproduce the prejudice, fear and stereotyping of dominant adults and media messages.

Sometimes, rejection is short-lived. Just as adolescents go through fads and fashions with clothes, eating habits, sleep, so there are language fashions. Language change may be temporary, reflecting peer-group culture, a symbol of growing emotional and social independence from parents and family life, growing self-assertiveness and the need for a distinct, independent self-identity from the family. Children often don't want to appear different. They want to conform to the status-giving behavior of the peer group. This may entail a temporary non-use of one of their languages. **Teenagers** also feel sensitive towards those who are excluded from conversations. When non-speakers of a language are present, they want to include them in all conversations.

 ## My teenage child is speaking the majority language more and more. What can I do?

During the **teenage years**, language influence is much less in the power of parents, and much more in the hands of the teenagers and the influence of the peer group and the mass media. During this period, conformity to the norms of the parents usually begins to change. If teenagers are to maintain both of their languages, it has to come from conviction rather than conformity. If pressure is placed on them by their parents to speak a language, the danger is that the child will react with hostility (in the long or the short term). When they begin to assert their language preference, parents can only act as **gentle persuaders**. They can encourage, offer opportunities and possibilities, but rarely decide, direct or drive the language life of the teenager.

What happens to bilingualism during adolescence, even if problematic, may not be long term. When teenagers reject one language, sometimes they come back to it later in life. As opportunities for travel, employment and new relationships develop, and sometimes a desire to find out about the history and roots of the family, so there may be changes in language tendencies. What was regarded during the teens as a language millstone round the neck, in later years may be seen as a lifebuoy that provides new opportunities. Those who temporarily abandoned one language as a teenager may pick it up again later.

To increase the chances of reversing the rejection of one language, parents can talk to the teenager in that language. The teenager may insist on responding in a different language, but at least 'passive' or 'receptive' bilingualism will be maintained by the child **consistently hearing** the other language. It makes it easier for them to speak that language again, later in life.

The following quote from someone who expressed some misgivings about bilingualism and biculturalism (see Glossary) during the teenage years is not untypical. In retrospect, the pleasure of being a bilingual shone through the cloud of teenage doubt.

I lift my hat every day to my parents for bringing me up bilingually. It is the greatest gift they have ever given me, and I lift off my hat to all other parents who have done, are doing, or thinking about doing the same. Bilinguals, don't worry if people think you are a bit different. Be proud of it. It may not always seem so but I suppose we are kind of special! (*Bilingual Family Newsletter* (1997), Vol. 14, No. 2, p. 6)

In times of language despair, parents need to have faith, hope and love. All parents can do is to **provide the conditions** in which an individual makes up their own mind about the future of their language existence. The gardener can prepare the ground, sow the seeds, provide an optimal environment for language growth. The parent cannot force the growth, change the color of the language flower or have control over its final blossoming.

The balance of my child's two languages seems to be shifting. How can I ensure one language doesn't disappear?

It is often the case that the strengths of a person's two languages tend to **vary** across time. As there is more or less exposure to one language, as different people such as brothers and sisters enter the family situation, as schooling starts and peer-group relationships grow, so does the language dominance (see Glossary) and preference of children for one of their two languages. A child may find it easier to speak English in some circumstances, Spanish in others and this may vary as practice and experience change.

Sometimes the shift will be large. A child may **stop speaking** one of their languages while still being able to understand that language. The teenage years sometimes witness such a change, although this is common as young as three and four years of age. Some children move towards speaking the majority language or their dominant language more and more, their minority language or less dominant language less and less. This is a naturally worrying event for many parents.

It is often impossible and unwise to compel a child to speak a language. Sometimes, bilingual parents try to achieve conformity without conviction. For example, a parent may say to their children that they do not understand them speaking the majority language. Unless this is handled tactfully and skillfully, the result is that children learn that language is an imposition, a part of authoritarian power. It is unwise to control dogmatically children's language preference. This is not to say that one shouldn't try to **influence** it tactfully and more latently. Manipulation rather than domination tends to achieve more in the long term.

When children are younger, one possible solution is to **extend the range of language experiences** in their less preferred language, for example, staying with grandparents or cousins, visits to enjoyable cultural festivals, a renewal in the language materials and other language stimuli in the home for that weaker language (e.g. videos, pop records, the visits of cousins). If both parents read to, or listen to the child reading before bedtime, or if the language of family conversation at the meal table is manipulated to advantage, then subtly the language balance of the home may be readjusted.

There need to be principles followed by pragmatism. If there is an underlying **principle**, it is to attempt the impossible task of providing a relatively balanced language diet for the child, considering all the different contexts, people and occasions where the two languages are used. If the minority language is being used decreasingly, it may demand decisions about increasing the contexts and occasions where the minority language is spoken. If the child's second language does not seem to be progressing, then decisions need to be made about how best to stimulate further development in that language. **Pragmatism** is also necessary to avoid language life in the home developing rigid rules. There are always occasions when communication needs, friendships and fun make exceptions justifiable.

There are times in a bilingual's life history that allow little intervention from parents. When **teenagers** reject a language, negative reactions by parents will often only harm future bilingual prospects and undermine the good that has already been achieved. Just as in teaching children and teenagers manners and morals, values and beliefs, parents have to let go the reins slowly and trust in an ultimate goodness embedded in their child, so with bilinguals. There comes a point in the teenage years when parents can have little influence on language usage and dependent children must grow into independent adults.*

* See page 73

Should the teenager reject one language the parent has still provided sufficient growth for passive bilingualism (see Glossary) to change into active bilingualism later. It is surprising how some reluctant teenagers return later in life to bilingualism. In their 20s, 30s and 40s, a person who has not actively spoken or read a language for 10 or 20 years will still find it relatively easy to **relearn** and become an active bilingual again. The long-term benefits in speaking two languages are not easily visible to teenagers. During early and middle adulthood, the value of two languages and two language cultures can be reawoken. Therefore, a positive message is possible even in the most negative situation. There are long-term possibilities dormant in short-term failure.

The parent has been successful in providing the conditions for later growth. Not all flowers bloom early. Some flowers that bloom late in the summer, even in the autumn, retain all the beauty promised in the sowing of the seed.

Will my child learn two languages only half as well as a monolingual child?

C6

The answer to this question is a definite 'no'. There is no known limit to a child's language learning capacity. It is not the case that the monolingual has one well-filled language balloon and the bilingual two half-filled language balloons.*

* See page 39

The child has enough capacity in the brain for learning two or more languages. Some two-thirds of people in the world are bilingual and these show that bilingualism and trilingualism are perfectly possible.

It is usual that the bilingual child will not have as large a **vocabulary** in each language as the monolingual child. Generally, a child's total combined vocabulary in two languages will far exceed the monolingual's in one language. Bilingual children usually have enough vocabulary to express themselves easily and fluently in either language. They also tend to have sufficient proficiency within specific contexts to operate successfully. There may be occasional periods when the bilingual child seems a little behind the monolingual in learning a language. However, this **lag** is usually temporary. With sufficient exposure and practice, the bilingual child will go through the same language development stages as the monolingual child. Occasionally, the speed of the journey may be slightly slower, but the route through the developmental stages is the same.

Will my child's thinking be affected by being bilingual?

The answer is yes, and probably for the better. The presence of two languages in the operating system of the brain is likely to produce a more richly fed thinking engine. There are various reasons for this. **First**, a bilingual child is less centered on the sound and form of a word. The bilingual tends to be more aware of the arbitrary nature of language. For example, the concept of the moon is not the same as the word 'moon'. Having two languages or more seems to **free** the child from constraints of a single language, enabling the child to see that ideas, concepts, meanings and thoughts are separate from language itself.

Second, a bilingual child can look at an issue or a problem through either language. The different associations of vocabulary in either language, the variety of meanings may give the child an extra **breadth** of understanding. Take a simple example of a child who has two different words for 'folk dancing'. The associations about 'folk dancing' are different in Swahili, Swedish, Scots Gaelic or Spanish. This wider set of associations provides the bilingual or multilingual child with a broader vision and a more comprehensive understanding.

Third, a bilingual child may be more sensitive in communication. Since bilinguals have to know when to speak which language, have to separate out languages, constantly monitoring which language to use with which person in which situation, they appear to be more sensitive to the needs of listeners than monolinguals. Being slightly more conscious about language may make the bilingual more interested in efficient and **empathic** communication. If the bilingual is slightly more aware of what is going on beneath, above and inside language, the bilingual may be more in harmony with the needs of the listener in conveying meaning sympathetically.

Fourth, there is evidence to suggest that bilinguals are relatively more **creative**

and more imaginative in their thinking. Having two or more words for each object and idea tends to mean that many bilinguals are more flexible and fluent in their thinking, more divergent thinkers. Bilinguals appear more able to move outside the boundaries of words and establish a wider variety of connections and meanings. The proviso is that a bilingual's languages are both relatively well developed.

Fifth, research evidence from Canadian, Basque, Catalan and Welsh bilingual education reveals that many children who can operate in two languages in the curriculum tend to show superior **performance**. This is probably partly related to the thinking advantages of bilingualism mentioned above.

Negative thinking effects will only arise in a small minority of cases when a child's two languages are both underdeveloped. When a child cannot cope in the **curriculum** in either language, a child's thinking may be disadvantaged. When a child has one language that is well developed and the other language that is less well developed, it is likely that the child will show no difference in thinking or educational achievement from the monolingual child.*

* See page 44f

The good news for bilingual parents is that when two languages are well developed, there are **advantages** rather than disadvantages in thinking. This is the figurative New Testament and not the Old Testament that highlighted problems of bilingualism. The Old Testament idea of the Tower of Babel, of confusion of tongues, is replaced by the New Testament idea that speaking in tongues is a gift. The new testament of bilingual research is that bilingualism has thinking advantages for children and does not produce mental confusion.

Does bilingualism have an effect on the functioning of the brain?

C8

A variety of studies have examined the brains of bilinguals. We know from recent research, for example, that a bilingual's two languages are always active. Even when speaking one language continuously, the other language is instantly available.

A frequently asked question is whether a bilingual's brain functions differently compared with a monolingual's brain? How is language organized and processed in the brain of a bilingual compared with a monolingual? Research is at an early stage and recent reviews show that **few conclusions** are warranted. For example, in one study, a man was regressed by hypnosis to the age of seven. Under hypnosis, the man spoke fluent Japanese. When he returned to his adult self, he could not speak Japanese. This indicated that a language learned early, but not maintained, is dormant in the brain. However, other studies have not replicated this finding. Therefore, no conclusion is currently possible.*

* See page 33f

In most right-handed adults, the left hemisphere of the brain is dominant for language processing. Some authors have suggested that bilinguals may use the right hemisphere more than monolinguals for first and second language processing. The idea is that the second language of a bilingual will use the right hemisphere of the brain for language processing more than the first language. However, as proficiency in the second language grows, right hemisphere involvement might decrease and left hemisphere involvement increase. This assumes that the right hemisphere is concerned with more immediate, pragmatic and emotional aspects of language. In contrast, the core aspects of language processing are assumed to reside more in the left hemisphere.

However, recent reviews tend to suggest that monolinguals and bilinguals are little different from each other in use of the right and left hemispheres of the brain. The left hemisphere tends to dominate strongly language processing for both monolinguals and bilinguals. Differences between monolinguals and bilinguals appear to be the exception rather than the rule.

There is currently no strong evidence that bilingualism has negative effects on the everyday functioning of the brain. In terms of efficient and effective use of the brain, storage in the brain and processing in the brain, bilinguals do not seem particularly different from monolinguals.

Will my bilingual children have a problem of identity with two different cultures?

At one end of an 'identity adjustment' dimension are children who learn to switch between two cultures as easily as they switch between two languages. They are Spanish in Spain and English in England; a Hebrew-speaking Jew in Israel, a Yiddish-speaking Jew in the home in New York and an English-speaking American at school. For some, there are few problems of cultural mixing or identity. Theirs is **biculturalism** (see Glossary) fully flowered, easily exhibited and much admired by all who view. They are not a hyphenated person (e.g. Irish-Canadian) but are fully Irish and Canadian.

Then there are those who celebrate being 'hyphenated'; a blend of two or more national identities, for example, the Anglo-French, Swedish-Finn, Chinese-American bilingual. This hyphenated variety is neither purely French nor English, nor solely Finnish or Swedish, neither Chinese nor purely Canadian. The bilingual, bicultural child has a broadened repertoire of custom and culture that allows high self-esteem, a positive self-concept, and a potential for choosing for oneself which cultures to accent in the future.

Close to this are those whose identity is securely rooted within their **language culture**. Welsh speakers, for example, primarily belong to their language minority (see Glossary) and belong to a larger group (e.g. British or European) sometimes with reluctance, sometimes marginally. Welsh speakers often regard themselves as Welsh first and foremost, English definitely not, British possibly and European increasingly. For such people there is little identity crisis as there are strong roots in a minority language culture.

At the other end of the 'identity adjustment' dimension are those who experience rootlessness or **dislocation** between two cultures. For example, with older in-migrants, there is sometimes a passive reaction, **isolation**, numbness and loss of a rooted identity. In younger in-migrants, there can be an aggressive reaction, having lost the identity of home and heritage, and finding it difficult to penetrate the thick walls to enter the new host culture. For some in-migrants, there may be a sense of rootlessness, confusion of identity, feeling neither one ethnic identity (see Glossary) nor the other. This can lead to hopelessness, an ambiguity of cultural existence, or feeling lost in a cultural wilderness.

If there are anxieties and struggles, bilingualism is unlikely to be the cause. It is not language *per se* that causes an **identity crisis**. Rather, it is typically the social, economic and political conditions surrounding the development of bilingualism. Such conditions tend to be economic (e.g. material poverty), political oppression, racism, social exclusion, discrimination, hostility and powerlessness.

Identity concerns are present in young children and teenagers. Ethnic identity, for example, begins around three to five years of age. By the age of seven or eight, it is well established and continues to develop. In the teenage years, ethnic differences may become increasingly conscious and considered. Overt and covert racial discrimination, racial abuse and harassment, color, religion, dress and dietary differences surface to increasingly focus ethnic awareness, identity and inequity. Bilingualism is not the cause of the discrimination.

Typically, identity is not static but **ever changing**. For example, immigrants often produce vibrant, pragmatic, new ethnic identities and are not easily classified into existing cultural, ethnic or linguistic groups. Young people growing up in multilingual urban settings (e.g. Utrecht, London, New York) are too simplistically considered as Turkish-Dutch, Somali-British or Cuban-American. They may be seen by others as Dutch, British or American, but the self perception of identity may be of a new, dynamic, multiple, overlapping and situationally changing nature. New varieties of English are heard in multilingual communities in England, especially in the multiple identities found in youth culture. These differ from their family identities, and allow membership of different networks, plus shared (not divided) loyalties.

Language identity among those who move between countries to live is ever changing. In Europe, ethnic and linguistic identity is dynamic as mass immigration, technology (e.g. air travel, satellite, Internet), religion, post-colonialism, mythologizing the past, ongoing enlargement of the European Union, feminism, intercultural marriage are some of the interacting modern trends that create **ever-changing, hybrid language identities**. This is found in the use of English in Europe. In Germany, Germans want to sound like Germans when they speak English, not like North Americans or the British.

It is natural for a child or adult to have **different identities in different contexts** which change across time. Identities are about becoming rather than being. It is not only 'who we are' or 'where we have come from' but also 'how we are represented' and 'what we might become' and 'what we cannot be'. Cultural, ethnic or language identity is often about making sense out of our past, present and future.

We are like actors and actresses on a stage. As the script changes so does the role we play. Fathers and mothers take on different identities in different situations with different people. There are the varied and different identities displayed at home, at work, in the church or mosque, in the cafe or bar, as a parent and when acting in a public capacity.

As we move in and out of **different roles**, we naturally have different identities. The child assumes different identities (and role-playing behavior) in school with teachers, in the playground with friends, in the street in the evening and at weekends, in church or the mosque, being Granny's little girl or little boy, being the sophisticated socialite at parties or the dazzling dancer at discos. With different people and in different situations, the child, particularly the teenager, learns to play different roles, wear different 'costumes' and harmonize with a different set of players. It is important that such roles and resultant **sub-identities** integrate into a satisfactory harmonized whole. We need coherence and wholeness around those sub-identities. From this consideration, something important can be said about bilingualism and self-identity.

This discussion of sub-identities and playing different roles suggests two things. First, that a child needs experience of, and exposure to playing different roles successfully. Acting on a new stage with different people with unusual props is difficult for any of us. Harmonization in the multiple roles we play is helped when there is plentiful experience of new scenery, changing actors and actresses and a different play. Therefore, a child needs plenty of exposure and **experience of the cultures that go with their languages**.

Second, if the language culture is to be retained within the child, **continuous participation through that language** is desirable. Otherwise, in the teenage years in particular, there may be a break away from that language and culture. Exposure to a strong majority language culture is usually automatic and almost takes care of itself. Cinema and television, newspapers and magazines, sports and shops, the World Wide Web and pop music all contain powerful, pervading influences that ensure majority language and culture are experienced.

 ### Will my identity change if I raise children to be bilingual and bi(multi)cultural?

Our individual identity is **not fixed**. It changes with life experiences and through daily negotiation of meanings and understandings. So expect your identity to retain much of the past but always be changing. Such changes are often caused by marriage, child-rearing, new networks of friends and not least changing language experiences.

We speak a language or languages, and they often identify our origins, history, membership and culture. But that identity is daily reauthored, reimagined, reconstructed and displayed. Language is a symbol of our identity, conveying our preferred distinctiveness and allegiance (e.g. Irish). However, language does not by itself define us. It is one feature or marker amongst many that makes up our constructed and shifting identity.

We do not so much own an identity as changing **multiple identities**. Our languages are just one aspect of our identities. Our views of our gender, age, ethnicity, race, dress, nationality, region (e.g. county, state), locality, group membership (e.g. religion, politics), socio-economic class, for example, provide us with a host of complementary, diverse, interacting, ever-changing, negotiated identities. A parent may speak English and Spanish, be a Moslem, Democrat, see herself as American, San Francisco Californian and Mexican, with identify as a teacher and trombonist. As our situations change (e.g. expanding the family, travel, moving country), so our identities are reframed, developed, sometimes challenged, sometimes in conflict. Therefore, raising bilingual children is likely to be just one effect among many on your identity.

In this century, ethnic and linguistic identity is dynamic as mass immigration, technology (e.g. air travel, satellite, Internet), religion, post-colonialism, feminism, and intercultural marriage are some of the interacting modern trends that create ever-changing, hybrid language identities. Yet politicians and members of the public sometimes portray bilingualism as being caught in-between two languages, with a resulting **conflict of identity**, social disorientation, even isolation and split personality. An old Irish poem talks of the struggle to express Irish identity in the language of the English oppressor: Who ever heard / Such a sight unsung / As a severed head / With a grafted tongue.

However, if you experience anxieties and struggles, bilingualism is unlikely to be the cause. It is not language that causes an identity crisis; rather, it is often the social, family, economic and political conditions surrounding the development of bilingualism. Such conditions tend to be economic (e.g. material poverty or the need for wealth), political oppression or distrust, religion or racism, social exclusion, discrimination, hostility and powerlessness. Languages tend to be bridge-builders rather than dividers.

What will happen to our identity if we move to live in another country?

When moving to another country, there is often a process of **reconstruction of identity**, particularly in children. After initial worries about adaptation and acclimatization (including worrying about losing the old identity), often comes a period of recovery and transformation that goes through stages of: emulation of others' voices, emergence of a new identity, reconstructing the past to merge with the present, and continuous growth into new understandings and identities.

Reactions among those who move countries include (sometimes in approximately this order):

- a brief honeymoon period when there is great **optimism**, pleasure in new surroundings and much hope for the future;
- a period of **confusion, frustration and strain**, when previous friends, familiarity and roles have been lost, expectations are lowered, dreams become changed with realities, and even barriers to full integration become apparent. New roles and behaviors are being shaped;
- a period of **fear, even rejection**, when there is concern that wrong decisions may have been made (internalized anger) or other people are preventing access to integration, friendships and success (externalized anger). Followed occasionally (for a few) by
- a period of **isolation**, when pessimism is dominant. Or
- wanting to identify with a new language and culture. A person may even suppress the home language, concentrating on being a citizen of the new country. Or
- **adaptation and integration** which means retaining all that is best from the past and adding on all that is good in the new way of life. Or
- **conforming without conviction** to allegiance to a new country and culture.

Adjustment among those who move to live in a new country thus takes many different forms: happy integration, uncomfortable assimilation (see Glossary), isolation, rejection and anomie (see Glossary). Bilingualism is greatly affected by the outcomes of adjustment. For the increasing numbers of people that move between countries with their employment, then adaptation is relatively fast and successful, partly due to optimism, prestige and a strong awareness that bilingualism and multilingualism are increasingly badges of success and help in acclimatization and adjustment.

There is the dual task in such adjustment. There is the need to retain a **continuity of cultural experience** with the past. For the family recently settled in a country, dislocation from the home and the previous culture for some children may mean an initial identity tension.

At the same time, a **gradual transition** needs making into the host culture. For example, to be successful in school or work, the family often needs to learn the lines of a new play, and become comfortable with a new script, different people, props and scenery. This is not always easy. Sometimes, the host actors and actresses do not want to let newcomers join their drama. As much as the newcomers may want to integrate, they may be barred from entry into privileged circles.

In the situation described above, **conflicts of identity** can arise. Wearing different dress, speaking a different tongue, having a different ethnic identity and religion, may make the establishment of a new identity (or adding onto the existing repertoire) a difficult drama. There are no rehearsals; only a stage with a potentially sceptical audience.

To help, parents may wish to look for opportunities for their children to **integrate** into the host culture while retaining the old culture. If there are particular playgroups, weekend or evening activities, churches and mosques where harmonization can occur without sacrificing the home language and culture, a child may be encouraged to adapt their identities. The **school** can play an important role in helping resolution of this paradox: retaining the child's home language, identity and culture, while allowing that child entry into the host language and culture. The school has the task of ensuring that there is addition and not subtraction. An effective school has the responsibility of developing a harmonic integration of identities within the child and not a division of identities that makes a child feel lost or in despair.

The identity of a bilingual is a particularly Western issue. In many African, and Asian language communities for example, bilingualism (or multilingualism) is accepted as the norm. The oddity in that region is the person who is monolingual and monocultural, who cannot switch between different cultures and language communities. In many countries, linguistic diversity within society and within an individual is accepted as natural, normal and desirable. The good news is that the Western world is catching up such that operating in multiple languages, and fostering more complex identities, is becoming more accepted and even attractive.

Reference for further reading

Carder, M. 2007, *Bilingualism in International Schools*. Clevedon: Multilingual Matters.

Will bilingualism have any adverse effect on my child's personality?

C12

A variety of research in the past has tried to locate **personality differences** between bilinguals and monolinguals. Overall, research has not found particular differences. Bilinguals and monolinguals do not generally differ in their degree of extroversion, introversion, anxiety, self-confidence, self-esteem, shyness, sociability, need for power, need for achievement, conscientiousness or cheerfulness.

Where personality differences between bilinguals and monolinguals do exist, they will be due to factors other than language. For example, where bilinguals are in-migrants and are suffering hostility and racial discrimination, it is not language but prejudice and hostility surrounding in-migrancy that are likely to be a major cause.

While bilingualism and biculturalism may superficially appear to have a detrimental effect on **personality**, bilingualism is not likely to be the cause. That is, it is not language that causes personality problems. Rather, it is often the social, economic and political conditions surrounding bilinguals that generates such problems. Where the bicultural community is stigmatized, seen as socially inferior, economically underprivileged, and where there is symbolic or physical violence towards the minority language community, personality problems within children may arise. It is not the ownership of bilingualism, but the condition in which that language community lives that may be the cause of the problem. Where language communities are oppressed and downtrodden, it is the prejudice and discrimination by other communities, and not bilingualism, that may affect identity and personality.

At the other end of the spectrum, where bilinguals appear more confident or accepted, this is not usually due to their dual language advantage. Rather such bilinguals may come from elite groups (e.g. from geographically mobile middle-class parents) or homes with successful child-rearing practices. **Bilingualism**, in and by itself, does **not** seem **a major cause of different personality characteristics**.

What does affect a child's personality is expressed in the wonderfully wise words of Dorothy Nolte:

If children live with criticism, they learn to condemn.

If children live with hostility, they learn to fight.

If children live with ridicule, they learn to be shy.

If children live with shame, they learn to feel guilty.

If children live with tolerance, they learn to be patient.

If children live with encouragement, they learn confidence.

If children live with praise, they learn to appreciate.

If children live with fairness, they learn justice.

If children live with security, they learn to have faith.

If children live with approval, they learn to like themselves.

If children live with acceptance and friendship, they learn to find love in the world

---

Will bilingualism have any adverse effect on my child's friendships and social development?

Overall, bilingualism is likely to be an **advantage** in social relationships. Children will be able to increase the variety of their friendships and make bridges with children from different language groups. One joy of bilingual parents is seeing their child interact with different children from different language groups, using either language to form friendships.

When visiting grandparents, uncles and aunts and cousins in a different country, one of the joys of bilingual children is to see them **communicate** so **easily**. They are at home in foreign parts. Having traveled a long distance physically, there is no distance to be traveled in language.

Bilingualism helps dismantle social barriers, enables more fluent growth of friendships with children from two or more language communities, widening the child's social, cultural and educational horizons.

The type of problem that sometimes arises is when a minority language child is confronted by majority language children. If that child's majority language skills are still developing, other children may deride the child's language skills and show **hostility** to the child.

That a child is not fluent in one language does not seem a problem in very young children's friendship formation. Through body language such as plenty of pointing and gesticulating, young children rarely seem conscious of language barriers. As children enter middle childhood and the teenage years, rivalries and competition sometimes prejudice, and peer group conformity contrive, to make language a barrier. This is an argument for early bilingual development.

When language becomes a barrier to friendship, or when **prejudice** arises due to language communication problems, the parent and teacher need to strike a very delicate balance between protection, and facilitating transition into a new friendship group, while maintaining a child's dignity and self-esteem. Over-protection of the child, and overexposure to negative experiences are both to be avoided by the child, the parent and the teacher.

There is an increasing responsibility for educationalists, teachers as well as **curriculum** planners, to ensure that majority (and minority) language children are given courses in language awareness. The responsibility for breaking down barriers to friendship which language and cultural differences might create, lies partly within a school curriculum. Through role playing, language awareness lessons, prejudice reduction activities, discussions in the classroom, the naturalness and value of language diversity in the world needs teaching in schools as much as any curriculum subject.

In helping a child to deal with problems of friendships, the parent needs to be a friendly listening ear, a suggester of possibilities, and occasionally a protector. At the same time, a parent needs to **communicate** with teachers when major problems arise, and gain the support of other parents with similar problems. A language problem shared is a bilingual's problem halved.

My child seems to have learning difficulties. Is this due to bilingualism?

If a child is slow in learning to read in school, or is placed in the lower half of their class in mathematics, people too quickly move to bilingualism as the first explanation. **Rarely is bilingualism a cause of learning difficulties**. Learning difficulties occasionally occur within bilingual children. This is totally different from bilingualism being the cause of their learning difficulties.*

Almost the only occasion when a learning difficulty of a bilingual child is attached to bilingualism is when a child enters the classroom with **neither language sufficiently developed** to cope with the higher order language skills demanded by the curriculum. In this rare case, the problem is not really with bilingualism but with insufficient language practice in the home, in the nursery school or in the outside world. Here we are talking not about bilingual deprivation, but about deprivation in any language.

If a child has lower ability than most in the school, well-meaning friends, teachers and speech therapists sometimes suggest that one language only should be developed. However, Canadian research tends to show that less able children are surprisingly capable of acquiring two languages early on. Just as their mathematical ability, literacy and scientific development may occur at a slower pace, so the two languages will develop with less speed. The size of vocabulary and accuracy of grammar may be less in both languages than the average bilingual child. Nevertheless, such children acquiring two languages early, will usually be able to communicate in both languages, often as well as they would communicate in one language (e.g. Down's syndrome children and adults).

My child seems to have an emotional/behavioral problem. Is this caused by bilingualism?

There is no evidence that bilingualism in itself causes emotional or behavioral problems. However, bilingualism is sometimes wrongly associated with emotional and behavioral difficulties because it is connected with some economically underprivileged, racially harassed and financially impoverished ethnic groups.

If children from such underprivileged groups experience problems in emotional or social adjustment, the **cause is not language**. Causes of emotional problems need searching for in, for example, the economic, political and financial

Learning difficulties are caused by a variety of possibilities, almost none of them aligned to bilingualism. Six examples of causes follow:

(1)   The standard of education: poor teaching methods, a non-motivating even hostile classroom environment, a dearth of suitable teaching materials, or clashes with the values and beliefs of the teacher.

(2)   Sink or swim situations. If a child is being taught in a second language and the home language is ignored, then failure and perceived learning difficulties may result. One example is various Spanish-speaking children in the United States. Such children are often placed in English-only classrooms on entry to school. They must operate in English. Some swim; others sink and may be deemed to have a deficiency.

(3)   By being assessed in their weaker second language rather than in their stronger home language children may be labeled as in need of special or remedial education.

(4)   Little self-confidence, low self-esteem, a fear of failure and high anxiety in the classroom.

(5)   Failure caused partly by interactions among children in the classroom. For example, where a group of children reinforce each other for fooling around, have a low motivation to succeed, or where there is bullying, hostility or social division rather than cohesion among children in a classroom, the learning ethos may disrupt the child's development.

(6)   Where there is a mismatch between the gradient of learning expected and the ability level of the child. Some children learn to read more slowly than others, still learning to read well, but after a longer period of time. Less able children can learn two languages within the (unknowable) limits of their ability. Other children experience specific learning difficulties (for example, dyslexia, neurological dysfunction, 'short-term memory' problems, poor physical coordination, problems in attention span or motivation). None of these specific learning difficulties or other language disorders are caused by bilingualism. At the same time, bilingual children will not escape from being included in this group. Bilingual families are no less or more likely to be affected than other families.

characteristics of the language minority group, or in the quality of child development experiences provided in the home, community and school. There is nothing emotionally damaging or restricting about owning two languages. On the contrary, bilingualism opens the door to wider emotional experiences from the different language cultures.

My child has a specific diagnosed problem (e.g. severe learning difficulty, language disorder, emotional problem). Should we change to speaking one language to the child rather than two languages? What language should I speak to my child?

Bilingualism in a family neither increases nor reduces the chance of experiencing language difficulties and language disorders. The bilingual child may, for example, be diagnosed as dyslexic, aphasic, partially hearing or with a low IQ score. Hopefully, the **specialist** making the diagnosis will have both experience with bilingual children and have studied bilingualism in professional training. If so, the diagnosis will include an assurance that bilingualism is typically not the cause of the problem.*

* See page 86

The communicative **differences** of language minority children must be distinguished from communicative **disorders**. Bilingual children are different from monolingual children in their language experience. For example, when a child is learning a second language, some temporary incorrectness is to be expected. It is not a sign of language disorder. Language disorders include specific items that are separate from the temporary lags and inaccuracies sometimes observed in bilinguals. Examples of symptoms of language disorders are: great difficulty in producing certain sounds; a considerable lack of understanding (or use) of familiar words; great difficulty in remembering new words despite a great deal of exposure to them; great difficulty in expressing needs and wants without use of gestures.

Such problems are too quickly attributed to bilingualism, partly because bilinguals are 'different'. Research tells a very different story. Bilingualism will **coexist** with, but will **not be the primary cause** of such problems.

A particular problem that illustrates the wrongly attributed link between bilingualism and developmental problems is '**language delay**'. Language delay occurs when a child is very late in beginning to talk, or lags well behind peers in language development. Estimates of young children experiencing language delay vary from 1 in 20 to 1 in 5 of the child population. Such varying estimates partly reflect that some delays are brief and hardly noticeable. Others are more severe. Language delay has a variety of causes (e.g. partial hearing, deafness, autism, visual impairment, severe subnormality, cerebral palsy, physical differences (e.g. cleft palate), psychological disturbance, emotional difficulties, a high degree of social or emotional deprivation). However, in approximately two-thirds of all cases, the precise reason for language delay is not known. Children who are medically normal, with no hearing loss, of normal IQ and memory, are not socially deprived or emotionally disturbed, can be delayed in starting to speak, slow in development or have problems in expressing themselves well. Such cases need specialist, professional help. Speech and language therapists, in particular, but clinical psychologists and educational psychologists may also give such advice and treatment.

Parents of bilingual children with such problems should not believe that bilingualism is the cause. Sometimes, well-meaning professionals make this diagnosis. Having a bilingual background is widely believed to produce language delayed children. The evidence does not support this belief.

A key consideration for a parent is whether removal of one language will improve, worsen or have no effect on a child's bilingualism. Given that the cause of the problem may be partially unknown, intuition and guesswork rather than 'science' often occurs.

One issue is which language to concentrate on if a major language or emotional problem is diagnosed. The danger is that parents, teachers and education administrators will want to accent the perceived importance of the majority language. In the United States, the advice is often that the child should have a solid diet of English – the language of school and employment. The advice too frequently given is that the home, **minority language** should be replaced by the majority language. Such an overnight switch may well have painful outcomes for the child. The mother tongue is denied, the language of the family is buried, and the child may feel as if thrown from a secure boat into strange waters. The solution is likely to exacerbate the problem.

It is more **important that the anchor language is retained**. The home language gives assurance and a feeling of security when there are stormy seas. Even if the child is slow in sailing in that language with progress delayed, it is the boat known to the child. Being forced to switch to the majority language will not make the journey faster or less problematic. It is more important to learn to sail in a familiar boat (the home language) in **minority language** situations.

Even when parents and professionals accept that bilingualism is not the cause of a child's problem, moving from bilingualism to **monolingualism** is seen by some as a way to help improve the problem. The reasoning is usually that the 'extra demands' of bilingualism, if removed, will lighten the burden for the child. While the cause of the problem is not addressed (often because the cause is unknown), one part of the context (i.e. bilingualism) where the problem occurs is changed to attempt a solution. Is this right?

There are many occasions when changing from bilingualism to monolingualism will have **no effect** on the problem. For example, if the child is exhibiting temper tantrums, seems slow to speak without an obvious cause or seems low in self-esteem, dropping one language is unlikely to have any effect. On the contrary, the sudden change in family life may exacerbate the problem. In most cases, it is inappropriate to move from bilingualism to monolingualism.

However, it is dangerous to make this advice absolute and unequivocal. To give only 'stick with bilingualism' advice is unwise and too simplistic. When there is **language delay**, for example, there will be a few family situations where maximal experience in one language is preferable. For example, where one language of a child is more secure and better developed than another, it may be sensible to concentrate on developing the stronger language. When a child has severe educational needs or is severely cognitively challenged, then ensuring a solid foundation in one language first is important.

This does not mean that the chance of bilingualism is lost forever. If, or when, language delay disappears, the other language can be reintroduced. If a child with **emotional problems** really detests using or even being spoken to in a particular language, the family may sensibly decide to accede to the child's preference. Again, once problems have been resolved, the 'dropped' language may be reintroduced, so long as it is immediately associated with pleasurable experiences. Stuttering (stammering) is also an example where occasionally the temporary dropping of a weaker language may help to move the child through a transitory stage of cognitive 'difficulty'.*

Any **temporary move** from bilingualism to monolingualism should not be seen as the only solution needed. A focus on such a language change as the sole remedy to the child's problem is naive and dangerous. For example, emotional problems may require other rearrangements in the family's pattern of relationships. Language delay may require visits to a speech therapist for advice about language interaction between parents and child. **Temporary monolingualism** should be seen as one component in a package of attempted changes to solve the child's language or emotional problem.

There are other occasions where changing from bilingualism to monolingualism is unnecessary and wrong. If someone who has loved, cared for and played with the child in one language suddenly only uses another language, the emotional well-being of the child may well be negatively affected. The language used to express love and caring disappears. Simultaneously, and by association, the child may feel that the love and care is also not as before. Such a language change is often drastic with its own negative after-effects and consequences.

For advice on Dyslexia, see Section D13, p. 115.

To conclude. When major language or emotional problems arise:

(1)   Don't rush to **blame** bilingualism. Bilingualism is very unlikely to be a cause. Don't rush to change to monolingualism as a solution. You may only make matters worse.

(2)   **Discuss** the problem with trusted friends, particularly those who may have experienced a similar problem. This also helps to clarify one's own thinking.

(3)   **Consult** professionals but check first if they have training and experience in dealing with bilingual children.

(4)   If you do adopt monolingualism as a solution, think about this as a **temporary** solution. Bilingualism can be reintroduced later.

(5)   Be extra **vigilant** that language doesn't become associated in the child's mind with anxiety, complications or unhappiness.

---

* See page 91

Reference for further reading

Laversuch, I.M. 2006, Bilingualism and severe educational needs. *Bilingual Family Newsletter*, Vol. 23, No. 1, pp. 4–5.

My child stutters. Is this caused by bilingualism?

For a short temporary period, many children (about 20% of all children) stutter (stammer). Stuttering is about three or four times more common in boys than girls and tends to run in families. This hints that a key cause may be genetic. Bilingualism does not increase the chances of stuttering. A study of some 800 stutterers speaking 52 native languages found that there was no difference in monolingual or bilingual speakers in the chances of experiencing stuttering. Bilinguals are equally as likely to be stutterers as monolinguals. Bilinguals are neither immune nor more prone.

Stuttering includes repeating sounds or words (e.g. p-p-p-play with m-m-me; I've got to – got to – got to go now); lengthening sounds (e.g. ffffish); time gaps between words (e.g. I'm going . . . home now); and unfinished words or phrases. Around three and four years of age, such stuttering is particularly common. Many older children and adults under pressure lose fluency. In addressing a large audience, the speaker may be so tense as to stutter.

The causes of stuttering are not well understood and seem multiple and varied. Some **neurophysiological** theories locate the problem in brain activity, others in a feedback problem between the ear and the brain. Further theories attempt a **psychological** explanation in terms of personality traits, and particularly anxiety (e.g. caused by impatient, over-corrective parents). None of these theories can explain all cases of stuttering.

One **linguistic** theory sees the cause as a difference between the language that is available (potential) and control over speech apparatus (production). Another linguistic theory sees 'cognitive overload' as the cause (e.g. the child's capacity for fluency exceeds the demands placed on the child). Some researchers have argued that coping with two languages around the age of two to four may cause a few children 'cognitive overload'.

The case studies suggest that any problems due to 'cognitive overload' are **temporary** in bilingual children. As language competence in the two languages increases, stammering usually disappears. It is also not clear from such research whether the causes were purely cognitive. Emotional problems (e.g. anxiety) may have been a prime cause; such anxiety derived from sources other than bilingualism.

Parents of bilingual children tend to focus on bilingualism as the cause of stuttering, rather than looking for other better explanations. Evidence tends to suggest that bilingualism is rarely a direct cause of stuttering.

Methods of treatment of stuttering also hint that bilingualism is rarely a cause. Developing a stutterer's breath control, learning to speak more slowly, tension reduction and relaxation techniques are examples of treatments. Parents cannot do anything about some potential causes of stuttering (e.g. brain activity). If potential causes are more about specific anxieties, nervousness, worries about speaking, or more general worries and fears in the child's life, the parent can help. Parents who criticize a child for stuttering, or who exhibit anxiety when they do so, only increase the child's nervousness and frequency of stuttering.

When stuttering first occurs, it is not necessary to seek immediate psychological or clinical advice. Merely showing and sharing anxiety, highlighting to the child that a problem exists, correcting the child and being impatient may only make the condition worse. Stuttering is frequent in many young children, both monolinguals and bilinguals. It is usually temporary, and reappears when a child (or adult) is particularly agitated and excited. If stuttering continues for a longer period, it is wise to seek **advice** from experts in child development or clinical psychology.

When the problem first occurs, it is important for parents to surround the child with greater love, greater relaxed care and attention. Be very patient. Focus on what the child wants to convey, not on the language being used. Concentrate on the function of the conversation and not on the form of language. If the sources of tension and anxiety in the child can be located, reduced or swept away, stuttering is quite likely to be a **temporary problem**. For a very small number of children, however, stuttering will be a continuous characteristic.

Stopping children speaking one of their languages could be counterproductive. It will not change the stuttering. Rather such an act will focus on language. This will increase children's anxiety about their language production.

If a child stutters considerably in their first language, then introducing a second language needs caution. For example, will second language learning produce more anxiety about speaking in the child? Sometimes, delaying the introduction of second language learning is wise, placing less cognitive, social and emotional demands on that child.

This discussion of stuttering conveys an important message to parents about their monitoring of their child's dual language development. If parents are anxious, constantly on edge about their child's bilingual development and this is relayed to the child, the child may internalize such anxieties. Stuttering is one possible consequence of the internalization of parental anxiety. It is therefore important that bilingual development is an enjoyable and pleasurable experience for the child. If a happy and positive atmosphere surrounds bilingual language development, bilingualism is very unlikely to cause stuttering.

Further reading

Laversuch, I.M. 2006, Stuttering and bilingualism. *Bilingual Family Newsletter*, Vol. 23, No. 2, pp. 6–8.

A child is autistic or has Asperger's syndrome. Should we use one language only with the child?

Children diagnosed with a specific autism spectrum disorder have a greater or lesser degree of impairment in language and communication skills, as well as repetitive or restrictive patterns of thought and behavior, with delays in social and emotional development. Such children use language in restricted ways, expecting much consistency in language and communication, and are less likely to learn through language. However, such children may experience the social and cultural benefits of bilingualism when living in a dual language environment. For example, such children may understand and speak two languages of the local community at their own level.

Like many parents of children with language impairment, bilingualism was frequently blamed by teachers and other professionals for the early signs of Asperger's, and a move to monolingualism was frequently regarded as an essential relief from the challenges.

There is almost no research on autism and bilingualism or on Asperger's syndrome and bilingualism. However, a study by Susan Rubinyi of her son who has Asperger's syndrome provides insights. Someone with the challenge of Asperger's also has gifts and exceptional talents, including in language.

Her son, Ben, became bilingual in English and French using the one parent–one language approach (OPOL). Susan Rubinyi sees definite advantages for a child

> who has challenges with flexibility and understanding the existence of different perspectives. Merely the fact that there are two different ways to describe the same object, concept, in each language, enlarges the perception of the possible. Since a bilingual learns culture as well as language, the child sees alternative ways of approaching multiple areas of life (eating, recreation, transportation etc.) (p. 20).

She argues that because of bilingualism, her son's brain had a chance to partly rewire itself even before Asperger's syndrome became obvious. Also, the intense focus of Asperger's meant that Ben absorbed vocabulary at a very fast rate with almost perfect native speaker intonation.

Reference for further reading

Rubinyi, S. 2006, *Natural Genius: The Gifts of Asperger's Syndrome*. Philadelphia & London: Jessica Kingsley Publishers.

People make fun of our speaking a minority language. How should I react?

It is often people who can't speak a second language who tend to poke fun at those who can speak two or three languages. Their poking fun may be a sense of their inadequacy in communication, their underlying jealousy, their worries about **exclusion** from the conversation, and meeting someone different from themselves.

For bilinguals meeting this situation, it is a matter of diplomacy, building bridges and breaking down barriers, keeping a good sense of humor, and trying to be tolerant. Pragmatically rather than idealistically, it is bilinguals who often have to forge improved relationships. Bilinguals have the role of **diplomats and not dividers**, showing that language diversity does not mean social divisions, that speaking a different language can still mean a harmonious relationship. Ironically, those who are the victims have to become the healers. The moral advantage, the character-building nature of such actions is built into many religions, and shines forth in the twentieth-century examples of Mahatma Gandhi and Martin Luther King.

It is important for speakers of a minority language to have high **self-esteem**. Minority speakers can form cohesive, self-confident networks which take pride

---

Cultural Differences

- The feelings that people have for their own language are often not evident until they encounter another language.
- People often feel their own language is far superior to other languages.
- It is necessary to know the language of a foreign culture to understand a culture in depth.
- Understanding another culture is a continuous and not a discrete process.
- Feelings of apprehension, loneliness and lack of confidence are common when visiting another culture.
- When people talk about other cultures, they tend to describe the differences and not the similarities.
- Differences between cultures are generally seen as threatening and described in negative terms.
- Stereotyping is probably inevitable in the absence of frequent contact or study.

Adapted from P.R. Harris & R.T Moran (1991)
Managing Cultural Differences. Houston, TX: Gulf Publishing Co.

in language vitality. Language minority speakers must not become islands but gather strength from being part of a language community. Sometimes, such a language community may be geographically close. At other times, the language community may communicate by phone, visits, letters, faxes, e-mail, swapping material for children's learning and annual festivals. Geographical isolation needs counteracting by creative means of communication to launch a **language community**. If there are self-doubts and derision by outsiders, there is strength to be gained from being part of a language community.

People around me are prejudiced and racist. Should we as a family switch to speaking only the majority language?

There are families whose language difference from surrounding families is joined by ethnic difference, color difference or religious difference. In many bilingual situations of the world, bilingualism exists alongside **racism**, deprivation, poverty, unemployment and **disadvantage**. For example, Spanish-speaking Mexicans in the United States, the Bengali speakers in England, the various in-migrant language groups in Germany are united by their minority language status, forming part of a cluster of differences in color, culture, creed, economic and social status. The prejudice may be about language, but also very much about color, and a different culture and lifestyle from the host country.

One response by some who experience such a reaction is to want to **switch** to the majority host language. Because they can't change their skin color and they do not want to change their creed, they nevertheless want to share in the economic affluence of the host country. For some, this is interpreted as the need to change language and change culture.

The weakness of this position is that it expresses the view that there has to be a suppression of the home language in order for the majority language to flourish. This is a monolingual position. A bilingual position is much more tenable. There is little reason why the heritage language and culture must be lost, with rootlessness as a possible outcome, rather than becoming bilingual in both languages.

Unfortunately, simply speaking the majority language will not cause a sudden change away from racism, discrimination and prejudice. Such negative attitudes by majority peoples tend to be based on **anxieties about** a different ethnic group, a fear of their economic privileged position being overturned, a fear of the unknown culture and a fear about loss of political and economic power and status. Becoming monolingual majority language speakers does not change economic disadvantage nor racial prejudice. Bilingualism that includes a well-developed fluency and literacy in the majority language has the equal advantage of allowing potential access to different economic markets and employment as well as retaining all that is good from the past. There is good reason for the family to become fluent in the majority language. This need not be at the cost of the first or minority language.

I'm a recent in-migrant to a country. Should I stop speaking my native language and switch to the first language of that country?

The answer is no. To deny the existence of your first language is to **deny** the **existence** of yourself, your past, your family history and traditions. You will want to learn the language of the country to which you have migrated. You will hope to communicate in the majority language with neighbors, shopkeepers, teachers and others in the community. You will also usually want your children to become fluent in the majority language of the country. This may occur in the home, in the local nursery school or when the children attend primary schooling.

There is little reason to stop using your native language (see Glossary) even when you and your children are proficient in the majority language. Retaining your native language in yourself and your children means retaining the rooted-ness of the past, maintaining values and beliefs, attitudes and culture that you and your family have held dear. In teaching a child your native language, you are **transmitting** something about **yourself**, your heritage and the extended family. You will be giving your child more rather than less, two languages and cultures rather than just one. As movement of peoples around the world becomes more possible with ease of communications, more likely with economic interrelation-ships between countries, so there will be an increasing need for people who can move with ease between countries, adapt to different cultures, make bridges and break down social and economic barriers. Bilinguals are well equipped for such roles.

My second language is not perfect. Should I speak it to my child?

This is a difficult question to answer simply. It really depends on how perfect or imperfect is the second language (see Glossary). One thing is for sure. If you are a bad **model** of language for your child, you should not speak that language to the child. If a child begins to learn incorrect linguistic structures or inexact expression from you speaking a second language, you may be under-mining rather than helping the child's language development. Instead, consider speaking the first language to your child knowing that many skills and com-petences learned in the first language (e.g. ideas, meanings, concepts) transfer easily to the second language.*

* See page 39

If you need to speak the second language to the child, why not try to avail yourself of language **practice** to improve your language or attend adult classes?

If you feel there is a problem with your second language, why not try to reduce that problem rather than pass the problem on to the child?

The language you speak to the child, particularly when the child is young, may be at the level where correctness is relatively assured. In speaking to young children, there is often a simplification of both grammatical structure and vocabulary. So it may be that you have **sufficient language competence** to be a valuable model to the child and your competence grows in a language along with the child.

The reality is that it is difficult for many mothers (and fathers) to speak a second language to their child. It feels restrictive and frustrating. The wealth of wise colloquial sayings, family stories, local jokes and colorful tales, are all stored and can only be authentically and intimately conveyed in the first or mother tongue (see Glossary). The transmission of the parents' heritage is best recounted in the mother tongue. That storage of experience in the mother tongue from birth to parenthood seems of low worth if a second language is used with the child.

One example of the pay-off for a parent using a minority language is when the children are in their teenage years. If a language minority mother or father has ignored their first language and speaks the majority language to her children, problems can arise. The majority language may be spoken with a 'foreign' accent (see Glossary), the language used may be perceived by the teenager as incorrect. One outcome might be that the teenager is embarrassed, the parent mocked and held in disdain, and the minority language hated. If such a language minority mother speaks her minority language instead, she may retain more prestige and credibility, and be more respected by the teenager.

Adults who have learned a second language often don't learn the language of children in that language. The appropriate expressions, the intimacy of personal expression may not be present in the second language. For this reason, many mothers and fathers naturally use their first language with their child.

A local professional (e.g. a doctor, psychologist, speech therapist, teacher) advised me against bilingualism. Is this correct?

Such negative advice occurs too often. One of the worst pieces of advice came from a Texas judge who told a mother that raising her five-year-old child in Spanish was 'abusive' and 'relegated her to the position of housemaid'. The *New York Times* (August 30, 1995) reported the judge as saying: 'Now get this straight. You start speaking English to this child because if she doesn't do good in school, then I can remove her [from the mother's home] because it's not in her best interest to be ignorant'.

The judge did not have the competence to give such language verdict. Similarly, a doctor or a teacher is not usually trained to answer questions about bilingualism in children. Yet the parent expects the professional to give an expert, highly informed judgment on the situation. Too often, well-meaning doctors and teachers tend to reflect in their answers the prejudices and negative beliefs of previous decades.

Such advice is contrary to current research and expert opinion about bilingualism. All too often, both members of the public and professionals tend to advise against bilingualism. To them, it is more natural for a child to be monolingual. Learning two languages would seem to exacerbate problems, seem to provide more worries, more of a chance for failure in language and cognitive development, educational development, identity formation and community integration. However well meaning, honest and professional, these people are not the ones to consult about bilingual problems.

If local **expertise** is sought, it may be found in the local linguistics department of a university or college, among specialist language teachers, among those in education specializing in bilingualism and bilingual education, among psychologists who have a special interest in languages or bilingualism, among teachers who have followed courses on bilingualism and bilingual education, and increasingly, among speech therapists who have taken a course in bilingualism as part of their studies.

Also, if advice is sought about bilingualism, have a look at the **References*** for further information. These references provide expert opinions and share information from recent decades of international research into bilingualism.

C24

Do teenagers suffer or gain if their parents come from different language and cultural backgrounds (mixed language marriages)?

One piece of Canadian research is well worth sharing to help answer this question. Two scholars investigated the effect on teenagers of mixed language marriages, testing them on their ethnic identity (see Glossary), identification with (or rejection of) one of their ethnic groups, their self-esteem and stability, perception of parents, peer relationships and attitudes and values.

In comparison with children from monolingual home backgrounds, bilingual teenagers had no problem in identifying with both their parents, nor suffered in self-esteem or stability. Such teenagers showed a positive attitude to both their parents' cultural groups. Children from monolingual homes tended to favor their own ethnic group.

The scholars concluded that mixed language background marriages were socially and emotionally valuable for teenagers. Such children showed no signs of personality disturbances, social disorientation or anxiety. Their self-concepts were positive and they saw their parents as giving them relatively more attention. The teenagers' values reflected the influence of both ethnic backgrounds. Rather than developing a divided allegiance or rejecting one of their dual language backgrounds, such teenagers had developed a dual allegiance. For the children of mixed language marriages, a double inheritance is much more likely than a division of loyalties.

This result concerns children from Canadian middle-class backgrounds where both languages and both cultures have status and prestige. In in-migrant situations in England and the United States for example, a slightly less rosy picture is sometimes found. When children come from language minority backgrounds, working towards an integration between their two cultures and languages may require more accent on the minority language, particularly in the early years. To counterbalance the effect of the dominant majority language, there may need to be two objectives. First, ensuring the child feels secure and confident in the minority language and culture. Second, to ensure that the child is taught the advantages of biculturalism (see Glossary), the value of harmony between cultures and languages, and not taught that conflicting competition is the inevitable outcome of two languages and cultures in contact.

References for further reading

Aellen, C. & Lambert, W.E. 1969, Ethnic identification and personality adjustments of Canadian adolescents of mixed English-French parentage. *Canadian Journal of Behavioural Science*, Vol. 1, No. 2, pp. 69–82.

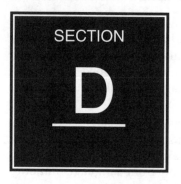

SECTION

D

Reading and Writing Questions

Should my child learn to read in one language first?

Reading has become increasingly essential to survival and success in society. Being illiterate or semi-literate has become a stigma of failure, personally, socially and economically. The consequences for low standards of literacy are as disastrous for the individual as they are for a community or country. For biliterate children and adults, this scenario can be turned upside down. Those literate in two languages may be more successful, more employable and be of increasing status in the global economy. In our internationally communicative society, those who can move easily between two or more literacies have market value.

Some children learn to read two languages **simultaneously** (although this is less frequent than sequential learning), which provides a successful route to biliteracy. Children acquire two reading systems at the same time. This is no different from children successfully acquiring two spoken languages from birth. There may be a short period of mixing the two systems (e.g. when two languages are similar), but this is temporary and transitory. The advantage of such early biliteracy is that it appears to develop a child's visual skills (e.g. searching for visual differences). Children as young as three years old can be aware of different scripts in the home (e.g. Arabic and English). Developing literacy in both languages simultaneously works best when both languages are relatively well developed.

A more common route is for the child to learn to read in one language first and in the second language a little later. **Sequential** rather than simultaneous learning to read in two languages tends to be frequent. When one language is much stronger than the other, achieving literacy in that one language first is preferable. The weaker language may be insufficiently developed to such an extent that learning to read more easily and quickly may be achieved in the stronger language first. This may also aid the child's motivation to learn to read, and develop more positive attitudes to literacy.

100

Developing literacy in a child's weaker language is often attempted with in-migrant children. For example, a Spanish-speaking in-migrant in the United States will be taught to read in the majority language of the country – English. Less success and slower development will usually occur than if the child is taught to read in the stronger language (Spanish) first.*

There are exceptions to this sequential pattern. In a **language majority** context, children sometimes learn to read in their second language. For example, in Canada, children from English-speaking homes take their early years of education through French. Hence, they may learn to read in French first, and English a little later. This usually results in fully biliterate children. Learning to read in French first will not impede later progress in learning to read English.

In this Canadian example, the second language will be well developed in speaking and understanding skills before introducing literacy. Also, the first language (English) will be well developed in the home and community, such that there will be additive and not subtractive (see Glossary) bilingualism and biliteracy. There is every chance that literacy will become as strong in English as in French.

Learning to read starts the day a child is born. Listening and speaking is a necessary **preparation for learning to read**. The vocabulary and language structures acquired in learning to talk are an essential foundation for reading. As soon as the child becomes aware of pictures and toys, it is time for the child to have some simple books to play with. As early as possible, the child needs the concept of a book and to value books in the home. Early in life a child can learn that a book has pictures and objects that are later understood as words. As parents move through the child's first year, it is time to start nursery rhymes, songs and relay wise sayings. By the time a child has reached the end of the first year, consider starting to read simple books to him or her. Children may not understand every word in the book, but they will often understand the story. They are learning that books are fun and that reading is a pleasure.

Reading can be encouraged before a child can read a single letter. As **parents** read to the very young child, they can gently hold a child's finger and show the movement of the words across the page from left to right (or right to left in some languages), in a rhythmical sequence. As favorite books are read night after night, a child will begin to recognize certain words and begin to associate meaning and word form. How many parents have laughed aloud when a young child picks up a book and pretends to read, having memorized some of the words on the page? The child is learning to love books, to love stories and to associate the printed word with competence and pleasure.

If it feels normal and natural, books in both languages can be introduced at an early age. In India, many children learn to read and write in three languages and three different scripts before they are eight without problems. Triliteracy (multiliteracy) is as possible as biliteracy.

* See page 103

Children's development in **reading in the second language is greatly helped by their learning to read in the first language**. Simply stated, there is much transfer between the first and the second language when learning to read.*

For example, if a child learns to read in English first, and later learns to read in French, the child does not have to begin to learn to read all over again when tackling French books or writing in French. Many reading skills (and attitudes) are simply **transferred** from one language to the next. For example, there is transfer of: learning to recognize that letters mean sounds, making sense of words as parts and wholes, making sensible guesses at words given the storyline, understanding the meaning of sentences from a string of words and moving left to right (or right to left) across the page.

Learning to read in a second language does not mean learning to read all over again. Far from it. Instead, there is immediate understanding that, in the second language: print is broken up into discrete words; words carry individual meaning; you can guess the meaning of words from the rest of the sentence often with accuracy; and that there are clues about words and meaning from previous sentences, pictures and previous experience.

This book does not tend to relate personal experiences in case they are particular or idiosyncratic. However, one of our children learned first to read in Welsh. Most books in his bedroom were Welsh language books. The plan was to establish, first of all, firm growth in minority language literacy. At the age of seven, he picked up a book written in English and began reading it. In sheer amazement, his mother called the family to the bedroom. With very little experience of English reading books, he moved across the page, sometimes decoding (see Glossary) correctly, sometimes guessing and gambling. After finishing the book, we questioned him, and he revealed a fine understanding of the storyline. His learning to read words in Welsh (which has many sounds of letters different from English), plus an ability to speak English fairly fluently, prepared him to read in English. Within a year, there was almost no difference in his ability to read English or Welsh books. **Learning to read in one language facilitates reading in a second language**.

Learning to read fluently, independently and critically takes **time**. Literacy skills do not occur in either language overnight but grow steadily and slowly through middle and later childhood, even into adulthood. Learning to read in one or two languages is a continuous, **gradual** development that extends to the teenage years and well beyond.

Learning to read in the second language is valuable for the development of that language. For example, reading in a second language will extend the vocabulary of that language and improve grammatical structuring of that language. Second language **reading develops speaking skills**, particularly when experience of that second language is not extensive. Second language reading also develops writing skills in that second language

Reading fluently has become increasingly essential in recent decades. Reading is a way of acquiring new vocabulary and different language structures. It expands the ways of communicating within a family and in school. Reading provides a means of acquiring information and expanding horizons (e.g. employment), manipulating and assimilating experience. It helps the development of new concepts, new ideas, encouraging empathy, enculturation and identity. Reading may also keep a language alive within an individual when there is a lack of opportunity to speak that language.

Will learning to read in a second language interfere with reading in the first language?

D2

Generally, learning to read in one language does not interfere with learning to read in a second language – rather the opposite. Learning to read in one language is preparing the ground for learning to read in another language. However, just as in learning to speak there is some mixing of words in a sentence, so with reading. A child may read a French word with English pronunciation, say a German word as if it is spelt in English. The irregularities of the English language can pose initial difficulties to those who learn to read in a language that is regular. Just as with oral language there is a steady movement away from language mixing, so with reading. Over time, a child learns that, for example, similar spellings in two languages can have different pronunciations.

Reading is not just decoding (see Glossary) sounds from pages of print, pronouncing letters, combinations of letters and words correctly. Such decoding skills are a means to an end, and must not be an end in themselves. The purpose of reading is to extract **meaning** from the page. Learning to read is learning to try to understand the message on the page. Reading is **making sense** of words, phrases, sentences, chapters and whole books.

Learning to extract meaning and sense from a page is a skill in itself. Guessing meaning, successfully struggling to understand the story is something that is learned and adults need to encourage. When a child learns such a 'making sense' strategy in reading, this **transfers** to reading in another language. The ability to understand the meaning of text, learned when reading in one language, becomes available when learning to read in a second language.

If the two languages have different scripts, will learning to read and write be a problem?

A typical query from parents is whether two languages with totally different scripts make it harder for a child to read and write in those two languages. For example, English and Arabic have two very different scripts, similarly Chinese and French. Children do **successfully learn** to read and write in two totally different scripts. The main difference is that there will be less transfer compared with two similar scripts.

Learning to read in a different script is still aided by learning to read in the first language. The act of character recognition, associating marks on the page with sounds and meanings, the strategy of sensible guessing, still transfer. However, there is **less transfer** of skills in learning* to read in two very different scripts. The child may have to learn to move in different directions, recognize totally different symbols, different constructions (as in Chinese and English), and different presentations in books.

* See
page
100

In the less cluttered brains of children, learning two different scripts can be made enjoyable and valuable. If children are aware that they are learning an important competence, their motivation may be heightened and their attitude made favorable.

 ## Can a child learn to be literate in three languages?

Many children who are trilingual or multilingual also become literate in three or even more languages. There is transfer from the two languages into the third in the same way that there is transfer between the first and second language literacies (see D1). Some children are trilingual but biliterate; others become literate in three languages.

As part of the contemporary concepts of multilingual literacies and multi-literacies, a person may, for example, speak Sylheti (a regional language of Bangladesh), read and write in Bengali (the standard language of Bangladesh) as well as English and French. Such a person may exhibit multiple literacies that have varied and different uses, varying levels of proficiency, different opportunities to use their multiliteracies (e.g. according to gender), changing over time with experience and opportunity, and are sometimes not used separately but in combinations with innovative blending (syncretism).

Such multilingual children do not remain in separate language and literacy worlds but acquire their multilingualism and multiliteracies simultaneously. However, teachers may not be aware of home literacies, with merger missing and much potential lost.

 ## When should a child begin to read in a second language?

Reading does not begin at the age of five, six or seven. Reading begins in the first year of life. If materials in both languages are available for the child to hold and glance through, and if books are read to the child in both languages, biliteracy is encouraged before a child begins to decode words on a page. The enjoyment of books begins when the child is in the first year of life. As children enter the nursery years, their enjoyment of books grows, their **curiosity** is aroused and they begin to handle books more and more. By the ages of four to seven, a child is usually beginning to read in one language, occasionally two.

During those first four or five years, there is no reason why books should not be available to a child in both languages. If parents decide to encourage reading in two languages at once, this will often occur around the ages four to six. If, on the other hand, parents decide to introduce one reading language first, the second language (see Glossary) may be introduced around age seven or later.

In some regions, it is more customary for children to begin to read and write when they first go to school (e.g. parts of Africa). Also, in some regions there is a dearth of books in the mother tongue. So learning to read is affected by culture and context, by availability and custom.

This **sequential strategy** is to encourage children to read in one language first and feel a growing competence in reading. When children start to read by themselves, they seem able to begin to read in a second language or begin to write in a different script. The key factor is that reading and writing must be a pleasure to the child. It is important to induce a long-term positive attitude to books and reading from the start.

How should I help my child to read and write in both languages? D6

Reading and writing experiences need to be fun. This occurs when reading and writing involve real and natural events, not artificial stories, artificial sequences rules of grammar and spelling, or stories that are not relevant to the child's experience. Reading and writing need to be interesting, culturally relevant to the child, belonging to the **child's experience**, allowing choice by the learner, giving children power and understanding of their world. Reading taught for its own sake is not fun. Going through a book of writing exercises following reading is not usually interesting or relevant to the child.

Children learn to read and write when there is a need to understand the **meaning** of a story, to chant a rhyme, to share the humor of a book. Books and other texts that are culturally relevant to the child imply that characters, contexts and experiences in a story are similar to their family and friends. Also, such characters talk in a related way to the readers' family and friends.

Writing is fun when it is **communication**. When reading and writing are contrived, and the form of words is put before their function, there is no encouragement for either activity. Reading and writing need to provide opportunities for shared language and shared meaning. A series of books that is based on how often words occur in a language, that tries very exactly to grade difficulty, moving from one level to another level slowly, might seem logical and sensible. Yet such books tend to have artificial stories, artificial language constructions and do not match or cultivate the child's experience.

Children need imaginative, vivid, interesting books that both relate to, and increase their experience, which make them laugh and stir their **imagination**, relevant to their world and their way of thinking. Children don't just need books on the shelf. Magazines and newspapers, directories and posters, signs in the street, packages and labels are all reading material. Children writing to each other (or to their grandparents in another country) are both valuable and authentic reading and writing activities. The rules of reading and writing are latently being taught.

Some homes and classrooms are full of literacy. There are words in the kitchen, on posters inside the child's bedroom, examples of the child's writing up on the wall to demonstrate literacy and its value. Children derive considerable pleasure from writing their own simple little books with lots of pictures. Advertisements in subways and metros, religious inscriptions, street signs and billboards, teletext and sports pages in the newspaper, are all ways in which children learn to read naturally.

Children learn to read by **constructing meaning** from books. They use their prior learning and experience to make sense of texts. Readers predict, select, self-correct as they seek to make sense out of print. They guess, sometimes wrongly, sometimes correctly. They monitor their reading to make sense of the print. Learning to read means struggling to make sense, because finding meaning is the purpose of reading. There is little intrinsically enjoyable in simply making the right sounds or writing with correct spellings. Reading and writing is about communication of meaning.

A child learns to write when they are writing for somebody with a **purpose** and a message. Efficient writing means making it comprehensible for an audience. Constantly highlighting grammatical and spelling errors is soul destroying for the child. Corrections concentrate on form and not function, on the medium and not the message. Conveying meaning is important in learning to write well. Learning to read is also learning to write. A child learns to spell when learning to read. The more children read, the more their writing improves.

In **school**, particularly with average and above average children, discussion of grammar (see Glossary) and spelling can accelerate language development. But this should not destroy the reason for writing and reading – which is communication of meaning. At school, there is a place for correction, consideration of the form of oral and written languages. There is less place for such a formal approach at home. In the home, language is usually a means and not an end, a vehicle and not a goal.

There is an analogy with a musician. It is the overall musical performance that is important. Sometimes there is a need to practice scales (octaves), arpeggios or trills as a separate skill to improve the overall standard of musicianship. Accurately playing scales is not a musical performance. More important is the overall combination of accurate playing, interpretation of a musical score, creating an ambience with a piece of music and communicating with the listener. Similarly with reading and writing. Sometimes a teacher will concentrate on specific skills (e.g. irregular words, punctuation, spelling, grammar). Specific skills are not reading or writing. The overall activity needs to be the central focus.

Reading and writing is about enjoyable participation and risk taking. It is important to use a child's internal motivation for wanting to read and wanting to write. Constant **correction** has little, if any value. For the parent, there can be great value in discussing reading with the child. Asking the child imaginative and creative questions stimulates both reading and speaking competences.

Developing competence in **writing** is **slower** than learning to read. At the start, the child's composition may simply involve dictating a letter to the parent who then reads it back to the child. A child may quickly learn to use the computer to enhance the look of the finished product. In writing (as in reading), it is important to build a pupil's level of self-confidence and encourage risk taking. Expressing ideas is initially more important than perfect spelling. At the beginning, a child's writing in either language will have so many spelling errors and be so minimal that even the child may not be able to understand what they have written.

However, developing writers quickly realize that **spelling** is important for understanding. The more pupils read and write, the less spelling mistakes tend to occur. Children's misspellings occur mostly with words they infrequently write or read. With increasing reading and writing experience, spelling errors decrease – although (as with adults) rarely completely.

When children learn to read and write, they begin to develop a sense of where to **punctuate** by self-monitoring. When children make mistakes in reading and writing, it is valuable for the child to **self-correct**. For example, ask the child to read the word again, or respell it. If an error still occurs, the parent needs to point to the correct form on the page. However, when there is constant correction, a child is learning the notes, but not the song. A delicate balance needs striking between reading the score and singing the song.

Parents can help their children to **enjoy writing** in two languages. Writing is essentially communication with someone else – to convey messages, persuade, make friends, express individuality, to question, explore, exercise the imagination, entertain, record events and for many other reasons. In writing, we reflect more deeply, learn to organize our thoughts and ideas, share our meanings and our understanding of the world with others.

Compare these aims of writing with parents and teachers who ask children to copy out a passage from a book in their best handwriting. Or when reading a child's writing, spelling errors are the main focus of feedback, alongside comments about neatness. Or the child is given a picture unrelated to their experience and asked to write one sentence underneath. In these examples, the wrong emphasis is given. While spelling and tidiness are important, neither constitute writing.

Helping a Child to Write in Two Languages

Parents can help a child learn to write in both languages, before going to school and while at elementary and secondary school. The list presents some ideas and suggestions. Cooperating with teachers is also very important.

(1)   Children initially write lots of squiggles over a page. There may be some letters, but there is much drawing that doesn't relate to adult forms of writing. Be proud, accepting and encouraging. The child has realized that writing exists, and there are varied shapes. Writing has begun.

(2)   Later, children write real letters from an alphabet, and increasingly whole words. However, children will usually be unable to read these back. Children expect the parent to be able to read and understand. Try to make sense of the text by reading it back to the child. Discuss what was written so the act of writing is seen as a sociable, pleasurable event. Encourage by sincere and measured praise. In this stage the child becomes aware that writing means conveying a message with meaning.

(3)   As children move towards adult forms of writing, they reflect, write in increasingly understandable forms and convey meaning more exactly. Children learn to write in different styles and for different audiences. There will be many spelling, grammatical and other structural **errors**. Try not to focus on errors at the expense of the meaning of the writing. Few adults are perfect spellers, yet unrealistically expect perfection from children at an early age. Able readers are often poor spellers. Such readers focus on the meaning of what they read rather than the form of each word. As a general rule, only focus on one or two errors at a time. Select what seems appropriate to the child's needs. Concentrate on what the child has almost got right and what will be used again. These corrections are more likely to be remembered.

(4)   Give your children their own private writing book to use as they wish. **Vary what the child writes** in the home: for example, helping to compose a shopping list, writing and rewriting a favorite family story together, writing a recipe to cook together later, keeping a diary, writing in a photo album that records family experiences, poetry, imaginative or personal stories, and writing jokes and cartoons.

(5)   Ensure the child has the opportunity to read and write in the **minority or heritage language**. Parents can write with their children the important wise sayings, folk tales, family history, and funny and important incidents told by previous generations and the extended family. A self-made, treasured family book can be jointly produced. The past is celebrated in the present; the contemporary is engraved in the history of the child.

Which approach to teaching reading works best? The 'look and say', 'phonemic awareness', 'phonics', 'whole language' or what approach?

The **look and say** approach suggests that children should learn to read and write whole words. Children are encouraged to focus on and remember the shape of a whole word (e.g. 'shop'). Words that are useful in everyday life are often highlighted (called Social Sight words – 'pay here', 'wet paint', 'subway'). Also highlighted are essential words that are phonically irregular (e.g. 'the', 'he', 'she', 'to', 'that'). Words that a pupil has difficulty with and constantly gets wrong are sometimes taught in this way (e.g. using home-made 'flashcards' where the word on card is 'flashed up' in front of the child). Generally, this method is not used by itself. It depends mostly on visual memory and can leave the child without the skills of decoding (see Glossary) longer and harder words and the ability to build a vocabulary of new words.

The **phonemic awareness** approach encourages children to break down the parts of the *spoken* word into their separate sounds. For example, the word 'shop' has three sounds: 'sh' forms one sound; the letter 'o' another; and 'p' the third. Children then piece together each word to create its overall sound. The teaching of phonemic awareness has to avoid constant repetitive drills. Rather, phonemic awareness needs to be taught in a fun way, through rhymes and games, for example. Some children learn to read fluently without being taught phonemic or phonic awareness (see Glossary). Other children rely so heavily on getting sounds correct that story meaning and enjoyment is lost.

A 'phonics' approach (see Glossary) is similar but different, in that phonemic awareness is about sounds in the *spoken* word, while phonics is about the sounds of *written* language. In phonics, children learn that there is a systematic relationship between spoken sounds and written letters (i.e. between phonemes and graphemes – see Glossary). The phonics approach teaches children the sounds associated with different letters and combinations of letters (e.g. 'sh', 'shr'). Phonemic awareness is thus a foundation before phonics. Most children are taught phonemic and phonic awareness as part of their reading repertoire. Successful, early readers tend to have 'decoding' skills. The strategy of phonemic awareness and phonics easily transfers from one language to another.

A phonic awareness approach is often used to teach English 'decoding' skills, (although over a third of English words are phonically irregular). Different languages will use different approaches to teaching 'decoding' skills (see Glossary). For example, a different strategy for teaching the 'decoding' of Spanish is used (i.e. a decoding of syllables). Such 'decoding' methods, if used exclusively, may result in a child reading without understanding. A child may recognize words and pronounce them correctly without comprehension. This is unsatisfactory and points to the need to move beyond a 'decoding' approach.

Both 'look and say', 'phonemic awareness' and 'phonics' are 'skills approaches' to reading and writing. Reading and writing are seen as constructed of independent skills that can be learnt in relative isolation.

The **whole language approach** emphasizes learning to read and write naturally, for enjoyment and purpose, for meaningful communication and for inherent pleasure. Generally, the **whole language approach** supports an holistic and integrated learning of reading, writing, spelling and oracy. The language used must have relevance and meaning to the child. The whole language approach is against basal readers (books that use simplified vocabulary – see Glossary) and phonics (see above) in learning to read. There is often a set order in reading basal books, moving from simple to more complex text in a gradually increasing gradient of difficulty. In a whole language approach, writing must be for real purposes. A child writes for somebody in a particular situation and for a defined reason. Writing means reflecting on one's ideas and sharing meaning with others. Writing can be in partnership with others, involving drafting and redrafting.

There is much current emphasis on skills approaches to reading, with a systematic approach to phonemic awareness and phonics being politically favored. For example, the US National Reading Panel Report (June 2003) provides parent-

---

A Typical Sequence (but not style) of Teaching Phonics in English

(1)   Learning to recognize the letters of the alphabet, in upper and lower case, their names, letter sounds, initial sounds at the start of a word, their sounds at the end of a word.

(2)   **Initial consonant blends** that occur at the start of words: e.g. **pl**od, **spl**it
        Two letters: pl, fr, dr, pr, tr, sk, cr, br, sn, cl, gr, gl, sp, fl, bl, sw, sm, sc, st, qu, sl, tw
        Three letters: spl, squ, spr, str, scr, shr

(3)   **Final consonant blends** that occur at the end of words: e.g. ra**mp**
        mp, st, nk, lt, nd, sp, nt, ng, sk, lp, ld

(4)   **Silent 'e' words** e.g. rude, fate, ev**e**
        u_e, a_e, i_e, o_e, e_e

(5)   **Vowel digraphs** e.g. c**ow**
        ow, oe, ar, ew, ou, aw, ue, oo, er, ay, ie, ea, ee, ur, oa, au, ai, oy, ir, or, oi

(6)   **Consonant digraphs** e.g. **wh**ip
        wh, ch, th, sh, ph, tch, shr, thr, sch

(7)   **Silent letters** e.g. **g**nat, knot, know
        g, k, w, u, h, b, gh, l, t

(8)   **Word endings** e.g. pict**ure**, vog**ue**, mis**sion**
        ure, ue, ion, ble, cle, fle, ple, sle, y, ge, tion, sion, ed, ous, re

readable analysis of five types of reading instruction: phonemic awareness, phonics, fluency, vocabulary and text comprehension. It is widely available on the WWW as *'Put Reading First: The Research Building Blocks for Teaching Children to Read'*.

Teaching children phonemic awareness and phonics is possible in the home. Many parents naturally break down words into component parts to help a child read increasingly difficult writing. A phonic approach helps a child read the words; a whole language approach helps the words come alive, and the sound of the language to resonate in the child.

A skills approach favors a conscious learning of the rules (e.g. in English 'when two vowels go walking, the first does the talking') and provides competence that will help with writing (e.g. spelling and grammar). But words have meaning in context, not in isolation. One possibility for parents is to **combine** a whole language approach with a phonemic awareness and phonics approach. Many teachers avoid a single approach and are eclectic in their reading and writing methods. A **combination** of a whole language, phonemic awareness, phonics and a structured element to language is an efficient and valuable way of accelerating learning.

Three Examples of Teaching Strategies that can be Used by Parents

(1)   Develop a 'sight' vocabulary first. For example, locate a child's favorite and often used words (e.g. ice cream, teddy, granny). Using pictures alongside these whole words, encourages the child to recognize and read these words. A sense of achievement will be felt by the child. It does not matter if the words are in two languages. It matters that the words are important to the child. A phonic approach is best introduced after the child has a small but central 'sight' vocabulary. This 'start up' vocabulary is the raw material on which a child can break down words into their sound components. Phonic analysis of words will be more interesting to the child if they operate on personal words.

(2)   Get your child to talk about an experience. One or more short sentences (or later, a story) is written down on card. A copy of the sentence is cut up and reconstructed by the child. The same activity is used later with sentences that need putting into a logical order. The activity centers on the child's own words and existing experiences to stimulate interest and motivation. Discuss the process with the child throughout the activity.

(3)   Children are given a story (especially to do with their own experience or something from their parent's past) with words missing. They are asked to guess the missing words and write them in the text. This is called 'Cloze procedure' or 'context cuing' and encourages comprehension and reading independence. Make the activity enjoyable.

Parents who listen to their children read are engaging in a most valuable activity. Both before the child goes to school and while in the early school years, reading with a child should be part of a daily ritual. Passive listening needs avoiding. **Parents** can do three things to make reading active. (1) Elaborate and explain the text to the child. This extends and deepens the experience of the story. (2) Relate the story to the child's own experiences. An interest in reading and understanding the meaning of the text occur if there is 'further information' to personalize the text. (3) Ask questions to ensure the child understands the story, thinks about the characters and plot, and extends their imagination.

One key aim for parents is to help their children become **independent readers** in both languages. Independent readers can monitor and correct themselves, search for cues and clues to make sense of unknown words and whole sentences. Children are surprisingly adept at doing this. Try them reading something like the following. It shows that they are clever reading detectives:

> I cluod not blveiee taht I cluod uesdnatnrd waht I was rdanieg. The phaonmneal pweor of the hmuan mnid, aoccdrnig to a rscheearch at Cmabrigde Uinervtisy, is that it dseno't mtaetr in waht oerdr the ltteres in a wrod are, the olny iproamtnt tihng is taht the frsit and lsat ltteer be in the rghit pclae.

> The rset can be a taotl mses and you can sitll raed it whotuit a pboerlm. Tihs is bcuseae the huamn mnid deos not raed ervey lteter by istlef, but the wrod as a wlohe.

Should I buy books for my child to read that contain two languages or just one language?

Most books in bilingual homes will be in one language or the other. However, there are books on the market where one page is in one language, and the other is an exact content replica, but in a different language. These books may be of some value for parents who, for example, are listening to a child reading in Spanish but cannot understand Spanish themselves.

Dual language books contain a story, folk tale, myth or information in two languages. Such languages may have a similar script (as in French and English, or Spanish and English) or different scripts (for example Chinese and English, Urdu and English, Bengali and English). There are many publishers and retailers selling dual language books. A search on 'dual language books' on the WWW provides many instant suppliers.

Some dual language books are professionally produced and published. Also, parents may work with children to produce these texts. Such books help children, both bilinguals and monolinguals, become aware that other languages have value and functions.

For children whose first language is not the majority language of the country, dual language books may serve as a bridge to literacy in, for example, English. Such children will read the story in Greek or German, Swedish or Spanish first of all. Subsequently, they may read the other language (e.g. English version) and, having already understood the storyline, be able to make sense of English words.

Dual language books are not without controversy. First, children usually only read one language in the book, and may ignore the other language. Having understood the story in one language, it may be tiresome reading the story in another language. The child ends up reading half the book rather than the whole book. Second the presence of a majority language such as English tends to remove the desire to read in a minority language. The different status of the two languages may mean that the child will only wish to read in the higher status language.

How can I locate books for my child to read in each language?

This question is often posed by parents for whom one language used in the home is not spoken in the region. For example, how does the Finnish mother living in England acquire sufficient reading material for her children to develop literacy in Finnish as well as English? A family can build up a **resource** of reading material in a particular language. When visiting on holidays, when relatives visit, by requests to those back in the native country to send material, it is possible to build up a store of material for children of different ages.

It is valuable to try to locate other parents in a similar situation. There is much strength in developing a **community**, not necessarily geographically close, whereby **experiences, materials and resources are shared and exchanged**. Not only does this provide support for literacy development, but also psychological, emotional and educational help within a group of like-minded people.

In some minority languages, finding suitable literature for children is difficult. The literature is sometimes scarce, sometimes mostly for adults, sometimes old-fashioned. Especially in the teenage years, children in such situations may prefer to read majority language books. One partial solution can be offered. Parents can write books in the minority language for the younger child – especially containing family stories. The traditions and culture of the family can be conveyed in such home-produced books

Will my child find it hard to write in two different languages?

Writing skills tend to develop later than reading skills. Given sufficient stimulation, encouragement and practice, there is little reason why children should not become literate in the written form in both languages. However writing is a harder skill to develop than listening and speaking. Whereas children often become readers in two languages, writing well tends to be a more difficult and **advanced** skill.

The development of biliteracy skills to fruition often requires **bilingual education** and not simply the education available in the home. Since reading and particularly writing develop through middle and late childhood into the teens, school often plays an important role in such biliteracy development. Parents of bilingual children do not always have access to such bilingual education. In such cases, literacy development in a second language takes place at home and requires commitment and effort by parents. Saturday and Sunday schools and religious instruction are alternative routes to biliteracy.

Studies of bilingual education show that it is easily possible for children to develop writing skills in both languages. However, fewer bilinguals become fluent writers in two languages than fluent speakers.

My child seems slow in learning to read. Is this due to bilingualism?

The answer is no. Some are quicker than others in learning to read. If your child is slower, this is very unlikely to have anything to do with bilingualism. Certainly, interest in learning to read is important. The child's readiness to read, and the desire to decode symbols on pages are both crucial in starting reading. Having an encouraging atmosphere in the home and the school for reading to develop is very important. Bilingualism has nothing to do with any of these situations.

The only possibility of bilingualism connecting with the speed of learning to read is when a negative **attitude** to languages, or a **lack of progress** in **either language** has occurred. If the child has learned to despise the minority language, learning to read may become problematic. If the language stimulation of the home is so inadequate that a child's language skills are well behind peers, learning to read may come later rather than earlier. Where parents have developed a positive attitude to language learning and to reading and writing, bilingualism will have no relationship to the speed of learning to read.

My child has problems with spelling. Is this due to bilingualism?

A frequent worry of parents is that learning to write in one language will interfere with learning to write in another. Spellings in one language seem **imitated** when writing the second. This is only a temporary stage that is ironed out as experience of reading and writing grows. If there are constant **spelling errors** (with dyslexia excepted), the primary cause is likely to be a lack of reading and writing practice and stimulation, rather than anything to do with bilingualism.

In the short term, there may be some transfer of spellings from one language to the other. From the child's point of view, this is creatively using their knowledge and experience to make headway in writing the second language. A child is making an intelligent, imaginative and thoughtful guess at spelling in the second language. This is sensible and **adaptive** behavior. As children increase their reading and writing in the second language, they learn to separate spellings in both languages. Few adults are perfect in their spelling, and bilinguals will be no different. Bilinguals are no better or worse spellers because of their bilingualism than monolinguals.

My child has been diagnosed as dyslexic. Should we develop reading and writing in one language and not two?

D13

Dyslexia is definitely not caused by bilingualism. There is no evidence that links dyslexia with being brought up as a bilingual or that ownership (e.g. from birth) of two or more spoken languages exacerbates dyslexia. This is the case irrespective of whether the child has mild, moderate or severe dyslexia. Wherever the child is placed on the continuum from mild to very severe dyslexia, understanding and speaking two or more languages does not trigger dyslexia.

Nevertheless, a dyslexic's problems will mean that decisions will have to be made about what language should be used to begin to learn to read and write. In one language or two? In the school language or a home language? In a majority language like English or in the minority language? In answering these questions (see below), it should be borne in mind that dyslexics have varied types and degrees of problem that will affect learning to read and write to a different extent.

First, parents of a dyslexic child are sometimes advised to concentrate on the child's school language particularly in learning to read and write. Sometimes (e.g. in Wales) this is advice to acquire literacy through a phonically consistent language (such as Welsh) rather than English (which is irregular and phonically inconsistent). For a dyslexic child, learning to read via a consistent phonetic language has advantages in ease and speed of learning.

An example is a language where the same letter or combination of letters always makes the same sound (e.g. Italian). The dyslexic child learns the 'sound rule' quicker than a language (e.g. English) that is irregular. In English, one letter can be pronounced in different ways (e.g. 'a' in cave and have; 'e' in her and here; 'i' in pint and mint). In English, a group of letters may change seemingly arbitrarily in their sound (e.g. 'ough' in tough, through, bough). For dyslexics, English is a particularly complex and more difficult language to learn to read and write.

This means that, where a child speaks two languages of which one is phonically inconsistent, if other things are reasonably equal, the better 'first language for learning to read' will be the phonically consistent one.

Second, if the only school language is English (or another irregular language), then it is usually sensible to concentrate on English reading and writing. If reading and writing in school is solely through English, then to ensure linguistic and intellectual development, English literacy must be stimulated. Reading is crucial for learning and study at school so the literacy of the school will be a major influence on the 'first language for learning to read'.

Third, once a child has achieved reasonable literacy skills in one language there are two effects. (a) The child has gained confidence in reading. For a dyslexic, such confidence is important for success to breed an expectation of more success (e.g. learning to read in a second language). When there is repeated failure in learning to read, it becomes disheartening for the child and increases the literacy problem. (b) Having acquired some skills in reading and writing in one language, there will be a transfer of skills into the second language: recognizing that letters mean sounds, decoding words as parts and wholes, making sensible guesses at words, understanding the meaning of a word in a sentence from the whole sentence, and that there are clues about words from previous sentences and pictures.

This means that a dyslexic child should not be banned from becoming biliterate. It implies that, once there is a solid foundation of reading and writing in one language, the other language can be introduced, particularly when there is sufficient self-interest, self-confidence and educational support. Often, the dyslexic child itself triggers an interest in acquiring second language literacy.

Fourth, should a dyslexic learn to read in two languages simultaneously in the initial stages? The answer is typically 'no'. For a dyslexic, learning literacy skills in one language is often slow and very difficult. Being taught two different systems at the same time from the outset will usually compound difficulties in acquiring the skills to read each language, developing at a fast enough rate to support curriculum learning, and developing confidence as a competent reader and writer.

However, if the environment is biliterate (e.g. with street signs and packaging in two languages), many inquisitive children will want to engage with both languages when they see them. Helping them to remember key words visually without necessarily learning the whole phonic system in the more complex language in the early stages may be satisfying for them, can be fun, and may lay the basis for later development of a broader range of reading and writing skills including biliteracy.

Reference for further reading

Cline, T. 2003, Bilingualism and dyslexia. *Bilingual Family Newsletter*, Vol. 20, No. 2, p. 4.

Education
Questions

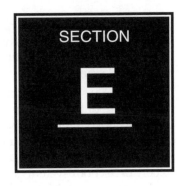

SECTION

E

BASIC EDUCATION QUESTIONS

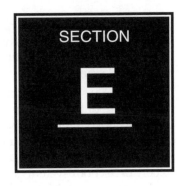

How can a pre-school playgroup or nursery school support children's bilingualism?

The answer to this question will only center on the language aspects of nursery schools. It will not discuss the possible benefits of nursery education in general. It is initially important to highlight situations where it may not be wise to send a child to a nursery school. If the family is attempting to raise the child in the minority language, and the nursery school runs through the medium of the majority language, parents need to make a careful decision about when to introduce the majority language. Many parents in **minority language situations** prefer to send their children to minority language nursery schools. If the minority language is threatened and in need of maintenance in the community, parents may wish their children to develop in the minority language before introducing the majority language.

Most children in **minority language** situations have little difficulty in acquiring the majority language. The majority language surrounds them in the mass media, as the common denominator in the street and playground, and as the dominant cultural medium in the teenage years. It is therefore quite usual for parents to wish to send their children to nursery schools using that minority language. Such nursery schools reinforce and extend the language development of the home.

If education through the minority language is not available, there is a danger in sending the child to a majority language nursery school. Exposure to the majority language at an early age may decrease the chances of the minority language retaining a strong place in the child's language life. Deferring entry to such a majority language nursery school needs to be considered, although pragmatically this is often impossible. Alternatives that will ensure the minority language is experienced fully in these formative years include: keeping the child at home, registered childminders, mother and toddler playgroups, and a group of carers meeting on an *ad hoc* basis.

A different situation occurs when a **majority language** parent wants the nursery school to help a child learn a **second language**. For example, there may be pre-school playgroups, mother and toddler groups, and nursery schools where children from English-language backgrounds attend (alongside Welsh speakers) and acquire the Welsh language. Apart from in Wales, there are experienced and expert pre-school systems in New Zealand, Ireland and Scandinavia. Similarly, the Dual Language Montessori approach provides immersion for the very young child in a second language (e.g. English and Spanish in the United States).

Through playing with other children, organized games and activities, children in a nursery school situation can easily and successfully pick up the basics of a second language. Depending on how many hours are spent in the nursery school, a child is likely to develop a good understanding of a second language. Speaking the second language fluently will come later than understanding.

An ability to **understand** a second language achieved at nursery school is an invaluable foundation for later blossoming in primary school. Sometimes parents find the nursery school seems to achieve little second language development success. They expect fluent speakers too soon. If such schools enable children to understand a second language, parents will find that primary education trans-forms passive understanding into active speaking quite quickly.

In an effective nursery school where children spend much of the day, and where adult language stimulation is well planned and delivered, fluency in a second language is possible. Such an immersion language situation is advanta-geous in producing a bilingual child.

In such a situation, the **majority language** of the home is **not at risk**. There will be sufficient exposure to the majority language in the home, in the outside environment, and later in formal schooling. Acquiring a second language in a well-organized and purposeful nursery school is usually straightforward and enjoyable. An early and valuable foundation is laid for bilingualism. Pre-school playgroups and nursery schools that are relaxed yet purposeful provide a context where children acquire a second language in a thorough manner.

What are the language features of an effective pre-school or nursery school to support my child's bilingualism?

At its best, bilingual pre-school education helps a child talk competently, con-fidently and clearly in two languages, using those skills to interact with adults and other children. Children will be helped to communicate thoughts, ideas and feelings to leaders and other children. Plenty of time and learning opportunities are planned to develop spoken language through conversations between children and adults, both one-to-one and in small groups.

Effective pre-school provision emphasizes communication, language and literacy that integrate with all the other important aspects of learning (e.g. personal, social and emotional development, mathematical development, knowledge and understanding of the world, physical development and creative development). Dual language development is encouraged through virtually every pre-school activity (e.g. when playing, role playing, eating, arriving and leaving).

An effective nursery or pre-school institution will be sensitive to the language levels of all children in their two languages and seek to encourage **individual development**. Sensitivity to personal needs and plans to linguistically develop each child are highly desirable. For example, giving instructions that each child understands, and using a level of language that sequentially enhances that child's language skills are important.

Equally valuable is giving the child plenty of **opportunity and encouragement** to practice their dual language skills. That is, each child needs the opportunity to be an active speaker and not a passive listener. This can be individual conversations, but also plenty of variety in singing, saying rhymes, collaborative play, group games and creative tasks, for example, allows language development across situations and activities, and in both languages. Young children enjoy stories, songs and short poems, and such oral experiences can soon be linked to literacy. A library of children's books in both languages, as well as DVDs, video, tapes and specialist computer programs will support early years' language learning. The wall displays and themes for each week or month can include two or more languages.

Thus an effective pre-school is a language-rich environment, in terms of teachers' communication and planned activities, material resources and stimulating play, and the encouragement of dual language use that provides a bilingual foundation not only for school but for life.

Should my child go to a bilingual school?

E3

Where parents have a **choice** of schooling, and this is not always the case, a **variety of factors need considering** when choosing an appropriate school for a child. The language (or languages) used in the school is an important part of that decision. Language should not be the only factor. Schools which support children's bilingualism range from the excellent, to the good, to the tolerable, and include the bad. A bilingual school is no guarantee of an effective or successful school. The ethos of the school, the commitment of the teachers, the success of the school in achieving literacy and numeracy, creativity in the expressive arts, a sound scientific foundation, moral development, a well-integrated and harmonious relationship between pupils, and effective cooperation with parents are just some of the factors that parents need to consider in deciding upon a suitable school.

In enquiring about the **language policy of the school**, it is important to hunt down the real language goals of the school. Schools are increasingly good at self-publicity, broadcasting visions and missions with regard to language and other policies. **Visits to classrooms**, careful questioning of the headteacher, principal, school administrator, and/or other teachers will reveal the language reality of the school and what a school actually achieves rather than what it says it hopes to achieve. Don't rely on the stated aims and objectives (or mission statement) of the school. Seek out the actual outcomes and track record of the school. Actions speak louder than words; performance is more important than promises.

Some schools have a **language policy** that encourages bilingualism. Yet close inspection reveals only a token use of the second language in the classroom. Other schools create linguistic and cultural diversity with ease and success, at no cost to their other aims and objectives.

Another situation is when there is **temporary bilingual support** given by the teacher or bilingual teacher assistants. For example, in some schools in England, children from Asian language backgrounds use their home language for one or two years with the help of a bilingual aide in the classroom. A similar pattern occurs with Spanish speakers in particular schools in the United States. Such bilingual support staff are valuable in cushioning the move from a language minority home to a majority language school.

Such schools may have a bilingual policy and may support bilingualism. However, the reality is that such schools aim for a quick transition from the Asian or Spanish language to working solely in the school language of English. Bilingualism is only temporarily supported for the child to feel 'at home' in the school. Children are soon encouraged not only in their development of English, but to operate solely in the curriculum in the English language. This is called transitional bilingual education.*

* See page 144f

In a **language minority situation** (see Glossary), the parent is likely to be interested in the minority language being present in the primary and the secondary school where possible. Sometimes called heritage language education, the aim of the school will be to support language development in the minority language. Literacy is encouraged in the minority language first. Around six or seven years of age, the majority language is likely to be introduced in the classroom. Once literacy in the minority language is well established, literacy in the second language – a majority language – soon develops. Generally, education through the minority language for a language minority child is the best option. A language minority child tends to be more successful in the curriculum than a similar child going to the majority language school.*

* See page 163

If the school supports the child's minority language, it is supporting the child itself, the child's home, the child's family and the child's heritage. Thereby, the school is maintaining the child's self-esteem and sense of self-confidence. If a child in a language minority situation is suddenly forced into using the majority language in school, their home, their parents and their self-image may be rejected. International research tends to show, in a variety of minority language situations, that children succeed better when educated through their home language. Such children still become fully bilingual and biliterate. A good heritage language bilingual school will ensure children can operate fluently and effectively in either language and become fully literate in both languages. Unless schools do this, they may not be giving their children an equal chance of employment, economic advancement and affluence in majority language-dominated economies.

When children are raised in the **majority language at home**, a different policy can be adopted about bilingual education. One example is Canada. In many parts of Canada, children who speak English in the home attend (from kindergarten onwards) schools that teach through the medium of French, called **immersion bilingual education**.* Children from majority language homes appear to be successful when **taught initially through a different majority language**. Eventually, such children are taught through both languages in the primary school. Through a gentle immersion at an early age in a second majority language, children become bilingual and biliterate with no loss to their academic performance. The essential point about such schools is that a child's home majority language is not replaced but added to (i.e. another majority language is gained). Children in such schools tend to start from the same basis – all are beginners in French.

* See page 145ff

A similar pattern is found with **majority language children taught through a minority language**. One example is Wales where increasing numbers of English-speaking parents opt to send their children to Welsh-medium primary and secondary schools. Particularly when such children start their education in Welsh at age four or five, their English language competence and curriculum performance does not suffer. Instead, they add a language and culture without cost to their home language and achievement in different school subjects.

What should I look out for in choosing a school for my bilingual child?

E4

If the school is known as a bilingual school, or as a monolingual (mainstream) school supporting bilingualism, it is important to seek out actual **use of**

languages throughout the curriculum. Is one language only taught for half an hour per day, or used to teach one subject such as Religious Education? How are two languages allocated in teaching the curriculum? How are languages separated in the school? A good bilingual school will have a detailed and thorough policy regarding the development of languages in the school and a policy about biliteracy. The school should have considered in detail the separation of the two languages both within the school curriculum and in the playground. Do teachers support the development of both languages – or is one language in reality given little status?

Another issue that needs considering is the status of **languages among children** in the school and the effects on what language children use most of the time. Do children constantly switch to a common denominator or high-status language such that the other language is insufficiently experienced in interaction between children? Does the numerical majority of children affect which language is most used? What language dominates, including in the playground? How does the school encourage development in the child's weaker language?

Part of language learning in the classroom and in the playground is the language interaction between children themselves. In primary school, when group work, project work, cooperation and discussion are particularly evident, and formal teaching by the teacher much less obvious than in secondary schools, the **informal language of the classroom** needs to be considered.

Where parents have no option for bilingual schooling, a chosen monolingual school also needs investigating. Have a look at **displays of children's work** in different classrooms. Are children's languages adequately represented on wall displays? Are the displays of children's work, posters, signs and information in the school monolingual, bilingual or multilingual? Have a look at the books and other language materials used in the classrooms. Is there an adequate supply of reading books, stimulating language materials, CDs, DVDs and work books to ensure that both languages can be developed in terms of oracy and literacy?

In choosing a school ask to see exam results and test scores. Such results are only one dipstick to measure a school. Many valuable aspects of a school evade simple exams and tests. Nevertheless, it is important to enquire about the language performance of the school in area-wide tests and exams. Can children follow both their languages to achieve 'passes' or graduation? Does the school encourage or allow children to take external exams for non-school languages (e.g. in Britain, Institute of Linguists exams for non-school languages such as Finnish)?

Ask about the **extracurricular activities** of the school. Will such activities support the child's bilingual development (e.g. dancing, singing, cultural festivals, discos, competitions, sport)?

Try to determine the **partnerships that exist between teachers and parents**. In an effective school, there is a close working relationship between parents and teachers, and time for discussion with parents about how to extend the child's education in the home. Effective schools aim for an integration of activity and purpose between home and school. This is important for an intercultural marriage (e.g. English–Finnish family). If a school understands the nature of an **intercultural family**, a child's self-esteem can be raised and dual cultural identity confirmed, even celebrated. Schools that are unable to support the child's home language (e.g. because only one child in the school speaks that language), should nevertheless have a positive attitude to the child's 'different' language. The bilingual nature of the child will be accepted, encouraged even celebrated in an effective school.

Bilingual schools will not have a bilingual policy just to support bilingualism or the maintenance of a minority language. They **support bilingualism because they support children**. Such schools are interested in the best interests of bilingual children. The ultimate language aims of the school must be the language interests of the child and not the fate of languages in society. A teacher once told me that she didn't teach through the medium of Welsh in the interests of the Welsh language and its future, but in the best interests of children. In bilingual education, such child-centered aims must be paramount.

The overall reputation and effectiveness of the school must be considered in a choice of school. Almost all parents would rather their child go to a stimulating and happy school than a school which is poorer in this respect but has a preferable language environment. A personal visit to the school and some 'intelligence gathering' is needed to make a sensible choice of schooling.

Should my child be taught bilingually in the primary school but not in the secondary school?   E5

Primary education often teaches children; secondary education often teaches subjects. While this is an exaggeration and an overgeneralization, there is a grain of truth that has implications for the way parents view bilingual education. Some parents find it quite natural for their children to be educated bilingually in the **primary school** because such schools are often **child-centered**. There is curriculum time and an informal, pleasant atmosphere for language acquisition to occur in the primary school. The primary years seem a time when language acquisition is a higher priority compared with the demands of later secondary school examination success. Some parents therefore see the primary school as the ideal arena where a child's bilingualism flourishes.

Sometimes, the same parents have different ideas for **secondary education**, which they consider a time to become serious about **subject learning**, examination success and readiness for university or the employment market. With the emphasis on mainstream subjects, a second language becomes an examination subject. Bilingual development for some parents does not become so important during the secondary years.

In countries where bilingual education flourishes successfully at the primary level, too often educational administrators, politicians and parents make bilingualism and bilingual education a lower priority in secondary schooling. One reason for bilingual secondary education is that it provides educational **language continuity**. Having been taught through two languages to the end of primary education, it is quite sensible for a child to continue the primary school language pattern in the secondary school curriculum. Research tends to suggest that dual use of language in the secondary school curriculum will not have a negative effect on progress and later success. Indeed, there may be a slight gain in achievement across the curriculum and, at the least, in **securing confidence and competence in a second language**. Bilingual secondary schools often produce children whose bilingualism and biliteracy are both well developed. One requirement is that children enter secondary education with sufficient language competence to cope with the language level used by teachers and found in curriculum materials.

Another requirement is that schools have appropriate curriculum materials in **both languages**. Quick translations from the majority language, poorly produced, photocopied worksheets and handouts are no substitute for professional, high-quality and up-to-date curriculum materials in the other language. This is expensive but fairly essential. Language minority secondary schools sometimes resort out of apparent necessity to glossy, majority language curriculum resources. In this circumstance, the relative status of the two languages is also projected and the minority language is shown to be deprived and inferior. This is an international problem found in many minority language schools.

I do not speak the same language of the school. How can I help my children with their homework?

This is one of the most frequently asked questions by parents who otherwise support bilingual education for their children, but do not speak the language of the school curriculum. They therefore fear their children will lose out. That parent believes (wrongly) that they cannot support the child with their homework and will not be able to monitor their child's progress. The parent worries that the child will suffer from not having help from home.

The advice is this. Ask the child to explain their homework in the parent's preferred language. If this is different from the school language there is a bonus. In translation, the child is often rethinking, reconceptualizing and digesting school learning. In translating for the parent, the child is valuably reprocessing, almost thinking out loud. If the child has understood it in two languages, they have really understood it. However, some specialist words (e.g. in Mathematics and Science) may need help from a dictionary.

Since understandings and explanations are being reconsidered and reprocessed, deeper learning may occur. The child is helping himself or herself; the parent is given the opportunity to advise, explain, correct and encourage. The outcomes can be remarkably enhancing for learning.

So rather than parents disadvantaging their children, the act of moving from one language to another will often advantage the child, and this can occur at elementary/primary school level and at secondary level. Secondary children whose two languages are both well developed usually have little difficulty in translating to help parents understand homework concerns. While it may take a little extra time to translate, the secondary school child and monolingual parent can interact and think through a homework problem together.

Children in secondary education can have their textbooks in one language with parallel or similar textbooks in a second language also available. Therefore, in mathematics and the sciences, children can have access to explanations and illustrations in both languages to help increase their probability of understanding.

The language of the university is different from that of the secondary school. Will my child suffer because they have not been educated in the language used at the university?   `E7`

Another objection by some bilingual parents to bilingual secondary schooling is that the language of universities and colleges is often a majority language. By the age of 16, 17 and 18, bilingual children seem so fluent at switching between languages that they can relatively easily adapt to working at university or college in either language. So long as the language to be used at university has been well developed and there is the depth of vocabulary and complexity of linguistic structure required in **higher or tertiary education**, there is little reason why a child cannot switch languages from school to college.

Increasing numbers of bilingual students, my own family included, take their university education in a different language to their schooling. Once they have acquired the technical language (e.g. in science and mathematics) in the 'university' language, they typically have no problem in succeeding at university. Understandings are available to the child through any language that they speak well.* To gain entry to university means bilingual students will often have high competence in academic studies. That is, they are intellectually ready for university studies.

For students linguistically competent in both languages, they can take their university courses in either language, or both. For students who will take their studies in a language that has not reached the standard required (specialized vocabulary excepted) to understand and learn at university level, then pre-sessional (and in-sessional) language courses may be valuable, even essential. For example, courses on academic writing or advanced English are very common in universities that operate through English and which attract international students. Pastoral and language support may also be available at an individual level to ensure a transition from school to university.

E8 Should older children not be placed in bilingual education?

As children and parents move from one area to another, so difficulties may arise in the language medium of the school. For example, when children are between the ages of seven and sixteen, and their language has not developed sufficiently to allow them easy entry into the language used in the curriculum of the school, what alternatives exist?

For **language minority children** (see Glossary), when there is a choice between attending a minority or majority language school, wise parents will usually opt for the minority language school. For a language minority child to switch suddenly to working in a majority language curriculum, is like pushing that child into the deep end of a swimming pool, expecting them to sink or swim. Some children do initially splash around and quickly learn to swim. Others are overwhelmed and become isolated or aggressive, losing self-confidence and status within the peer group and with teachers.

If a **minority language child** has to move into majority language medium education (e.g. due to moving to live in another country), the parent may wish to ensure a foundation for that child by increased exposure to the majority language before the child moves school. This may involve language lessons and using specific times and places in the home for increased exposure to the majority language. Such a switch requires discussions between parent and child about anxieties, so as to ease the transition. Parents also need to visit the new school to explain the language situation of the family to teachers to help them be more sensitive to the language needs of the child, and their transition into a new language environment, even to the extent of extra language support in the initial stages. Also, parents may be able to encourage friendships for their child with similarly placed families in the new locality.

If a **majority language** parent moves to a different language environment, the same advice applies. There may be supplementary language courses before, or as soon as the child enters the new school. For example, in Wales, there are language centers for majority language in-migrants into the area. The children spend 15 or more weeks in such minority language centers before entering primary school. The children are taught the new language in a lively and attractive way, and simultaneously, efforts are made to ensure that their work throughout the core curriculum is kept up to age expectations. When children are sufficiently fluent to understand the language in the classroom, they are transferred to a mainstream primary school.

In other cases, there are classes (e.g. withdrawal classes) within a school for children who are late entrants. While long-term use of separate classes tends to stigmatize children, in the short term there may be a language necessity for extra provision to be given.

Older children experience a more advanced curriculum and therefore require a more advanced language to cope. Hence, movement from one language medium to another tends to become more difficult as children progress through their school years. If sympathetically, sensitively and carefully handled by teachers, language transition is possible. After initial worries and concerns by children and their parents, children are resilient and adaptable to new situations, including new language situations. It is important that children are accepted, their self-esteem is preserved, their confidence in their academic ability is maintained and their first language is not the subject of derision and disparagement.

There are some situations when parents have the choice of moving an older child to a bilingual school and away from a monolingual school. Children entering middle or late immersion programs in Canada* learn through the medium of French and English. However, there are large numbers of children in the same situation making the transition easier.

* See page 145f

In a school which uses a different language **up to the age of seven,** there are usually **few transition problems**. After the age of seven, there is often a need for a child to quickly acquire **language competence sufficient for working in the curriculum**. If such language competence can be relatively speedily achieved, a switch to a different language medium is possible throughout the primary school years.

When a child will struggle in the long term (and not just short term) to catch up with the language competence required to cope, parents may need to consider the alternatives carefully. Parents' relative priorities in schooling (e.g. exam success, moral and social development) need weighing against language priorities. Maintaining a child's positive academic self-concept and positive achievement in the curriculum is essential to ensure that success breeds success.

Is there a 'critical age' when children shouldn't be moved to a school with a different language pattern in the curriculum?

E9

A critical age is when an aspect of development can *only* occur at one (usually very early) time in a person's life. In the 1960s, one viewpoint suggested that there was a particular critical period (see Glossary) in young children for language to develop easily. Research has since suggested that there are no critical periods within a child's language development. Advances in language are possible later in life if they have not occurred earlier. A second language can be successfully acquired from birth or in retirement years.

However, there are often **advantageous periods**. Acquiring a second language very early in life has advantages (e.g. for pronunciation). Developing a second language in the pre-school and primary school is advantageous, giving an early foundation and many more years ahead for that language to mature. In the early years of schooling, a second language is acquired rather than learnt. Such advantageous periods occur when there is a higher probability of language acquisition due to circumstances, time available, teaching resources and motivation.

The question points to an important decision for parents who **move to a different geographical area**. Children vary in their ability to adapt to a new language environment, and their attitude and motivation to picking up a new language quickly. The quality and quantity of practice in the new language available in the school and outside school also varies. However, as a rough guide, and with many children being exceptions to this guide, here is a suggestion. Up to the **age of seven**, there seems little problem with children quickly adapting to the new language environment of a school. The language used in the classroom in the infant years tends to be relatively simple and straightforward, and fairly quickly acquired. The infant classroom involves project work, plenty of action and role playing, and plenty of interaction with other children, all of which enable children to acquire a new language relatively quickly.

Between the ages of seven and eleven or twelve, children need support within and outside the classroom to enable them to acquire sufficient competence in a language to cope in the classroom. As curriculum areas become more complex, as present learning is built on prior learning, as ideas and concepts become more complex, a child's level of language needs to be more advanced. Such children will probably need extra language support.*

* See page 156ff

In secondary education, **after the ages of 12 and 13**, it becomes relatively more difficult for a child to face a completely new and different language pattern in the curriculum. The subject-based curriculum, the move to assessments and examinations, the increasing complexity of Science and Mathematics, Humanities, Social Sciences and Expressive Arts all make coping in a different language difficult.

* See page 145ff

In late immersion bilingual education,* the Canadians have shown that it is possible for children to learn through a different language in secondary education. The difference here is that children in late immersion bilingual education will all start from the same language point. There is homogeneity within children in the class, and children will have had French lessons in the primary/elementary school before moving into late immersion.

In the very **early years of secondary schooling** some children may adapt to being taught through a new language, if one or usually more of the following is provided: sufficient language support is given in the classroom; there are extra language classes outside the usual subject curriculum; the child is relatively optimistic and has a positive attitude and motivation to learning in a new language; and if there is much parental support and encouragement. However, in reality, after one or two years of secondary schooling, using a new language in the curriculum will be quite difficult. At this stage, parents need to consider alternative options – such as the child remaining in their current school, living with the extended family or friends, thereby retaining continuity in schooling.

My children can hold a conversation in a second language. Is that sufficient for them to be taught in that language at school?

E10

There is an important distinction between **conversational language and classroom language**. There are language skills required to hold a conversation in the shop, on the street and in the home. A different type of language competence is required to operate successfully in the classroom. The language of a classroom is more tacit, more complex and more abstract.

In the street, in the shop, on the television and at home, language is relatively simple. There are plenty of cues and clues in the environment, plenty of body language, pointing and gesticulating to convey messages and information. In the **classroom**, as children grow older, there are fewer contextual cues and clues. The language of concepts becomes more complex, requiring a higher level of language competence to decode the messages of the classroom.

One danger with bilingual children is when their level of language competence is not sufficient to cope in the more difficult language environment of the classroom. Children who have recently learned a language may not have the level of **language competence to enable them to understand the teacher's instruction**, the curriculum content of textbooks and discussions among peers. Thus, a bilingual whose second language is not so well developed as their first language needs monitoring to ensure that their second language skills are sufficiently advanced to cope in the more complex and abstract classroom language situation.

While conversational language and classroom language are typically different, the exact nature of language development required for classroom use remains elusive. Nevertheless, the distinction is important because it highlights a trap for teachers and parents. The trap is expecting children to work in the curriculum with insufficient development in their second language. Recognition of this distinction allows parent and teacher to attempt to establish such language competence as is needed for a child to cope in the curriculum, before presenting that child with overly complex curriculum material.

My child is learning through a second language at school. Should we change our language pattern at home?

If a child is coping well at school, including learning through a language that is not used in the home, a different language may be used at home. Only if the child is having real longer-term difficulties in understanding the language of the classroom should parents consider switching from the home language to the school language to help the child's educational development. Language is not like a switch with an 'on and off' button. Language patterns in a home tend to be well established. There is potential danger in changing abruptly. So generally, it is important to be **natural** in the language of the home, to establish continuity and a stimulating language environment.

If the **school** language is a majority language, there is usually no need to change the home language. There are sufficient hours in school and when doing homework to ensure development in that language. When a child from a minority language is studying through a majority language at school, wherever possible, parents should continue to support the minority language to support the child's psychological development.

When a **language minority** child in a majority language classroom has educational difficulties, parents may be placed in a difficult and paradoxical situation. To switch to the majority language in the home means denying part of the family reality and vitality, denying identity, distinctiveness and individuality. Such a child in the majority language school may be failing due to being submerged among children who can speak that majority language fluently. If minority language education is available, parents may decide to educate their children through that minority language, while ensuring that they become fully bilingual.

If the only available schooling for the language minority child is through the majority language, the temptation is sometimes to change to the majority language at home. Well-meaning professionals often advise the switch. The preference of politicians and public is often that language minority in-migrants, in particular, integrate and assimilate through dropping their language. This is a real dilemma that involves a careful calculation of priorities in family and educational life. Continuity of language and culture must be weighed against attempted language enablement and empowerment of the child to suit a dominantly monolingual school and a monolingual society.

Parents can provide out-of-school support for a child learning the majority language, particularly when there is slow development. Such support can be given by extra lessons, by using friends and neighbors, by parents involving themselves in their child's learning. The child needs to be thoroughly supported and encouraged in majority language school work. The attitude of the parents and a positive and facilitative environment in the home support the child through difficult acclimatization periods.

If parents do decide to use the majority language in the home to develop the child's majority language skills, they need to consider carefully how the family identity, heritage and culture can still be maintained so that there is sufficient bedrock and strength to establish family continuity.

How easy or difficult will it be for my children to find a job if they are bilingual?

E12

Although bilingualism and bilingual education provide no guarantee of employment, bilinguals seem increasingly required as international trade barriers fall and a more global economy grows. Bilinguals and **multilinguals** are currently needed in the international retail sector, tourism, international transport, public relations, mass media, banking and accountancy, information technology, interpreting (see Glossary) and translating, nursing, secretarial work, marketing and sales, the law, teaching and overseas aid work, for example.* The increase in screen-based and information-based labor has led to bilinguals and multilinguals being marketable and desirable. In the wake of 9/11, intelligence-gathering, diplomacy, foreign relations and national security has led to the need for those fluent in languages other than English. For example, the US Defense Language Institute in Monterey, California has around a 2500 student enrollment supplying the US army, navy, air force, Department of Defense, CIA and FBI with employees whose language skills are vital to their post.

* See page 184

Wherever there is a customer interface, then multilinguals have an advantage in employment and promotion. With patients in hospitals, buyers in competitive markets, and government services, the bilingual and multilingual can communicate in the language of the customer. Customer satisfaction, increased profits and effective service provision is then enhanced. If the customer is king, then speaking the language of the client is important in keeping the king satisfied and served. Research in Wales found that bilinguals tend to earn 8 to 10% extra because of their ability to work in two languages.

Bilinguals don't always work in high-status jobs. Moving country to find work or better employment has increased in recent decades. People of different nations often seek an alternative employment market in richer countries. Around half of the Irish population since 1820 has emigrated to find work. Germany and the Benelux countries (Belgium, Netherlands, Luxembourg) countries are particularly good examples of movement among workers. Such immigrants may still find that their degree of bilingualism and multilingualism is important in securing work. The ability to speak the majority language of the new country or region may be valuable in securing employment.

There is another variety of bilingual who may find their bilingualism an advantage in the employment market. As central international trade increases, there is also increasing concern about peripheral areas of countries. Where rural areas with scattered populations are in need of economic development, there is a growing European interest in assuring that economic advantage and affluence is shared as widely as possible. Therefore, in places such as rural Ireland and Wales, the highlands and islands of Scotland, there have been major attempts at economic regeneration where the minority language is strong. Among such marginalized language minority communities (see Glossary), there is an awareness that **language maintenance requires economic regeneration**. Unless there are jobs for minority language speakers in the area, they will migrate and lose their language.

Therefore, many **new rural enterprises and industries** have grown. There is more economic aid to areas where minority languages coexist with less economic growth, attempting simultaneously to support economic regeneration and language preservation. In other minority language communities, there are self-help, language minority group-generated industries and activities.

Some Asian communities in England are a particularly good example of a language minority creating and supporting their **own industries** (e.g. the clothing industry). The Chinese throughout the world also seem able to establish their own businesses and simultaneously engage in language preservation in local Chinese communities. Yiddish- and Hebrew-speaking peoples have also taken part in the strong Jewish tradition of economic vitality alongside religious and language vigor.

Bilingualism or multilingualism provides no promise of a job, of financial fortune or a high quality of life but there is a current indication that it may give the competitive edge, an extra qualification and sometimes an essential customer-friendly skill in employment and affluence in a rapidly changing economy.

TYPES OF BILINGUAL EDUCATION

What types of bilingual education exist?

There are many different types of bilingual school. The main types of bilingual schools will now be briefly introduced and then considered in detail in different questions in this section.

Dual Language schools are found in the United States. There are a variety of **terms** used to describe such United States schools: Two-Way Schools, Two-Way Immersion, Two-Way Bilingual Education, Developmental Bilingual Education and Dual Language Education. **International schools** teach through a majority language (usually English) and sometimes incorporate a local language(s) into the curriculum. The aim of International schools can be, but not always, bilingualism and biculturalism. English is usually the dominant language of the school. The **European Schools Movement** tends to celebrate multilingualism, using two or three languages for content learning. Each of these types of bilingual schooling are discussed in this section.

For language minority children, there are **Heritage Language schools** (with a variety of different names). Such schools are found in many areas of the world. A Heritage Language school seeks to deliver much of the curriculum in the child's minority language, whether it is an indigenous language or an 'immigrant' language. By the age of leaving an elementary Heritage Language school, children are usually bilingual in the heritage and a majority language as well as being biliterate.

In Canada, there are **Immersion schools** where English speakers are taught mostly or partly through the medium of French. Such schools have also subsequently appeared in Europe and Asia using two majority languages. The 'immersion' child already owns one prestigious language, and acquires another high-status language in school. Immersion children usually become bilingual and biliterate.*

* See page 145ff

Immersion schools, Heritage Language schools, International schools and Dual Language schools are **'strong' forms of bilingual education**. The promotion of two or more languages is attempted, as is biliteracy and biculturalism or multiculturalism. Each 'strong' type of bilingual school aims to enrich the child, particularly linguistically. There are also **'weak' or 'non' forms of bilingual education**. These 'weak' forms of bilingual education include: mainstreaming (see Glossary – also called submersion), mainstreaming with Withdrawal classes, Structured Immersion, Sheltered English and Transitional Bilingual Education. They are found in countries where the aim is to enable the language minority child to operate in the majority language of the country.* The intended outcomes of 'weak' forms of bilingual education often include monolingualism in the majority language of the country (or limited bilingualism) and **assimilation** (see Glossary) into mainstream culture, values and attitudes.

* See page 144f

In the United States, 'weak' forms of bilingual education attempt to submerse Spanish speakers, for example, in the English language, or provide a fast transition from dominance in Spanish to dominance in English. In England, the aim is to ensure that speakers of different Asian languages (and Greeks and Turks) are taught through the medium of English, to speak standard English and become patriotic citizens of Britain. The justifications, politics and problems of 'weak' forms of bilingual education are discussed below in succeeding questions.

What are Dual Language schools?

E14

Children in Dual Language schools learn through two languages. Some periods of teaching will use one language; other periods the second language so that children become bilingual and biliterate. Children from different language backgrounds (e.g. English, Spanish) are integrated for most or all of the timetable.

Mostly found among United States elementary schools, classrooms ideally contain a mixture of language majority and language minority children. For example, half the children may come from Spanish-speaking homes; the other half from English language backgrounds. A **language balance** close to 50:50% is attempted but not often achieved. If one language becomes dominant (e.g. due to much larger numbers of one language group), the aim of bilingualism and biliteracy may be at risk.

An **imbalance** in the two languages among students may result in one language being used to the exclusion of the other (e.g. smaller numbers of Spanish-speaking children having to switch to English to work cooperatively). Alternatively, one language group may become sidelined (e.g. Spanish speakers become excluded from dominant English-speaking groups). Segregation rather than integration may occur. In the creation of a Dual Language school or classroom, careful student selection decisions have to be made to ensure a **language balance**.

If an **imbalance** does exist, it may be preferable to have slightly more language minority children (see Glossary). Where there is a preponderance of language majority children, the tendency is for language minority children to switch to the higher status, majority language. In most (but not all) language contexts, the majority language is well represented outside of the school (e.g. in the media and in employment). Therefore, this external influence can be complemented by a balance towards the minority language in school (among student intake and in curriculum delivery). However, if there is a particularly high number of language minority children, the perceived prestige of the school may sometimes suffer (both among language majority and language minority parents).

There are situations where **attracting language majority students** to a Dual Language school is difficult. Where the monolingual mainstream school is as (or more) attractive to prospective parents, recruitment to Dual Language schools may be a challenge. For parents, the choice of such Dual Language Bilingual Programs for their children will be voluntary and not enforced. Hence, the good **reputation**, perceived effectiveness and curriculum success of such Dual Language schools becomes crucial to their continuation. Evidence from the United States suggests that while language minority parents are often support-ive of such a program, majority language parents may need more persuading. Community backing and involvement in the school is also important in long-term success.

The **aim** of a Dual Language school is not just to produce bilingual and biliter-ate children. To gain status and to flourish, such a school needs to show success throughout the curriculum. On standardized tests, on attainment compared with other schools in the locality, and in specialisms (e.g. music, sport, science), a Dual Language school will strive to show relative success. A narrow focus on proficiency in two languages will be an insufficient aim.

The **goals** of Dual Language schools may be couched in terms such as 'equality of educational opportunity for children from different language backgrounds', 'child-centered education building on the child's existing language competence', 'a community dedicated to the integration of all its children', 'enrichment not compensatory education', 'a family-like experience to produce multicultural children', and 'supporting Bilingual Proficiency not Limited English Proficiency'. Such Dual Language schools thus have a diversity of aims. These essentially include achievement throughout the curriculum, social integration of children in the school and community, a positive self-image in each child, and attempting equality of access to opportunity among all students. Such equality of opportunity is offered to recent or established in-migrants, and to those living in language minority or language majority homes.

One of the special aims of Dual Language schools (e.g. compared with mainstream schools) is to produce thoroughly **bilingual, biliterate and multicultural children**. Language minority students are expected to become literate in their native language (see Glossary) as well as in the majority language. Language majority students are expected to develop language and literacy skills in a second language. At the same time, they must make normal progress in their first language. To achieve these aims, a variety of practices are implemented in Dual Language schools.

(1)   The two **languages** of the school (e.g. Spanish and English, Chinese and English, Haitian Creole and English) have **equal status**. Both languages will be used as a medium of instruction. Mathematics, Science and Social Studies, for example, may be taught in both languages.

(2)   The **school ethos** will be bilingual. Such an ethos is created by classroom and corridor displays, notice boards, curriculum resources, cultural events, extracurricula activity using both languages in a relatively balanced way. Announcements across the school address system will be bilingual. Letters to parents will also be in two languages. While playground conversations and student-to-student talk in the classroom is difficult to influence or manipulate, the school environment aims to be transparently bilingual.

(3)   In some Dual Language schools, the two **languages** are **taught** as languages (e.g. aspects of spelling, grammar, metaphors and communicative skills – sometimes called Language Arts instruction). In other Dual Language schools, use of both languages as a medium of instruction is regarded as sufficient to ensure bilingual development. Children are expected to **acquire proficiency** in language informally throughout the curriculum. In both cases, reading and writing in both languages are likely to receive direct attention in the curriculum and literacy will be acquired in both languages either simultaneously or with an initial emphasis on native language literacy. Biliteracy is as much an aim as full bilingualism.

(4)   **Staff** in the dual language classrooms are often bilingual. Such **teachers**

use both languages on different occasions with their students. Where this is difficult (e.g. due to teacher supply), teachers may be paired and work together closely as a team. A teacher's aide, paraprofessionals, secretaries, custodial staff, parents offering or invited to help the teacher may also be bilingual. Language minority **parents** can be valuable 'teacher auxiliaries' in the classroom. For example, parents and grandparents may recount authentic stories, dances and recipes, and share the traditions and wisdom of previous generations. This underlines the importance of the cultural heritage of language minorities being shared in the classroom to create an **additive** (see Glossary) bilingual and multicultural environment.

(5)   The **length of the Dual Language program** needs to be longer rather than shorter. Such a program for two or three grades is insufficient. A minimum of four years extending through the grades as far as possible is more desirable to ensure a fuller and deeper development of language skills, and biliteracy in particular. Where a United States Dual Language program lasts for more years, there is a tendency for the curriculum to be increasingly taught in English.

A central idea in Dual Language schools is **language separation and com-partmentalization**. In each period of instruction, only one language is used. **Language boundaries** are established in terms of time, curriculum content and teaching. These will each be considered.

First, a decision is made about **when** to teach through each language. One preference is to use on **alternate days**. On the door of the classroom may be a message about which language is to be used that day. Alternately, **different lessons** may use **different languages** with a regular changeover to ensure both languages are used in all curricula areas.

There are other possibilities. The division of time may be in half-days, alternate weeks, alternate half-semesters. The essential element is the approximate distribution of time to achieve bilingual and biliterate students.

The amount of time spent learning through each language varies from school to school. Often, a 50:50% balance in use of languages is attempted in early and later grades. In other classrooms, the minority language will be given more time (60, 75, 80 and 90% is not uncommon), especially in the first two or three years. In the middle and secondary years of schooling, there is sometimes a preference for a 50:50% balance, or more accent on the majority language (e.g. 70% through English, 30% through Spanish).

Whatever the division of time, instruction in a Dual Language school will keep **boundaries** between the languages. Switching languages within a lesson is not officially acceptable. If language mixing by the teacher occurs, students may wait until there is delivery in their stronger language, and become uninvolved at other times. When there is clear separation, the Spanish speakers,

Young children develop bilingualism effortlessly and naturally through play. (Photo © Regina Cassidy).

Developing reading and writing skills in a second language is important in communication, enculturation, school achievement, employment and sometimes religion. (Photo © National Centre for Language and Literacy).

Modern technology enables children to communicate across the world, in voice and text, through whatever languages they choose. (Photo © Kathryn King).

Some of the reading skills in one language transfer to reading in another language. (Photo © National Centre for Language and Literacy).

Dual language books help bilingual children, supportive parents and small groups in school with learning to read. (Photo by John Dorricott).

A selection of groceries from a UK supermarket shows how world-wide trade has meant greater contact between languages. (Photo by John Dorricott).

Dual language schools in the USA date back to 1963. Coral Way Elementary School is one such school, developed by the US Cuban community in Florida. (Photo © Coral Way School).

Children of different first languages find bilingualism and multilingualism provide them with a common language. (Photo © National Centre for Language and Literacy).

for example, may help the English-speakers on Spanish days, and the English-speakers help the Spanish-speakers on English days. Interdependence may stimulate cooperation and friendship, as well as learning and achievement. The potential problems of segregation and racial hostility may thus be considerably reduced.

However, the two languages will sometimes be switched or mixed in the classroom (e.g. in private conversations, in further explanations by a teacher). Use of languages by children, especially when young, is not usually consciously controlled.*

There is an important **paradox** in Dual Language schools. Boundaries are kept between languages so that separation does not occur between children. English- and non-English speakers are integrated in all lessons through language segregation.

Second, bilingual **teachers** ensure they do not switch languages. Children hear them using one language (during the allotted session) and are expected to respond in that same language. When there is a shortage of bilingual teachers, a pairing of teachers may ensure language separation. A teacher using Spanish only will work in close association with a teacher who only uses English with the same class. Such teamwork requires teachers to be committed to bilingualism and multiculturalism as important educational aims.

Third, language boundaries can be established so that different parts of the curriculum are taught in different languages. For example, Social Studies and Environmental Studies may be taught in Spanish, Science and Mathematics in English. However, one danger is that the majority language becomes aligned with modern technology and science, while the minority language becomes associated with tradition and culture. This may affect the status of the language in the eyes of the child, parents and society. The relationship of languages to employment prospects, economic advantage and power thus need considering. Many Dual Language schools do not operate like this, but teach each curriculum area through both languages, but on different days (e.g. mathematics instruction is in Spanish on Monday and English on Tuesday).

Such Dual Language schools differ from **Transitional Bilingual Education*** and **Submersion/Mainstream/English Second Language** approaches by teaching through the medium of two languages over four or more grades, enabling children to achieve increasing proficiency in two languages.

Dual Language schools differ from **Immersion Bilingual Education*** in the language backgrounds of the students. Immersion schools normally contain only language majority children learning much or part of the curriculum through a second language, whereas Dual Language schools contain a balanced mixture of children from two (or more) different language backgrounds.

For further details about Dual Language schools, see: http://www.cal.org/twi/

What are Dual Language Peace schools?

In Israel and Macedonia, there are examples of bilingual education to attempt social and cultural change, particularly in strengthening the weak, empowering the powerless, and working for peace and humanity in the midst of war and terror. Such schools are particularly concerned with **peace initiatives**. The role of dual language schools in bringing peace is well illustrated by Dawn Tankersley in an article entitled 'Bombs or bilingual programmes?'. Situated in the recent ethnic conflict in the Balkans, she examines a Macedonian/Albanian dual language program. The program demonstrated success in aiding community rebuilding after the war and the growth of cross-ethnic friendships. The case study shows the potential for bilingual education to develop students' respect for different languages and cultures, and help to resolve ethnic conflict.

A similar dual language (Arabic/Hebrew) program with the aim of breaking down barriers of mistrust and building peace is located in a village (Neve Shalom/Wahat Al-Salam) in Israel. In this community, **Jews and Palestinians** attempt to live together harmoniously and cooperatively, maintaining respect for the culture, identity and languages of each group. This social engineering is attempted by two schools: an elementary school and the 'School for Peace', that create bilingual Hebrew–Arabic bilinguals, biculturals and students sensitive to each others' traditions, religions and customs. Jewish children learn through Arabic, and Palestinian children learn through Hebrew so as to increase intergroup sensitivity, respect and integration.

Yet such schools cannot be islands, and 'bottom-up' rather than 'top-down' initiatives are not always easy to sustain. **Peace schools** are inevitably part of a wider society, such that equality of languages can be difficult to sustain. Parents also have other dreams, such as English language fluency, high educational achievement and social mobility for their children, that make language and political dreams one component in a complex whole. Yet such initiatives symbolize that bilingual education can include a vision that goes beyond languages, with a vision of peace upon earth for our children.

Reference for further reading

Tankersley, D. 2001, Bombs or bilingual programmes?: Dual language immersion, transformative education and community building in Macedonia. *International Journal of Bilingual Education and Bilingualism*, Vol, 4, No. 2, pp. 107–124.

What are International schools?

International schools are a diverse collection of schools throughout the world. Numbering over 850, they are found in more than 80 countries, mostly in large cities. Parents pay fees for mostly **private, selective, independent education**. Some of the children in these schools have parents in the diplomatic service, multinational organizations, international businesses, and who are geographically and vocationally mobile. Other children come from the locality, whose parents want their children to have an internationally flavored education.

One **language** (sometimes *the* language) of the school is usually English. Such schools become bilingual when a local or another international language is incorporated in the curriculum. Sometimes the second language (taught for up to 12 years) is only taught as a language. In other schools, the second language is used as a medium to teach part of the curriculum. Some schools enable their students to acquire third and fourth languages. Generally, the languages of International schools are majority languages with international prestige.

The elementary and secondary **curriculum** tends to reflect United States, British, as well as the local curriculum tradition. The teachers are from varying countries, usually with a plentiful supply of British and American trained staff. Sometimes preparing children for the International Baccalaureate, United States tests or British examinations, most prepare their clientele for universities in Europe and North America.

References for further reading

Second Language Students in Mainstream Classrooms: A Handbook for Teachers in International Schools (1998), by Coreen Sears, is an excellent source of information as is Maurice Carder's *Bilingualism in International Schools* (2007). Both are published by Multilingual Matters: http://www.multilingual-matters.com/.

E17

What is the European Schools Movement?

The European Schools Movement **aims** to produce children who are multilingual and biliterate in languages of the European Union. The schools are located in various countries in Europe. Children learn through their home language and a second language. They are also taught a third language. Classroom time is allocated for activities to integrate children of diverse language backgrounds.

The **European Schools Movement** started in the 1950s and its schools are found in Belgium, Germany, Italy, the Netherlands and England. The schools were originally designed to provide education partly for the children of European Union workers. Sons and daughters of diplomats, civil servants, translators, technicians and domestic workers have priority of access. The original intention of the European schools was also for relatively open access to children of different nationalities who were not necessarily families of European Union officials. Thus places are made available to children within the locality, partly to balance the language mix of the school.

The schools are truly multilingual in character and cater for some 15,000 children from a wide variety of different European Union nations. Many languages of the European Union have **equal status** within the schools. Therefore, each school may have a variety of sub-sections reflecting the **first languages** of the children.

One central aim of the school is to support and extend the child's first language. In the primary years, much of a child's instruction is through their native language (see Glossary). Children become thoroughly literate in their native language and are taught its attendant culture (see Glossary). The schools also engineer the integration between children from different regions.

All children are taught a second language from the beginning of the primary / elementary school. The language is taught by native speakers and not the class teacher, to ensure excellent role models. Children who are native speakers of the vehicular language may also be present in the schools. In European Schools this second language is called a **vehicular language** or working language.

In the first and second grades, the second language will only be taught as a language. In these grades, no curriculum subjects will be taught through the second language. In the third, fourth and fifth grades, such language teaching continues. Physical education may also be taught through the second language. By the end of primary education, approximately 25% of the curriculum is taught through the second language. This proportion increases as the child goes through secondary education. In Grades 6 though 8, the second language will be taught as a subject as well as teaching the following subjects through it: Design Technology, Music, Physical Education and complementary activities. In Grades 9 through 12, History, Geography and options such as Economics and Social Sciences will be taught through the second language. For children coming into the school late, there are 'catching-up classes' and 'support classes' to increase proficiency in the second language.

While European Schools ensure the development of the child's first language and cultural identity, they also aim to promote a sense of **European identity**. Many centuries of rivalry and conflict in Europe have meant that national differences rather than a shared European identity are still common. With a considerable mix of different nationalities within a European School, teachers are on guard against prejudice and rivalry.

One form of integration is through **communal lessons** (see Glossary). The more the child progresses through the grades, the more lessons are taught to mixed language groups. In the primary school, these communal lessons are known as **European Hours**. Starting in the third year of primary education, there are three such lessons a week lasting two hours and fifteen minutes.

The primary aim is for children from different language sections to work and play together. As the lessons develop, children should become more aware of their similarities rather than differences, of their **common European heritage**, and of the importance of living peacefully and harmoniously together. In classes of 20 to 25 students, cooperative activities such as cooking are used to integrate children. Teachers are given freedom of choice of activity so long as such activity engages cooperation between children. All elementary school teachers are involved in the European Hours. However, teachers change classes during the school year to reinforce the multicultural and multilingual aspects of European Hours.

The classroom atmosphere and **ethos** of European Hours is regarded as essential. Enjoyable, motivating projects are used, with satisfying and attainable goals. Small multilingual groups work together to attain a goal. Cooperation is essential for a successful outcome.

Given that five or six different languages may coexist among students within the European Hours classroom, children act as translators for the teacher. If the instruction is given in French and the teacher cannot speak German, children who can speak both languages act as informal interpreters.

Two **European Hours** lessons per week are conducted in the classroom. The third European Hours lesson is a games activity with the same aims and processes. No child is forced to use a particular language in European Hours. Valuably, the circumstances create a hidden curriculum. The hidden message to the child is of the importance of cooperation between languages, of accepting multilingualism as natural and workable.

The nature of the **European Hours project** makes is cognitively less demanding than other subjects. The project also tends to be '**context embedded**' (see Glossary). That is, the activity does not depend on language alone, but actions can relay a lot of information between children. This teaches the child that harmony and cooperation can occur with relative ease and that languages are not barriers to cooperation. Does it work? In one research study, it was found that in the latter stages of secondary schooling, the majority of students had best friends in a language section *other* than their own.

Teachers are recruited from different European education systems and all are **native speakers** of a school language. They must also be **bilingual** or multilingual. No special teacher training or certification is required to work in a European School but a National Teachers Certificate is needed from that person's native country. There is currently almost no training in Europe for working in a multilingual or multicultural school such as a European School. Therefore, teachers learn 'on the job'. New teachers usually have two or three weeks observation before starting teaching and are placed in the care of an experienced 'mentor' teacher.

Communication with parents is multilingual. Meetings with parents are usually for that parent's language group only. When a large meeting of parents needs to take place, interpretation facilities will often be available. Parents who send their children to such European Schools tend to be bilingual or multilingual themselves. Therefore, their children start with an extra interest and accustomization to bilingual or multilingual settings. Many students come from literacy-oriented, middle-class homes, with a positive view of bilingualism.

Research on the **effectiveness of European Schools** suggests that there are usually no detrimental effects on academic achievement stemming from the bilingual and multilingual policies. Students tend to succeed in the European Baccalaureate examination and many go to university. The schools provide a fine example of the production of bilingual and biliterate children. They produce relatively privileged European children, secure in their own national culture and with a supranational European identity. However, there is the issue of whether it produces an educational and cultural **elite**. The schools may be reproducing families who already have a considerable bilingual advantage.

European Schools have many similarities with **immersion bilingual education**. Both forms of bilingual education tend to recruit from the middle classes and offer education through two majority languages. A major **difference** between the European Schools Movement and the Canadian Immersion program* is that the second language is taught as a subject in the European Schools *before* being used as a medium of instruction. In Canadian Immersion programs, the second language is used as a medium of instruction from the beginning. In the European Schools Movement, there is also relatively more emphasis on the second language being taught as a subject in itself.

* See page 145f

E18 What is Heritage Language Bilingual Education?

Heritage Language Bilingual Education is where **language minority children** use their native, ethnic, home or heritage language in the school as a medium of instruction and the goal is full bilingualism. Examples include education through the (minority language) medium of Navajo and Spanish in the United States, Basque and Catalan in Spain, Ukrainian in Canada, Gaelic in Scotland, Finnish in Sweden and Welsh in Wales. The child's native language (see Glossary) is protected and developed alongside development in the majority language. In New Zealand, the Maori language has increasingly been promoted in schools. In Ireland, Irish-medium education is often available for children from Irish language backgrounds. The students will learn English and Irish, and possibly other European languages. The language **aim** is **to protect the indigenous language** in school lest it wither and die among the all-pervading growth of majority languages.

Heritage language education is also found in schools and classes for established and recent immigrant language groups. For example, in the early 1980s in the United States, Joshua Fishman located 6553 heritage language schools (mostly private), with an impression that there were 1000 more not located. These schools were using 145 different mother tongues (see Glossary) of various

Typical features of Heritage Language / Developmental Maintenance Programs

(1) Many classrooms will tend to contain a varying **mixture of language majority and language minority children**. At the same time, the minority language may be the majority language of a local community. In certain areas of the US, Spanish speakers are in a majority in their neighborhood or community.

(2) **Parents** will often have the **choice** of sending their children to mainstream schools or to heritage language education. Ukrainian, Jewish and Mohawkian heritage language programs in Canada, for example, gave parents freedom of choice in selecting schools.

(3) The language minority pupil's home language will often be used for approximately half or more of **curriculum time**. The Ukrainian programs in Alberta and Manitoba allotted half the time to Ukrainian, half to English. Mathematics and Science, for example, were taught in English; Music, Art and Social Studies in Ukrainian. There is a tendency to teach technological, scientific studies through the majority language.

(4) Where a minority language is used for a majority of classroom time (e.g. 80 to almost 100% in Wales), the justification is usually that **children easily transfer ideas, concepts, skills and knowledge into the majority language**. Having taught a child multiplication in Spanish for example, this mathematical concept does not have to be retaught in English.

(5) The **justification** given for heritage language education is also that a minority language is easily lost, a majority language easily gained. Children tend to be surrounded by the majority language in daily life. Thus bilingualism is achieved by a concentration on the minority language at school.

(6) Heritage language schools are mostly **elementary schools**. This need not be the case. In Wales, for example, such schools are available to the end of secondary education and the heritage language can be used as a medium of study at college and university.

communities: Arabs, Africans, Asians, French, German, Greek, Haitian, Italian, Jewish, Polish, Japanese, Latin American, Armenian, Dutch, Bulgarian, Irish, Russian, Rumanian, Serbian, Turkish, Ukrainian and Yiddish. Such schools have been supported by foreign governments and religious institutions (churches, mosques, temples, synagogues). Some community-based organizations also foster after-school programs, Saturday schools, weekend schools and religion-based programs. These supplemental schools have grown, especially among the Chinese and Korean communities.

Day schools are typically fee-paying, private establishments. Hence the students tend to come from middle-class or relatively more affluent working-class backgrounds. For example, there have been over 130 Yiddish day schools in New York successfully teaching children to read and write English, Hebrew and Yiddish. This kind of school, mostly attended by the Jewish Hassidic Orthodox community, has increased in New York in recent years with its own association of Yiddish teachers and schools. In contrast, non-religious all day schools organized by ethnic groups have tended to become more English-focused. For example, many Greek schools in New York are now teaching in English, with Greek as a second language being taught every day.

The 'public school' United States instance of Heritage Language Bilingual Education is sometimes called **Maintenance Bilingual Education** or **Developmental Maintenance Bilingual Education**. These are few in number. In Canada, the term used to describe such education is **Heritage Language Education**.

In essence, heritage or maintenance language education refers to the education of **language minority** children through their minority language in a majority language society. However, majority language children (e.g. recent arrival to a town) may also be present. In most countries, the majority language will also be present in the curriculum, ranging from second language lessons to a varying proportion of the curriculum being taught through the majority language.

The heritage language (see Glossary) may, or may not, be an indigenous language. Both Navajo and Spanish can be perceived as heritage languages in the United States depending on an individual's perception of what constitutes their heritage language. The **term** 'heritage language' (see Glossary) may also be called 'native language' (see Glossary), 'ethnic language', 'minority language' (see Glossary), 'ancestral language', or, in French, *'langues d'origine'*. The **danger** of the term 'heritage' is that it points to the past and not the future, to traditions rather than the contemporary.

What is Transitional Bilingual Education?

In the United States for example, children from Spanish-speaking backgrounds have been frequently placed in what educationists call Transitional Bilingual Education. Rather than immediately submerging language minority children in an English language monolingual class, they are allowed to splash around in their home language for one or two years. The idea is to make a **relatively quick transition from the home language to the language of the school** – English. The value of such classes is that they provide a year or two's language buffer to mitigate the effects of the 'sink or swim' mainstreaming (see Glossary) approach. A temporary period of using the home language in Transitional Bilingual Education is better than none at all. Children are allowed a transition period that provides temporary support for their home language.

Such transitional classes deny, after one or more years, the minority language linguistic resources of that child. Children are mainstreamed and expected to behave linguistically, culturally and educationally as their monolingual, mono-cultural peers. Research in the United States has suggested that the longer a child is left in Transitional Bilingual Education classes (e.g. for up to four or five years and called Late Exit Transitional Bilingual Education), the more success the child will have at school. **The more children are allowed to use their home language in a school, the better will be their language and curriculum achievement**. These children still become fluent in the English language. There is sufficient support in school and in the community for them to become bilingual. In Transitional Bilingual Education the chance is lost of full development in the minority language, cultural pluralism, and a full immersion in the language diversity of society.

One paradoxical situation in England and the United States is that whilst such minority language children's home language is slowly eradicated in such schools, at the secondary stage such children are sometimes encouraged to learn a new European language. Second language learning has been viewed in these countries as a resource to promote foreign trade and world influence. Thus, the **paradox** is that while bilingual education to support minority languages has tended to be depreciated in the United States and England, the current trend is to appreciate English speakers who learn a second language. There is a tendency to value the acquisition of languages while devaluing the language minorities who have them. On the one hand, we encourage and promote the study of foreign languages (see Glossary) for English monolinguals at great cost and with inefficiency. At the same time, we subdue the linguistic gifts that children from non-English language backgrounds bring to school.

What is Immersion Bilingual Education?

E20

Immersion Bilingual Education derives from a Canadian educational 'experiment'. The movement started in St Lambert, Montreal, in 1965. Some dissatisfied **English-speaking,** middle-class parents persuaded school district administrators to set up an experimental kindergarten class of 26 children. The aims were for pupils: (1) to become competent speakers, readers and writers in **French**; (2) to reach normal achievement levels throughout the curriculum including the English language; (3) to appreciate the traditions and culture of both French-speaking and English-speaking Canadians. In short, the aims were for children to become bilingual and bicultural without loss of achievement. The latent agenda was possibly that such children would be very marketable. Bilinguals who could switch between the French- and English-speaking communities in Canada would be able to find good employment, have varied job opportunities, and have an edge in the promotion and advancement market.

Immersion education is an umbrella term with variations in:

(1)   **Age** at which a child commences the experience. This may be at the kinder-garten or infant stage (**early** immersion), at nine to ten years old (delayed or **middle** immersion) or at secondary level (**late** immersion).

(2)   The amount of **time** spent in immersion in a day. **Total** immersion usually commences with 100% immersion in the second language, after two or three years reducing to 80% for the next three or four years, finishing junior schooling with approximately 50% immersion. **Partial** immersion provides close to 50% immersion in the second language throughout infant and junior schooling. **Early total immersion** is the most popular program, followed by late and middle immersion. The following histogram illus-trates **early total immersion**.

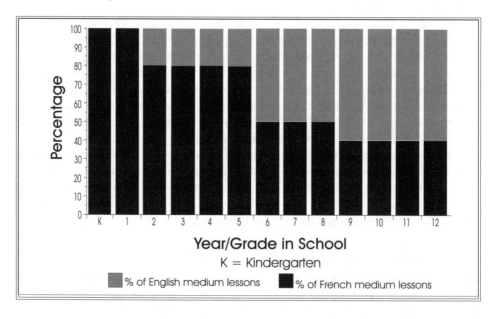

The St Lambert experiment suggested that the aims were met. Early immersion pupils are eventually able to read, write, speak and understand **English** as well as youngsters instructed in English in the mainstream English medium schools. For the first four years of **early total immersion**, pupils tend not to progress in English as do monolingual English pupils in mainstream classes. Reading, spelling and punctuation, for example, are not so developed. Since such children are usually not given English language instruction for one, two or three years after starting school, these results are to be expected. However, the initial pattern does not last. After approximately six years of schooling, early total immersion children have caught up with their mono-lingual peers in English language skills. By the **end of elementary schooling**, the early total immersion experience has generally not affected first language speaking and writing development. Parents of these children believe the same as the attainment tests reveal.

Indeed, when differences in achievement between immersion and main-stream children have been located by research, it is often in favor of immersion pupils. This finding links with the possible thinking (cognitive) advantages consequential from bilingualism. If bilingualism permits increased linguistic awareness, more flexibility in thought, more internal inspection of language, such cognitive advantages may help to explain **the favorable English progress of early immersion pupils.**[*]

* See page 150f

In addition, and at no cost, immersion pupils can also read, write, speak and understand **French** in a way far superior to English pupils who are taught French as a second language. Most students in **early total immersion programs** approach native-like performance in French in receptive language skills (listening and reading) at around 11 years old.

Partial early immersion pupils tend to lag behind for three or four years in their English language skills. Their performance is little different from that of total early immersion pupils, which is surprising since early partial immersion education has more English language content. By the end of elementary schooling, partial early immersion children catch up with mainstream peers in English language attainment. Similarly, **late immersion** (see figure below) has no detrimental effect on English language skills.

If immersion education results in children becoming bilingual in French and English, the question is whether this is at the cost of **achievement in other curriculum areas**. The reviews of research suggest that **early total immersion** pupils generally perform as well in these subjects as do main-stream children.

The evaluations of **early partial immersion education** are not quite so positive. When children in early partial immersion learn Mathematics and Science through the medium of French, they tend to lag behind comparable mainstream children, at least initially. This may be because their French skills are insufficiently developed to be able to think mathematically and scientifi-cally in their second language. The results for **late immersion** are similar. An important factor appears to be whether second language skills (French) are suf-ficiently developed to cope with fairly complex curriculum material.

Overall, the results suggest that bilingual education by an immersion experience need not have negative effects on curriculum performance. Indeed, most children

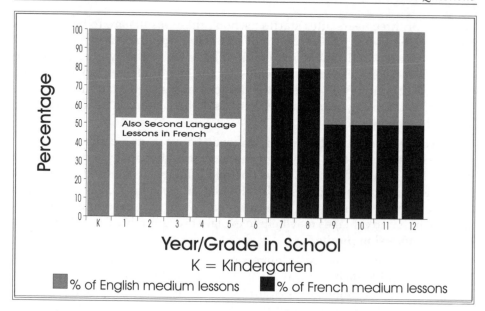

gain a second language without cost to their performance in the curriculum. However, one **key factor seems to be whether their language skills have evolved sufficiently in order to work in the curriculum in their second language**.

What are the essential features of Canadian immersion education? **First**, immersion in Canada aims at bilingualism in **two prestigious, majority languages** (French and English). **Second**, immersion bilingual education in Canada has been **optional not compulsory**. Parents choose to send their children to such schools. The convictions of parents, capabilities of children plus the commitment of the teachers may aid the motivation of pupils. There is respect for the child's home language and culture (see Glossary). This relates to the **additive** bilingual situation (see Introduction* and Glossary). Parents have generally been seen as partners in the immersion movement and some dialogue has existed between parents, administrators, teachers and researchers.

* See page xx

Third, children in early immersion are often **allowed to use their home language for up to one and a half years for classroom communication**. There is no compulsion to speak French in the playground or dining hall. The child's home language is appreciated and not belittled.

Fourth, immersion teachers are competent bilinguals. However, they initially appear to the children as able to speak French but only understand (and not speak) English.

Fifth, the **content** of the curriculum becomes the focus for the language. Perpetual insistence on correct communication is avoided. Learning second language French in early immersion becomes incidental and subconscious, similar to the way a first language is acquired. Emphasis is placed on understanding French before speaking French.

Sixth, the pupils **start immersion** education with a similar lack of experience of the second language. Most are monolingual. Starting with relatively homogeneous language skills not only simplifies the teacher's task. It also means that pupils' self-esteem and classroom motivation is not at risk due to some pupils being linguistically more expert.

Seventh, pupils in immersion education experience the same curriculum as mainstream 'core' pupils.

One of the **limitations of immersion** bilingual education is that for many students, French can become a school-only phenomenon. Outside the school walls, immersion students tend not to use French any more than 'drip feed, 30 minutes a day' second language students. Immersion students are competent in French, but tend not to communicate in French in the community. Lack of spontaneous or contrived French language opportunity and a dearth of French cultural occasions to actively and purposefully use the second language may partly be the explanation. Immersion programs have been criticized for being strong on language, but weak on widening immersion students' cultural horizons.

Various other possible **limitations** in immersion education need sharing. **First**, immersion students do not always become grammatically accurate in their French. They also tend to lack the social and stylistic sense of appropriate language use which the native speaker possesses.

Second, there is difficulty in pinpointing the crucial factors that create an effective immersion experience. Is it immersion as a system that leads to relatively successful outcomes or (or as well as), factors such as student motivation, teachers' preparation, parental attitude, community vitality and amount of time studying different curricula? **Intensity of language learning**, for example, hours per day and the number of language learners, is likely to be as important as the length of language learning (e.g. the number of years of second language learning).

Third, immersion programs can have **effects on mainstream schools**. For example, effects may include: a redistribution of classroom teachers and leaders, a change in the language and ability profile of mainstream classes, and discrepancies in class size with increasing numbers of mixed-age classes.

Fourth, it is important not to view immersion education in Canada in purely educational terms. Behind immersion education are political, social and cultural beliefs and values, moving towards a different kind of society. By promoting bilingualism in English speakers, immersion education in Canada may support French language communities, increase the opportunities for Francophones outside Quebec and help promote bilingualism in the public sector (and debatably in the private sector).

Immersion education is seen as a Trojan Horse of further English assimilation (see Glossary) by some Francophones, who question whether an increase in bilingual Anglophones will simply deprive them of their historical advantage in occupying bilingual jobs. This is linked to the finding that children from higher socio-economic backgrounds tend to be over-represented in immersion programs. Thus immersion education may act to reproduce elite groups, giving Anglophone children with bilingual abilities an advantage in the jobs market.

Fifth, there is danger of generalizing from the Canadian experience to elsewhere in the world. In Canada, immersion concerns **two major high-status international languages**: French and English. In many countries the situation is different. Often the context is one of a majority and a minority language (or languages) coexisting with differences in status and power between them. Yet many European countries have adapted immersion bilingual education as the title for their form of bilingual education due to the association of 'immersion' with this prestigious Canadian movement.

Canadian immersion bilingual education has been an educational experiment of unusual success and growth. It has influenced bilingual education in Europe and beyond.

What are the main classroom features of successful immersion programs?

First, the **minimum time** the second language needs to be used as a medium to ensure 'receptive' (listening and reading) second language proficiency is four to six or seven years. **Second**, the **curriculum** tends to be the same for immersion children as for their mainstream peers. Thus, immersion children can easily be compared with mainstream children for levels of achievement.

Immersion needs to attempt to cultivate empathy for the new language **culture** (e.g. French culture in Canada). The immersion curriculum needs to have distinct components in it that develop **participation** in that language's distinctive culture. The danger is then that French becomes the language of school, and English the language of the playground, street and vocational success. The English language cultural influence is often so strong and persuasive that French immersion children are in danger of becoming passive (see Glossary) rather than active bilinguals outside the school gates.

* See page 136f

Third, studies of bilingual education indicate that it may be preferable to **separate languages in instruction** rather than to mix them during a single lesson.* Sustained periods of monolingual instruction will require students to attend to the language of instruction, both improving their language competences and acquiring subject matter simultaneously.

The **fourth** issue is how much **time** should be devoted to the two languages within the curriculum? A typical recommendation is that a minimum of 50% of instruction should be in the second language. Bilingual schools need to ensure that, through school instruction and school learning experiences, majority language proficiency and literacy is monitored and promoted. Such majority language instruction may range from a minimum of 10% for seven year olds, to 70% or more for those in examination classes at secondary level schooling.

Fifth, immersion education has been built around the twin towers of teacher enthusiasm and parental commitment. French immersion **parents** in Canada tend to be middle class, involved in school teacher–parent committees, and take a sustained interest in their children's progress. Immersion education in Canada has, from its beginnings, been powerfully promoted by parents. Since then, the Canadian Parents for French organization has been a powerful pressure group for the evolution, recognition and dissemination of immersion education. Parents in other countries have also been powerful advocates at the grass-roots level for other 'strong' forms of bilingual education (e.g. Wales). Through localized pressure groups, schools which give native language medium teaching have successfully developed.

Teachers in Canadian immersion classrooms tend to have native or native-like proficiency in both French and English. Such teachers are able to understand children speaking in their home language but speak to the children almost entirely in French. Teachers are thus important language models through their status and power role, identifying French with something of value. Immersion teachers also provide the child with a model of acceptable French pronunciation and style.

Most **immersion teachers** are particularly committed to bilingual education, enthusiastic about bilingualism in society, acting as language missionaries. In the equation of a successful bilingual school, such enthusiasm and commitment may be an important and often underestimated factor in success. There is a danger of seeing success in bilingual education as due to the system (e.g. immersion) and use of two languages in school. The commitment of bilingual teachers, and the special skills that a bilingual teacher uses beyond those required of a monolingual teacher, may be underestimated in the equation of successful bilingual schooling.

Sixth, the French immersion approach allows a relatively **homogeneous language classroom**. For example, in Canadian early total immersion, all children are beginners without French proficiency. This makes the task of the teacher relatively easy. Children can grow in the French language under a shared teaching and learning approach.

On a comparative education note, the term 'immersion' is used in Wales and Ireland. In these Celtic situations, there is often a **classroom mixture** of those who are fluent and those who are less fluent in the classroom language.

The Irish and Welsh experiences tend to suggest that most children whose home language is English will cope successfully in **minority language immersion** classrooms. For such children, the language context is additive rather than subtractive (see Glossary). The danger is that the majority language of English, being the common denominator, will be the language used between pupils in the classroom, in the playground and certainly out of school. A balance towards a greater proportion of language minority speakers may help to ensure that the 'common denominator' majority language does not always dominate in informal classroom and playground talk.

Seventh, immersion provides an **additive bilingual environment** (see Introduction and Glossary). Students acquire French at no cost to their home language and culture. Such enrichment may be contrasted to subtractive bilingual environments where the home language is replaced by the second language, and negative rather than positive effects may occur in school performance and self-esteem. This highlights the term 'immersion education' as best reserved for additive rather than subtractive environments. The term 'immersion education' is appropriate only when the home language is a majority language and the school is adding a second minority or majority language.

What language strategies are used in immersion classrooms?

Immersion education is based on the idea that a first language is acquired relatively subconsciously. Children are unaware that they are acquiring a language in the home. Immersion attempts to copy this process in the early years of schooling. The **focus is on the content and not the form of the language**. It is the task at hand that is central, not conscious language learning. In the early stages, there are no formal language learning classes, although simple elements of grammar (see Glossary) such as verb endings may be taught informally. In the latter years of elementary schooling, formal consideration may be given to the rules of the language (e.g. grammar and syntax).

Immersion also tends to assume that the **earlier a language is taught the better**. While teenagers and adults may learn a second language fluently and proficiently, young children typically acquire authentic pronunciation better than adults. In this respect, a young child is more plastic and malleable.

In the early stages in Early French immersion classrooms, the teacher concentrates on **listening comprehension skills**. Oral skills are given more importance in kindergarten to Grade 3; reading and writing skills, even though started as early as Grade 1 (age 6), are stressed in Grades 4 to 6. Students are not made to speak French with their teacher or with their peers in the initial stages. Children will initially speak English to each other and to their teacher, without any penalty. Immersion teachers do not force children to use French until they are naturally willing to do so. Early insistence on French may inhibit children and develop negative attitudes to the French language and to education in general. Over the first two years, immersion children develop an understanding of French and then begin to speak French, particularly to the teacher.

The most frequent grade in which **English** becomes part of the formal curriculum in Early Total French Immersion is Grade 3. Other practices include introducing English at an earlier grade or kindergarten, and at Grade 4.

In the early stages of immersion, it is crucial that the **teacher is comprehensible** to the children. The teacher needs to be sympathetically aware of the level of a child's vocabulary and grammar, to deliver in French at a level the child can understand, whilst simultaneously pushing forward competence in French. The teacher will be aiming to push back the frontiers of a child's French by ensuring that messages are both comprehensible and are slightly ahead of the learner's current level of mastery of the language.

The language used to communicate with the child at these early stages is often called **caretaker speech**. For the first year or two in immersion, the vocabulary will be deliberately limited. There will be a simplified presentation of grammar and syntax. The teacher may be repetitive in the words used and the ideas presented, with the same idea presented in two or more ways. The teacher will deliberately speak slowly, giving the child more time to process the language input and understand the meaning. This tends to parallel the simplified talk of mother to child (**motherese**) and **foreigner talk** (a person deliberately simplifying and slowing the language so a foreigner can understand). During this caretaker stage, the teacher constantly questions the child to ensure that understanding has occurred.

A teacher may also present the language to be used before a lesson topic is presented. When new words and new concepts are being introduced into a lesson, the teacher spends some time in introducing the words and clarifying the concepts. Such teachers may also be sensitive to **non-verbal feedback** from students: questioning glances, losing concentration and a glazed look. A student may be encouraged to question the teacher for clarification and simplification when understanding has not occurred.

These strategies cover two different areas: the importance of **understandable instruction** and the importance of **negotiating meaning**. The worst case is when neither the teacher nor the pupil is aware that misunderstanding (or no understanding) has taken place. A more effective classroom is when pupils and teachers are negotiating meaning, ensuring that mutual understanding has occurred. Not only is the negotiation of meaning important in language development and in maximizing achievement throughout the curriculum, it is also important in aiding motivation of children within the classroom. Patronizing such children and oversimplifying are two of the dangers in this process. Therefore, constantly presenting students with ever-challenging and advancing learning situations is important in classroom achievement.

Immersion classrooms usually have a particular view about **language errors**. Language errors are a typical and important part of the language learning process, not a symptom of failure. With time and practice, these knots can be removed. Language accuracy tends to develop over time and with experience. Therefore, immersion teachers are discouraged from overcorrecting children's attempts to speak a second language. Constant error correction may be self-defeating, negatively reinforcing language acquisition and disrupting communication and content learning in the classroom. Language accuracy tends to develop over time and with experience. When a child or several children constantly make the same errors, then appropriate and positive intervention may be of value.

In the early stages of immersion, there will be a natural **interlanguage** among children (a simplified 'mixed' language used initially by a second language learner). A child may change round the correct order in a sentence yet produce a perfectly comprehensible message. A child may put the pronoun or a preposition in the wrong order: as in 'go you and get it'. **Interlanguage** is not to be seen as error. Rather it indicates the linguistic creativity of students who are using their latent understanding of the first language to construct meaningful communication in the second language. Interlanguage is thus an intermediate, approximate system. It is a worthwhile attempt to communicate and therefore needs encouragement. Seen as a halfway stage in-between monolingualism and being proficient in a second language, interlanguage becomes part of the journey and not a permanent rest point.

The immersion teacher will assume that proficiency in the first language contributes to proficiency in the second language. Concepts attached to words in the first language will easily be **transferred** into the second language. The acquisition of literacy skills in the first language tends to facilitate the acquisition of literacy skills in the second. However, not all aspects of a language will transfer. Rules of grammar and spelling may not lend themselves to transfer. The closer a language structure is to the second language structure, the greater the transfer there is likely to be between the two languages. For example, the transfer between English and Spanish is likely to be more than Arabic to English, due to differences in syntax, symbols and direction of writing. However, the system of meanings, the conceptual map and skills that a person owns, may be readily transferable between languages.*

An immersion classroom will not just enable children to acquire the second language in a subconscious, almost incidental manner. Towards the end of elementary education, the experiential approach may be joined by a meaning-based focus on the form of language. Children may at this point be encouraged to **analyze their vocabulary and grammar** (see Glossary). At this later stage, some lessons may have progress in the second language as their sole aim. After early sheltering with language, the development of vocabulary and grammar may be dealt with in a direct and systematic manner.

Ten specific techniques used by immersion teachers

(1) Providing plenty of contextual support for the language being used (e.g. by body language – plenty of gestures, facial expressions and acting).

(2) Deliberately giving more classroom directions and organizational advice to immersion students. For example, signaling the start and the end of different routines, more explicit directions with homework and assignments.

(3) Understanding where a child is at, thereby connecting the unfamiliar with the familiar, the known with the unknown. New material is linked directly and explicitly with the child's present knowledge and understanding.

(4) Extensive use of visual material. Using concrete objects to illustrate lessons, using pictures and audio-visual aids, giving the child plenty of hands-on manipulative activities to ensure all senses are used in the educational experience.

(5) Obtaining constant feedback as to the level of a student's understanding. Diagnosing the level of a student's language.

(6) Using plenty of repetition, summaries, restatement to ensure that students understand the directions of the teacher.

(7) The teacher being a role model for language emulation by the student.

(8) Indirect error correction rather than constantly faulting students. Teachers ensure that the corrections are built in to their language to make a quick and immediate impact.

(9) Using plenty of variety in both general learning tasks and in language learning tasks.

(10) Using frequent and varied methods to check the understanding level of the children.

(Adapted from M.A. Snow (1990) Instructional methodology in immersion foreign language education. In A.M. Padilla, H.H. Fairchild and C.M. Valadez (eds) *Foreign Language Education: Issues and Strategies*. London: Sage.)

What is the new form for Intensive Second Language Immersion at the end of elementary schooling?

E23

A new form of immersion education has recently been introduced in Canada. It is called **Intensive French** and was piloted in Newfoundland and Labrador from 1998 to 2001. It has since spread to other Canadian provinces and territories (and to Wales, UK). In contrast to 1000 hours of 'drip feed' French lessons from Grade 4 to Grade 12 in mainstream programs, and in contrast to 6000 to

7000 hours of French instruction in early immersion, Intensive French operates in Grade 5 or Grade 6 for a five-month intensive period of language learning.

In one school year, the first five months may be devoted to the concentrated learning of French; the following five months are devoted to achieving necessary learning outcomes in the regular curriculum. Sometimes, the final five months of the school year are devoted to intensive French. Either way, the overall aim is to produce fluent speakers who can communicate spontaneously in French by the end of elementary schooling, and who are ready for bilingual education in a secondary school.

In this program, between 50 and 80% of each school day is devoted to learning French. Although no subjects are taught in French (as in immersion), the time allotted to some other subjects is reduced (e.g. Social studies, Health, Science and particularly English). The time allocation to Mathematics is not normally reduced. Early findings show linguistic and educational success and expectations of expansion in the future.

What is a Withdrawal class for extra language support?

Induction classes, Withdrawal classes, Transition classes, Reception classes or whatever name is given them, provide **language support** for a child moving from the home language to the language of the school. Such extra language help before a child enters a mainstream classroom seems valuable and important. Taking a child out from lessons for a few periods a week, or placed in a special class for a few months, may provide the language confidence required for the child to swim in the complex language pool of the classroom. However, there are possible negative outcomes, nothing to do with language.

What educationists have spotlighted is the **non-language effects of such classes**. Children placed in these classes may feel stigmatized, segregated and ostracized, feeling that they have a deficiency in language. Entry into usual peer-group relationships may be made difficult. This leads many educationists to argue for language support **within** the class. Providing bilingual resources for teachers, parent help and team teaching in the classroom may be ways in which language support is given more subtly to particular children, with less stigmatization and more sensitivity.

Potential problems of a psychological nature that may be caused by extra language help should not detract from language help being given. Particularly where minority language children attend a mainstream majority language school, there is often a need for supplementary language help in the classroom. Such **language support** is often essential. How such support is given to minimize the risk of a loss of face and self-esteem for that child requires careful planning. For minority language children, this often means that Withdrawal classes may not always be the best method. A special track or stream in the school for such children, particularly when there are color, racial and ethnic differences between streams, is best avoided. Integration and inclusion of children in school is a high priority. This means that support, where possible, needs providing in a positive, sensitive and diplomatic way in the mainstream classroom itself (e.g. assistant teachers, support teachers, parents as helpers).

When language minority children are integrated in the classroom, majority language children can be used to help them by acting as language models and mentors. Such cooperation may succeed in providing a more integrated and harmonious classroom.

Withdrawal classes or language centers are more defensible for majority language children learning a new, majority or minority language. Such children may have fewer problems of stigmatization, prejudice or integration because they own a majority language and culture that has high status and prestige.

When a large number of children with a majority language are placed in a minority language school, there is a tendency for minority language children to **switch** to the majority language. The teacher may also switch from using the minority language to using the majority language much of the time. When majority language in-migrants, for example, change the language balance of a hitherto language minority school, there may be an argument for temporary separate provision for those in-migrants. Some induction into the minority language may be considered before attending schools operating in that minority language.

What does Scaffolding mean, and why is it important in supporting language learners in school?

E25

Many bilingual children attend mainstream 'monolingual' schools and operate as quickly as possible through a **second language**. They are expected to learn a new language, engage in subject learning and develop thinking skills all at the same time. Teaching and learning will be in that new language and will increasingly become more complex, abstract and require a different register (see Glossary) from informal conversation.

When children are older (e.g. in the later years of primary education, or in secondary school), they do not learn a new language solely through content instruction. Their second language proficiency may be too underdeveloped to understand Mathematics or Social Studies. Hence, such children need **language support** if they are to succeed in the classroom. The key issue is how that teacher supports the child by a careful use of understandable language. This is termed '**scaffolding**'.

Rather than simplifying a task, the teacher provides the 'scaffolding' so that the child is successively enhancing their knowledge, skills and competences. **Scaffolding** is thus a temporary device to enable understanding of content.

When learning is successful, that support is removed as the child can then complete the same task independently.

Scaffolding occurs when a teacher ensures: (1) that a child has enough prior experience or prior knowledge to make a task understandable; (2) the child is made familiar with the purpose, structure and linguistic features of the task; (3) the teacher and the child work together on the process, content and form of learning; and (4) children will eventually be able to do the task independently, with the scaffold being gradually removed. They have moved from the familiar to being stretched, from **guidance to independence**.

When bilingual children need language scaffolding, the following school attributes are also important:

- Teachers build on the prior knowledge and experience of children that has often built through the minority and not just the majority language.
- Peer-support systems are used in the classroom so that language support is possible through friends.
- Language minority children are well integrated into the mainstream operation including practice in speaking with majority language native speakers.
- Linguistic and cultural diversity is valued and celebrated.
- High expectations are communicated to language minority children.
- The curriculum is carefully paced so that children comprehend, but is ever challenging and enriching, not compensatory or remedial.
- Linguistic competence and conceptual understanding are not confused. For example, a child's proficiency in second language English is not a measure of the quality of their thinking.
- Teachers relate instruction to meaningful student experiences, including experiences from their language minority homes and communities.

 What kind of education should I give my child if we regularly move to different countries?

This type of question tends to come from those parents who, as part of their employment, have to move regularly across regional and national borders. For example, diplomats, those working for large international companies, those involved in marketing and commerce in a variety of countries, and academics increasingly move across borders. Children are resilient and adapt to new circumstances and situations with an ease that many adults do not predict. Nevertheless, for all children, there is a **transition period**, of adapting to new environments, new friends, a new school and a new pattern of living. The home and family become an important source of stability, strength and continuity for the child.*

Children differ in their accommodation of new circumstances, a new school and new friends. At one end are those who meet the challenge with interest and confidence, learning to adapt and enjoy fresh stimulation. Some children enjoy change and the benefits from it. At the other end, there are those who lack confidence in their ability to cope in new circumstances, quickly become apprehensive of a change of circumstances, and require much greater support in the home and in the school. Such differences between children not only emanate from child-rearing practices, but also from personality, prior experiences in schools and age. Race, gender, color, creed and language may also play a part in this.

For parents in this situation, there are sometimes **choices**:

(1)   Sending a child to a boarding school where the home language is used. This may be in the home country.
(2)   Alternatively, there are schools in some large cities that teach through international languages.
(3)   Another alternative is to leave a child with the extended family or other carers in the home country. This will establish continuity of schooling whilst allowing the child to return to the family at vacation times and school breaks.
(4)   Another option is sometimes for children to accompany their parents as they move. Children attend the local school. This may mean a switch of language. When children are very young, for example under the age of seven, there is usually little problem in switching schools where a different language is used. However, as children become older, adapting to a completely new language environment becomes more difficult in terms of speedy language learning, obtaining sufficient skills in a language to cope in the classroom alongside first language speakers, and understanding a relatively complex curriculum.

Therefore, into the **decision equation** comes:

• the age of the child (younger children can linguistically and educationally adapt more easily than older children);
• a decision about children living in the home or being away at boarding school or remaining at home with friends and carers;
• the personality and adaptability of the child to a new situation;
• how effective the new school and the teachers will be in providing a sensitive transition period for the child and accommodating the language profile of the child;
• will the school provide supplementary help and language support;

* See page 22

- the time and effort parents are prepared to put in so as to help their child's transition to a new language and culture;
- the language support that parents and those around them can offer the child;
- and parents' own goals and wishes for the educational and language development of their child.

What are Saturday Schools and Voluntary Schools outside regular school hours, and how valuable are they in the development of a minority or second language?

When parents speak a minority language, Voluntary Schools and Saturday Schools may be a path parents choose, where available, to extend that minority or native language (see Glossary). For example, many minority language communities in Britain have locally supported Saturday Schools so that children can supplement their education through their heritage language.

The reason for such schools is that children will be taking their education through the medium of the majority language. Parents want the **home language** to be **supported** and extended, for the culture attached to the language to be taught in such schools, and for their children to understand curriculum areas through their native tongue.

So long as such schools are a joy rather than a burden, a pleasurable experience for the children rather than making large inroads into their playtime, such schools have great value. A child becomes more bilingual and more bicultural (see Glossary).

Many such schools are important in literacy development in the home language. This highlights an increasing recognition that such Saturday Schools and Voluntary Schools need to cooperate and integrate with a child's mainstream school for maximal benefit for the child. When there is congruence, mutually understood and harmonious activity, one school system helps the other in a bilingual child's educational growth in literacy and general cross-curriculum achievement.

Such Saturday Schools and Voluntary Schools work particularly well when they support and extend the language, or one of the languages of the home. When such schools are **effective**, they may increase the motivation of both the children and parents. However, if they are seen as an imposition, as depriving children of time for sport, friends, and personal hobbies and interests, such schools may serve to work against their aims. One **danger** is that the child will see such extra schooling as a negative accompaniment of their minority language and culture. Therefore, such schools need to provide an enjoyable and pleasurable experience for the children.

While many Saturday Schools and Voluntary Schools are enterprising and effective, unfortunately in some schools the education is not progressive in style or content. Typical problems include: a lack of trained, qualified teachers; poor working conditions and facilities; outdated, imported materials (e.g. books); large classes; poor attendance and demotivated children; rote-learning rather than activity methods; dogmatic teaching; and few financial resources to pay teachers and buy equipment.

Such Saturday and Voluntary Schools also exist to teach a language for religion and worship (e.g. Arabic, Hebrew, Greek or Russian). When Islam, Judaism or Orthodox Christianity requires an understanding of a different tongue from the home and school, such schools may have the purpose of ensuring children can understand the Koran, the Talmud, the Bible and understand the sacred language of worship in temple, synagogue, mosque or church. Given that such schools provide strong links with the child's nuclear and extended family, links with the child's roots and tradition, history and heritage, and teach morals and values, attitudes and beliefs, such schools have great value. The high premium that many Jews place on Hebrew, and Moslems on Arabic, shows the key place that language plays in maintaining religious tradition and ensuring an enculturation that links the past with the present.

ACHIEVEMENT AND UNDERACHIEVEMENT QUESTIONS

Will my child's performance in school be affected by being bilingual?

E28

This is an important question. Take the child who is bilingual via the home and attends a monolingual school. There is no evidence to suggest that children will be handicapped in their school performance by being bilingual. Bilingual children attending a monolingual school may have some advantages **in thinking***. However, this answer needs refining. When children are dominant in a **minority language** and attend a school through the majority language, and where their peers are mostly majority language speakers, there may be potential problems.

* See page 42

Studies in the United States tend to show that children from **language minority homes** whose bilingualism is not valued by the school, who are forced to operate alongside majority language peers in a majority language, can fall behind. Their linguistic skills are being denied. The level of fluency, power of thinking, even literacy skills in the minority language are not recognized by the monolingual school. Children are expected to learn through a weaker language. They may feel that their minority language, their parents, their culture, their home and family are being rejected by the school's rejection of their minority language. Their self-esteem, self-confidence and belief in their learning ability may suffer in this situation.

Such a school is failing to build on the language minority children's current level of understanding or level of **intellectual development** by not using their minority language. Therefore, such children's education may suffer and they may fall behind. Initial failure may breed further failure rather than 'success breeding success'. This provides a strong argument for minority language children being educated through their minority language.

When **majority language** children are **educated in a minority language or a second majority language**, international evidence suggests that their achievement does not suffer in school. The first majority language is not under threat, nor is their self-esteem, status, or academic competence. In such an **additive bilingual environment** (see Glossary), majority language children tend to benefit from bilingual schooling, either in a minority language or a second majority language, without negative effects on their achievement. There may be a **temporary lag**. When the child is learning a second language, Canadian research suggests that any such lag between approximately the ages of six and ten years of age is temporary. Children taught through a second language catch up. Indeed the Canadian research tends to suggest that some bilingual children surpass their monolingual peers in performance in the curriculum, perhaps due to the advantages in thinking and self-esteem that two languages give.*

* See page 1ff

If there is an essential **principle** to ensure a child's performance is not being negatively affected by their bilingualism, it is that parents and the school must ensure that a child's language development is sufficiently advanced for that child to be able to **cope with an increasingly complex conceptual level in the curriculum**. In the early years of primary education, the language complexity of the classroom makes relatively few demands on the child's language skills. As a child proceeds through school, there is a reduction in actions, physical demonstrations and body language. Learning is increasingly through abstract words and ideas, and less through object lessons. Therefore, the **bilingual child's language has to be matched to the complexity level of the curriculum in the classroom**. This either means ensuring that the child has sufficiently well-developed language to cope in the curriculum. Or, the teacher needs to adapt to the language level of the child, encouraging language development while making sure that over-complex and over-abstract curriculum learning is not introduced too early.

* See page 66f

Problems may arise when older children are placed in a classroom and are expected to work in a **language** that is **underdeveloped** or below the level demanded in curriculum activity.*

If the child is placed in a school which is unable to give language support for the child's home language, the degree of **determination** of the **parents** will be vital in maintaining the language. Such determination and interest in the child's language learning can have a positive knock-on effect. The child's overall motivation to succeed and desire to achieve may be stimulated by parental interest and encouragement. The latent message is that the child is capable: capable with languages, therefore capable in general learning at school.

Are there positive effects of learning through the medium of two languages?

E29

The bilingual has the **advantage** of operating in two languages compared with the monolingual. This usually means later success in two languages when assessed as a curriculum area. For example, the child who is fluent in French and English will usually be highly successful in French in the British, Irish or North American secondary school. It may also mean an increase in employment prospects, cultural biliteracy, and being able to operate in two language groups and two language cultures. In this sense, a child educated bilingually may be more sympathetic and sensitive to language and ethnic diversity in the world, have a wider world view and have more cultural 'costumes' and understandings than the monolingual child.

Canadian research also shows that there may be small performance advantages among 'balanced' or well-developed bilinguals in school. Those **children who can work in either language in the curriculum** often show a marginally improved performance in the curriculum. If there are cognitive benefits attached to bilinguals,* this may bring success in the classroom. If a child has permeated the two cultures attached to the languages, there can be more breadth of understanding, appreciation and sensibility that can enhance performance in subjects such as History and Geography, Social Studies, the Creative Arts and the Language Arts.

* See page 42f

My child is learning through a new language. Will this affect attainment at school?

E30

If the **switch** has been **from a minority language to a majority language**, there is a possibility that attainment will suffer in school. If children feel their minority language, their parents, their home and heritage and culture have all been rejected, such children may feel rejected as well. In cases where the minority language has been replaced by another, educational performance may suffer.

This pattern of **potential failure** is found in some mainstream schools in the United States. When Spanish-speaking children enter such schools, their Spanish is either denied or only allowed for a short period (such as a year). The expectation is that they move as quickly as possible into the majority language. When they are placed in the mainstream alongside monolingual English speakers, many become low achievers, become segregated and are labeled as deficient or limited in their language proficiency. The official United States term for such bilinguals is Limited English Proficiency children.

Wherever possible, **language minority** children need their language to be represented in the school and to learn through the medium of that language for as long as possible. Research tends to suggest this produces maximal performance.

* See page 145ff

Where a **language majority child** enters a school and learns through a new language, particularly when this language is learned from an earlier age, attainment is unlikely to suffer, as the earlier example from Canada shows.* Where both their languages are well developed, there are possible curriculum advantages to being bilingual. Another example is when a family moves to a different country. Language majority children, particularly when young, usually adapt to the new language school situation.

Two cases may be less positive in outcome. First, when a **language minority** child moves to a school or different geographical location where their minority language is not valued, the imposition of a majority language may create lower self-esteem, lower academic motivation and lower school performance. Second, when an **older child moves school**, the danger is that they will not be able to cope with increasingly complex concepts in the curriculum in a 'new' language.*

* See page 126f

Part of the equation of success in school is that a child achieves a positive academic self-concept which derives, to some degree, from self-acceptance (e.g. feeling that the home language and culture is valued in school and in society). In this **additive** language environment, the child may become aware that two languages are better than one, that bilingualism means addition rather than subtraction, multiplication rather than division. Hence academic attainment in the primary school and secondary school is unlikely to be different from monolinguals. While there may be a temporary lag in primary school attainment compared with the monolingual, as the child learns a new language, this is unlikely to continue beyond a two- to four-year period.

E31 My child's school teaches through the minority language. Will this affect my child's development in the majority language?

Children who learn through the minority language usually pick up the majority language with a degree of ease. There are two main reasons for this. **First**, what a child learns in one language can easily be **transferred** into a second language and does not have to be relearnt in the majority language. So long as the child has the vocabulary in the majority language, what is learned at school is usable in that majority language. For example, a child who has been taught to read a clock does not have to be retaught that skill in their second language.

Second, a child's majority language fluency and competence is often well represented through other **experiences in the environment**. On television and the Internet, street signs and posters, in music and magazines, comics and catalogs, majority languages are all well represented. Also, many children are exposed to the majority language in the playground, in the street and with the growth of the peer group. Often, the majority language is the common denominator language to such an extent that the minority language speakers are expected to switch when only one person is present who cannot understand the minority language.

Out-of-school experiences help children develop in the majority language. Therefore, if the diet of the school is mostly in the minority language, and there is a diet outside school partly in the majority language, children often become bilingual. However, it is also important in school that time is allocated to ensuring fluency and literacy in the majority language. **Over-balancing** towards the minority language and too little development of the majority language is rarely in the best interests of the child. Literacy in the majority language is usually essential for the minority language child (e.g. employment).

Speakers of our home language are often poor and unemployed. Should we ensure our child is educated in the majority language to aid employment prospects?

E32

In some countries of the world, **bilinguals** are over-represented among the poor, underprivileged, unemployed and disadvantaged. With in-migrants, guest workers, refugees and indigenous languages in remote rural areas, there is a pattern of deprivation, unemployment and poverty. While there are many examples of bilinguals in elite positions (e.g. in Europe, working for the Council of Europe or European Union and working in transnational companies), many other bilinguals do not tend to live in such privileged circumstances.

Speakers of languages that are aligned with poverty, unemployment, less power and political influence, often wonder if **moving to the majority language** will give them more access to advantage, employment and affluence. It is as if changing language might change life fortunes. Bread on the table is more important than bilingualism. It is important for minority language speakers to become fully fluent and functional in the majority language. To compete against majority language monolinguals, it is important to be able to start on relatively equal terms as far as language goes. Access to employment may require a high degree of competence in the majority language. The opportunity to compete for jobs increases when a person has majority language skills.

However, this is an **argument for thorough bilingualism**. It is not an argument for majority language monolingualism. Families and schools can ensure that children are thoroughly competent in the majority language while retaining their minority language. One language need not be removed to improve another. Languages don't exist in a balance: the higher the one, the lower the other. Rather two languages (and more) can be accommodated within the thinking systems of individuals. Retaining the minority language while ensuring that majority language competence is high enables a bilingual child to have more rather than less. If the majority language overtakes the minority language at home, much will be lost. Heritage, family identity, and the cultural cement that holds minority families together, will be lost. Gaining fluency in the majority language while retaining the minority language will be a multiplication of language skills and culture.

E33 My child seems to be underachieving at school. Is this because of bilingualism?

Many parents believe their children are underperforming, at least at some point in their educational careers. What might be the causes of such underperformance?

* See page 38f

First, parents of bilingual children too quickly assume the blame can be attributed to the child's **bilingualism** in causing cognitive confusion. This is very rarely the case. An explanation is that a bilingual's brain has two engines working at half throttle, while the monolingual has one well-tuned engine at full throttle. Such an explanation is incorrect.* Where two languages are well developed, then bilingualism is more likely to lead to cognitive advantages than disadvantages. Only when a child's two languages are *both* poorly developed can 'blame' be attributed to bilingualism itself. Even then, the blame should not go to the victim, but to the societal circumstances that create underdeveloped languages.

Second, where underachievement exists, the reason may be given as a **lack of exposure to the majority language**. In the United States and England, failure or below average performance is attributed to students having insufficiently developed English language skills to cope with the curriculum. Those who use Spanish or French or Bengali at home and in the neighborhood are perceived as struggling at school due to a lack of skills in the dominant, mainstream language. Thus mainstreaming and transitional bilingual education attempts to ensure a fast conversion to the majority language.

A **fast conversion** to the majority language stands the chance of doing **more harm than good**. It denies the child's skills in the home language, even denies the identity and self-respect of the child itself. Instead of using existing language skills, the 'sink or swim' approach attempts to replace those skills. The level of English used in the curriculum may also cause the child to show underachievement, with consequent demands for more of the same medicine (more English language lessons).

Underachievement in majority language education (e.g. mainstreaming and transitional bilingual education) may be combated by allowing the language minority child to operate in their heritage language in the curriculum. The evidence suggests that success rather than failure results. Such success includes becoming fluent in the majority language (e.g. English). Thus **lack of exposure to a majority language** (e.g. English) is a popular but **incorrect explanation** of underachievement. This explanation fails to note the advantages of education in the minority language for achievement. It inappropriately seeks an answer in increased majority language tuition rather than increased minority language education that would be more beneficial.

Third, when bilingual children underachieve, the attributed reason is sometimes a **mismatch between home and school**. Such a mismatch is seen as not just about language differences but also about dissimilarities in culture, values and beliefs. As an extreme, this tends to reflect a majority viewpoint that is assimilationist (see Glossary), imperialist and even oppressive. The child and family is expected to adjust to the system, not the system to be pluralist and incorporate variety. For such an assimilationist viewpoint, the solution is in the home adjusting to mainstream language and culture to prepare the child for school. Past advice by some professionals has been for language minority parents to raise their children in the majority, school language.

The alternative view is that, where practicable, the school system should be flexible enough to incorporate the home language and culture. A mismatch between home and school can be positively addressed by 'strong' forms of bilingual education for language minorities. By bilingual education, through the inclusion of parents in the running of the school, by involving parents as partners and participants in their child's education, the mismatch can become a merger.

Fourth, underachievement may be attributed to **socio-economic factors** that surround a language minority group. Typical circumstances are in-migrant and refugee children leading a life of urban poverty or rural isolation. In some cases bilingual children live alongside abuse, malnutrition, poor health, ignorance and neglect. Their circumstances reveal a life of ethnic stigma and low status.

Socio-economic status is a broad umbrella term that points to a **definite cause** of language minority underachievement. It provides an example of the importance of not blaming the victim, but analyzing societal features that contribute to underachievement. Such features may be **economic deprivation**, material circumstances and living conditions as well as psychological and social features such as discrimination, racial prejudice, pessimism and immobilizing inferiority.

While socio-economic factors are a proper partial explanation of language minority underachievement, caution must be sounded. Socio-economic status doesn't explain why different language minorities of similar socio-economic status may perform differently at school. **Beliefs, values and attitudes** vary between ethnic groups. Sociocultural factors within and between ethnic groups and not simply socio-economic status must be assessed to begin to work out the equation of language minority achievement and underachievement.

This raises another caution. Underachievement cannot be simply related to one of several causes. The equation of underachievement is going to be complex, involving a number of factors. Those factors will **interact** together and not be simple 'stand-alone' effects. For example, umbrella labels such as socio-economic status need deconstructing into more definable predictors of underachievement (e.g. parents' attitude to education). Home factors will then interact with school factors to provide an enormous number of different routes that may lead to varying school success and failure. The recipes of success and failure are many, with varying ingredients that interact together in complex ways. However, socio-economic and sociocultural features are important ingredients in many equations of underachievement.

Fifth, part of the language minority achievement and underachievement equation is the **type of school** a child attends. The same child will tend to attain more if placed in education that uses the heritage language as a medium of instruction than in programs which seek to replace the home language as quickly as possible. Therefore the system of schooling needs scrutiny. A system that suppresses the home language is likely to be part of the explanation of individual and ethnic group underachievement where such underachievement exists.

Sixth, types of school is a broad heading under which there can exist superior and inferior schools, outstanding and mediocre schools. Where underachievement exists, it is sometimes too simple to blame the type of school rather than digging deeper and locating more specific causes. Some of the attributes that affect the **quality of education** for language minority children include: the supply, ethnic origins and bilingualism of teachers, balance of language minority and language majority students in the classroom, use and sequencing of the two languages across the curriculum over different grades, and reward systems for enriching the minority language and culture.

* See
page
86, 88

Seventh, underachievement may be due to **real learning difficulties*** and the need for some form of special education. It is important to make a distinction between real and apparent learning difficulties. Too often, bilingual children are labeled as having learning difficulties which are attributed to their bilingualism. The child is perceived as having learning difficulties when the problem may lie in the subtractive (see Glossary), assimilative education system which itself creates negative attitudes and low motivation. In the 'sink or swim' mainstreaming approach (see Glossary), 'sinking' can be attributed to an unsympathetic system and to insensitive teaching methods rather than individual learning problems.

Apart from system-generated and school-generated learning problems, there will be those who are bilingual and have genuine learning difficulties. The essential beginning is to distinguish between real, genuine individual learning difficulties and problems which are caused by factors outside the individual.*

Such a distinction between the real and the apparent, the system-generated and the remediable problems of the individual, highlights the alternatives. When underachievement exists, do we blame the victim, blame the teacher and the school, or blame the system? When assessment, tests and examinations occur and show relatively low performance of language minority individuals and groups, will prejudices about bilingual children and ethnic groups be confirmed? Or can we use such assessment to reveal deficiencies in the human architecture of the school system and the design of the curriculum rather than blame the child? As this section has revealed, underachievement often tends to be blamed on the child and the language minority group. Often the explanation lies in factors outside of the individual.

* See page 88

Should my child be placed in a Bilingual Special Education Program?

E34

Categories of special education vary from country to country but are likely to include areas such as: visual impairment, hearing impairment, communication disorders, learning disabilities (e.g. dyslexia **(see Section D13)** and developmental aphasia), severe subnormality in cognitive development, behavioral problems and physical handicaps.

In the United States, the Office of Special Education has estimated that nearly one million children from language minority backgrounds (see Glossary) are in need of some form of special education. Can we be sure that such a categorization is valid and just, and that such children will benefit from a placement in special education?

The danger is that many children from language minorities may be wrongly regarded as having a 'disability' and, as such, incorrectly placed in special education. The communicative differences of language minority children must be distinguished from communicative disorders. This occurs because **common errors** are made. The child is often assessed in a weaker, second language thereby inaccurately measuring both language development and general cognitive development. Thus such children are classed as having a 'language disability' and perhaps a 'learning disability'. Instead of being seen as developing bilinguals (i.e. children with a good command of their first language who are in the process of acquiring a second, majority language), they may be classed as of 'Limited English Proficiency' (LEP in the United States – see Glossary), or even as having general difficulties with learning. Their below average test scores in the second language are wrongly defined as a 'deficit' or 'disability' that can be remedied by some form of special education.

When language minority children are assessed, it is important that three different aspects of their development are kept distinct: (1) language proficiency, (2) second language proficiency, and (3) the existence (or not) of a physical, learning or behavioral difficulty. This distinction means that there will be two different groups of bilinguals with regard to special education.

The first comprises those who are bilingual *and* have a physical, neurological, learning, emotional, cognitive or behavioral difficulty. Such children may need some kind of special education or intervention. One estimate in the United States is that one in eight (approximately 12%) of language minority students will fit into this category. Similar figures are quoted in other countries. Most of these children will **benefit considerably from bilingual special education** rather than monolingual special education.

When bilingual or language minority children have been accurately assessed as having special needs, many educators will argue that education solely in the dominant, majority language is needed. In the United States, the advice is often given that Latino children (see Glossary) with special needs should be educated in monolingual, English special schools. The argument is that such children are going to live in an English-speaking society. When there is **serious mental retardation**, it seems sensible that a child should be educated monolingually. Such a child develops very slowly in one language.

For other special needs children, the **benefits of bilingual special education** are many. One example is the recently arrived in-migrant, special needs child. Placing such a child in a class where he or she doesn't speak the language of the classroom (e.g. English in the United States) may only increase failure and lower self-esteem. To be educated, the child preferably needs initial instruction mostly in the first language, with the chance to become as bilingual as possible. Most children with special needs are capable of developing in two languages. Many do not reach levels of proficiency in either language compared with peers in mainstream classrooms. Nevertheless, they reach satisfactory levels of proficiency in two languages according to their abilities. Becoming bilingual does not detract from achievement in other areas of the curriculum (e.g. Mathematics and Creative Arts).

Children in bilingual special education share the benefits of those in other forms of bilingual education: dual language, educational, cultural, self-identity and self-esteem benefits.

The second group comprises those who are bilingual and do **not** have a physical, learning or behavioral difficulty. This is the great majority of language minority children. Such children will usually prosper in bilingual rather than special education. The optimal education for such children is where their first language is used as a medium of instruction. At the same time, the child learns the second (majority) language, gradually reaching competence in both languages. After a foundation of education in the first language, the second language is developed to the level where the child is able to work in the curriculum through either language.

Separation of these two groups shows that the child's second language proficiency is different from potential problems in an individual's capacities that require specialist treatment (e.g. hearing impairment, stammering). Neither the language and culture of the home, nor socio-economic and ethnic differences should be considered as handicapping conditions. The child's level of functioning in a second language must not be seen as representing the child's level of language development. The child's development in the **first language** needs to be assessed (e.g. by observation if psychological and educational tests are not available) so as to paint a picture of proficiency rather than deficiency.

The movement of a bilingual student to special education should only occur after a conclusion is reached that the child's needs cannot be met by a regular (mainstream) school. In most countries, **inclusion** in mainstream education is preferred to separation in special education.

One example not discussed so far is when a child is **failing** in a mainstream school due to his or her language proficiency not being sufficient to operate in the curriculum. For example, in the United States, some Spanish-speaking children are in mainstream schools (a 'submersion' experience) and, although of normal ability, fail in the system (e.g. drop out of school, repeat grades, leave high school without a diploma) because their English proficiency is insufficiently developed to comprehend the increasingly complex curriculum.

This situation creates an apparent dilemma. By being placed in some form of **special education**, the child is possibly stigmatized as having a 'deficiency' and a 'language deficit'. Such special education may be a separate school (or a special unit within a larger school) that provides special ('remedial') education for bilingual children. Such schools and units may not foster bilingualism. Often, they will emphasize the importance of children becoming competent in the majority language. Such segregation may allow more attention to the second language but results in ghettoization of language minorities. While giving some sanctuary from sinking in second language submersion in a mainstream school, special education can be a retreat, marginalizing the child. Will children in such special education realize their potential across the curriculum? Will they have increased access to employment? Will their apparent failure be accepted and validated because they are associated with a remedial institution?

The ideal for many children in this dilemma is education which allows them to start and continue learning in their first language. The second language can be nurtured as well to ensure the development of bilinguals who can operate in mainstream society. In such schools, both languages are developed and used in the curriculum. Such schools avoid the 'remedial' or 'compensatory' associations of special education. Such schools celebrate the cultural and linguistic diversity of their students.

Bilingual education is sometimes in danger of being seen as a form of special education. Even when the 'language delayed' are separated from those who are in the early stages of learning the majority language, the danger is that the latter will still be assessed as in need of compensatory, remedial special education, including being allocated to bilingual education.

In the United States, Public Law (94-142) gives the **right** to free public education, to tests that are not culturally discriminatory, to tests in the child's native language, to multidimensional 'all areas' assessment to all 'handicapped' students. The misdiagnosis of language minority students for special education has led to court cases (e.g. Diana versus California State Board of Education). Such court cases revealed how language minority students were **wrongly assessed** as in need of special education. In some cases, teachers were unsure how to cope with a child whose English was relatively 'weak' and on this basis only, wanted special education for the 'Limited English Proficient' child.

The litigation showed the importance of separating bilinguals with real learning difficulties from those bilinguals whose second language (e.g. English) proficiency is below 'native' average. It also showed the wrongs done to language minority students: misidentification, misplacement, misuse of tests and failure when allocated to special education.

Unfortunately, the fear of litigation by school districts can lead to an **under-identification** of language minority pupils with a real need of special education. In the early 1980s, the trend was (in California, for example), for assuming too many language minority students were in need of special education. Towards the end of the 1980s, this had been reversed. The tendency moved to underestimating the special needs of language minority children. This makes accurate assessment very important.* However, accurate assessment and placement in different schools is not enough. The development of **effective instruction strategies** and an appropriate curriculum is crucial. So is the need to train teachers for bilingual students in special education.

E35

My child is suffering in school because other children tease him/her about speaking another language. What can I do?

Just as many children are teased about their color, clothes, religious beliefs, creeds and ethnic identity (see Glossary), so there are occasions when children are teased about their language. It is of little solace to the child, but teasing about language skills often reveals a deficiency in the teaser and not the teased. The problem lies in the perception of the person ridiculing, rather than the one who is ridiculed. Such a situation is experienced by many minority language children. Such ridiculing may be part of a **fear** about difference. When language difference resides alongside color, creed and cultural difference, there is often a fear of the unknown, a fear of the different, and a fear of the 'not understood' in the person making the negative comments.

For parents and children, apart from suffering silently and explaining and discussing where possible, there is often no permanent solution to the immediate cause of the teasing and ridicule. Wherever possible, if bridges of **friendship** can be made with the ones doing the teasing, the abuse may decrease or disappear. Bilinguals often have to be the ones who make the bridges of friendship with those who oppose them. The ridiculer is rarely directly concerned about language difference but concerned about the distance it may place between two people. Not understanding a conversation and feeling excluded may be the cause of the ridicule. The bilingual therefore has to be the eternal **diplomat** in breaking down barriers of communication, harmoniously integrating a peer group, and using their two languages to ensure good relationships with both communities of speakers. Part of being a diplomat is the ability to inject humor and forgiveness into the situation. Humor and kindness, even when not deserved, are routes to barrier breaking.

Parents can also educate their children as to why teasing and bullying occur. While this does not change the situation, it allows understanding. If a child has some understanding of the illogical, irrational motives and reasons behind teasing and bullying, it provides a small shield and a little psychological defense, enabling the child to tolerate some teasing. However, this is no substitute for the real remedy: the education and modification of the behavior of the perpetrators.

There is an important role to be played by **teachers** and education in the furtherance of multiculturalism, linguistic diversity and the increase of understanding between different groups of people. For example, getting the monolingual to 'role play' a bilingual in a contrived situation may allow the monolingual to understand the situation of the bilingual. When sensitivity and empathy are taught and caught in the classroom, divisions between languages, cultures and ethnic groups may be helped. Increasingly, education has become important in **anti-racism and prejudice reduction** drives, in teaching about language awareness, and encouraging children and teenagers to see the beauty of language diversity in the world.

A poor solution to teasing is to return the ridicule and abuse. No positive headway is made if a spear is met with a sword. Continuing antagonism, embattled positions and warfare will only be generated. As difficult as it is, hate needs to meet with love, confrontation with information, abusing by the defusing of an emotional situation. There are no quick fixes or certain solutions. There is only a chiseling at the edges of envy and evil. Teasing and taunts are never simply erased or ended. Civilized progress unfairly rests with those who have been wronged – often language minority speakers.

LANGUAGE IN THE CLASSROOM

Will my child be able to learn a new language thoroughly in the school system?

One route to **second language and foreign language learning** used in many countries is approximately one half-hour language lesson per day over five or more years. Even when children have 12 years of such a diet, from primary school through to secondary school, the general finding in Canada, United States and Britain is that few become really fluent in the second/foreign language. While some do achieve fluency in French, German, Spanish or Italian, and can use the language with ease in a foreign country or study that language at university, the majority fall by the wayside. The seed sown takes root, but does not flower.

Despite many hundreds of hours of second/foreign language learning lessons, it is the few rather than the many who become functionally bilingual. It tends to produce a small percentage of people who can just about communicate with native speakers in the learned language. Only an elite learn that language thoroughly. Such **drip feed language teaching** tends to produce children who do not use their second/foreign language out of school, and soon lose that language.

In contrast to the United Kingdom and the United States, in some European countries, children seem much better at learning languages through the school system. In countries such as the Netherlands, Belgium, Denmark, Finland, Sweden, Austria, Slovenia and Germany, children seem to learn languages via the school with more ease. Sometimes, this is out of necessity, for employment prospects, for use in a different community, and for frequent travel. Often such students find plenty of second **language support out of school** (e.g. television programs in the second language) to support their incipient bilingualism (see Glossary). Such learners also find opportunities to practice (their English and French for example) in their community with in-migrants, travelers from abroad and guest workers. One special example of successful second and third language learning is the **European Schools Movement.***

* See page 139

A higher probability of learning a new language and becoming bilingual occurs when the new language is also a language of the curriculum in the school. When language learning is joined by that language becoming a **medium of instruction** in a school, a greater depth and width of experience in that second language will be gained. This is the difference between bilingual education (in its strong sense) and second language learning. Second language learning is a thin diet of language lessons in a school. Language is taught as a subject in itself. Bilingual education means language learning, plus using that second language as a medium to learn a variety of subjects in the curriculum. In such a way, the second language becomes more embedded, has more use and function, and is more likely to lead to bilingualism.

One important question is **how early or late a child should begin learning a language in school**. Considerable research suggests that neither young children nor older children have an overall advantage in learning a language. Young children tend to learn a new language more slowly, and older children more quickly and efficiently. However, with young children, the language may become more embedded, with pronunciation more correct and with the potentiality of more years of language learning.*

* See page 31

Overall, it is more valuable for a child to begin learning a second language as **early** as possible in school. With young children in the primary school, language is acquired informally, subconsciously, almost accidentally. There is no focus on language as in language learning lessons in the secondary school. In the primary school it can be a by-product of play, projects and participation in singing, drama and games. If such language activity occurs throughout schooling, primary and secondary, and where possible with some medium teaching in that language, the child stands more chance of being bilingual. At the same time, there are 50, 60 and 70 year olds who have successfully learned a language and become bilingual. No age is too late.

How should two languages be distributed in a bilingual classroom?

Particularly in the early years of primary education, bilingual educators often regard it as important that two languages used in the classroom are compartmentalized. Clear boundaries are needed to keep **languages separated in school**. For example, in **Dual Language schools** in the United States, the policy is sometimes 'one language one day, the other language on the next day'. An **alternating pattern** by day or half day is strictly adhered to by teachers in order for both languages to be given equal practice, equal status and equal instruction time. This means that all curriculum areas will be taught in both languages. For example, Mathematics will be taught in Spanish one day, English the next day. Spanish songs will be sung one day, English songs on the next day. On the door to such dual language classrooms, a notice or a picture indicates the language of that day.

Inside dual language classrooms, there is often a **separation of languages** on the wall displays. The idea is not only the equality of status of languages and equality of exposure, but also teaching the child to keep their two languages separate. This is the same principle as the one parent–one language approach to raising young children bilingually.

The **reality** of Dual Language schools tends to be slightly different. On English days, children naturally speak Spanish to each other just as on Spanish days, a

Spanish child may speak English to a friend who is dominant in English. It feels natural and normal for the child, and to keep that naturalness and avoid imposing punishments, the teacher may allow such variation. Also, the teacher will sometimes switch languages to reinforce an idea, ensure understanding by all children in the classroom, to stress a point and sometimes compare and contrast the languages as interesting information in itself. On wall displays in such Dual Language schools, there are times when both languages appear side by side. In Dual Language schools, there is also a tendency to teach Science and Mathematics increasingly in the English language. This will be discussed in a later question.

In **minority language schools**, the separation that occurs will ensure the minority language dominates, particularly in the early years. The aim is a strong and steady development of a potentially weaker plant. The teacher may accept what the language majority child is saying in their majority language, but always responds in the minority language. In the early years of minority language education, it is usual for all, or almost all the curriculum to be taught through the minority language. The majority language will be introduced often around seven years of age, sometimes around eight or nine years of age. In such minority language schools, the teacher may teach one topic a day through English, or have English language lessons. Increasingly, the children are allowed to work through the medium of English as they proceed through the primary school.

Often, in such minority language schools, when children reach the ages of 11 and 12, they are expected to be able to work in **both languages in the curriculum**. At this age, the child may be able to work in Mathematics in either language, and read school textbooks in both the majority and the minority language. Minority language schools often have an 80 to a 100% minority language curriculum at the start of schooling. This will gradually change, increasing the use of the majority language to approximately a 50:50% distribution. In other minority language schools, the minority language dominates in the curriculum (including literacy development) in all year groups (e.g. two-thirds in the minority language, one-third in the majority language).

Where **secondary school bilingual education** is available through the medium of the minority language, some 50 to 80% of the curriculum may be taught through the minority language. The aim is still to produce fully bilingual and biliterate children. The policy of developing the minority language in school is partly to balance the dominance of the majority language outside the school gates.

Where a **majority language** is introduced as a new language to a child at the start or middle of primary education, the majority of or all the curriculum will initially be through that new language. For example, in the Canadian immersion bilingual education programs, children from English-speaking backgrounds learn through the medium of French for 100% of the curriculum at the start of primary education. They slowly move to around a 50% distribution between French and English by the end of primary education. The aim is to build up the second language strongly at the start of primary education.

By the end of primary education, the child should be approximately equally fluent and biliterate in both languages. Some degree of balanced bilingualism (see Glossary) in individual children is encouraged by a thorough immersion in a second language at the start of schooling. This is followed by a slow and gradual movement to using both languages in the curriculum by the end of the primary school years. One special European case is the **European Schools Movement** where children from different European language groups are taught through their home and another language in a European School.*

Should Science and Mathematics be taught in an international language such as English?

In many minority language, dual language and bilingual schools, there is a trend towards teaching **Sciences, Technology and Mathematics through the medium of English** – or another majority, international language. The rationale is that most science text books, scientific information, college and university studies of Science and Technology (and lots of other 'ologies', such as Sociology, Psychology, Geology) are in English. For example, in Kuwait University, Art students are taught through Arabic, and Science students through English. In Dual Language schools in New York, Science and Mathematics are often taught in English only. In Welsh-medium secondary schools, where much of the curriculum is taught through the medium of Welsh, it is not unusual to find Science and Mathematics taught in English. This may reflect the textbooks that are available, the preference of English language-educated Science teachers, the preference of some to think mathematically in English, or simply the tradition of teaching Science and Mathematics in English.

The **problem** is in the associations that accompany teaching Science and Mathematics through a majority language such as English. Scientific culture is seen as Anglo-American, and increased status is given to the English language. French in France is following a crusade against the scientific dominance of English terminology.

Is the hidden message that the **minority language** is not up-to-date, isn't capable of scientific and mathematical usage, hasn't the vocabulary to enable scientific and mathematical teaching? Is the minority language therefore connected with history, culture, tradition, folk lore and heritage? Is the majority language connected with modernity, the high status and powerful aspects of Science and Technology? Does this make one language more internationally valued and the other language less so?

In Spain and Wales, for example, there have been **movements** to try to ensure that science teaching, science textbooks and science thinking can all operate in a minority language (such as Catalan, Basque and Welsh). Considerable attempts have been made to show that a minority language can adapt to being a modern language. New vocabulary needs inventing, sometimes providing extra meaning to a scientific concept, at other times borrowing (see Glossary) from the English, Greek or Latin languages.

The language of Science, Technology and Mathematics is a **controversial area** among parents and educators. It tends to split those who fervently seek language minority revitalization and those who argue that English is *de facto* the international language of Science and Mathematics, Technology and Computing. It tends to separate those who argue for basic language principles and planning from those who are language pragmatists and 'free market language economists'.

My child's school doesn't support bilingualism and there is no bilingual school nearby. What should I do?

Many bilingual parents find themselves in an environment where a **monolingual school** has little regard for their child's bilingualism which seems neither to be noticed nor valued and celebrated. The affection, care and support the child has received at home has been transmitted through the home, minority language. The monolingual school sometimes regards that minority language as worthless. The child's lifestyle, culture, religion, eating and dietary habits, even the 'foreign' names of in-migrant children are belittled. The child's self-esteem, sense of dignity and self-confidence often suffer. A school**'s attitude to bilingual** children should certainly be one factor when there is a choice of schools.

However, there are also many schools that have a positive attitude to linguistic diversity and cultural diversity. Some schools are particularly good at celebrating the variety of languages and cultures within their school, making them a learning experience for all, and generally reducing prejudice and racism (see Glossary) in the locality. An effective school accepts and celebrates bilingual children and their home and community backgrounds. A visit to the school will often reveal whether there are high expectations for all children irrespective of linguistic and cultural background. A vital issue is the extent to which the school provides an ethos which fully accepts children of different cultures and languages.

Effective schools value **parent–teacher cooperation**. When a school is sensitive to the wishes and needs of the parents, and is prepared to treat children as important individuals rather than as whole classes, the school often has much vitality. Explain to the teacher that your child can speak two languages or comes from an intercultural marriage or from a minority language group. Ask, for example, if the child can sometimes take a book in the non-school language to read in the school. Suggest that occasionally the child be allowed to display something on the classroom wall that is in the non-school language. Sometimes, parents are invited to the school to help the teacher. For example, language minority parents listen to children reading or help the teacher organize classroom activities. This is an important way that bilingual parents help bilingual children in a monolingual school. When the door is open to parents to come and help the teacher in the classroom, this opens up opportunities for other languages than the school language to be supported in the classroom.

A crucial role is played by headteachers and other leaders within a school. Therefore an important question is the extent to which such professional leadership is aware of the nature, needs and nurturing of a bilingual child. A visit to a school is very important, and will reveal whether pupils are accepting of each other, especially when there is linguistic and cultural diversity. Effective schools engineer an environment where pupils are accepting and supportive of each other. In colorful classroom displays, special celebrations and activities, linguistic and cultural diversity can be acclaimed and esteemed by teachers and children alike.

There is a difference between schooling and education. Education doesn't just occur at school, it continues from cradle to grave, from the second of waking in the morning to the second of going to sleep at night. Therefore, **parents** may have time during the latter part of the day and at weekends to add to the educational experience of their children. During these times, a child's second language or non-school language can be fostered, enhanced and celebrated. During **school holidays**, there may be opportunities for bilingual children to join similar others in the locality to play, paint and participate in educational activities through a language not used in school. In Saturday or Sunday schools, Voluntary schools outside formal education and vacation camps, children may participate through their non-school language, enabling that language to develop as a tool of thinking, enculturation and socialization. Trips abroad to family and friends may also achieve such language development and enhancement.

Which language should be used to test/assess/counsel a bilingual child? What should be the nature of such assessment?

* See page 169

The answer to a question on Bilingual Special Education highlights how essential it is for the psychological and educational assessment of bilingual children to be fair, accurate, valid, broad and extensive.* Too often, tests given to bilingual children only serve to suggest their 'disabilities', supposed 'deficits' or lack of proficiency in a second language. Assessment can too easily legitimize the disabling of language minority students. Here are some **guidelines** as to how the assessment of bilingual children can be more fairly achieved:

(1)   The **temporary difficulties** faced by bilinguals must be distinguished from relatively more permanent difficulties that impede everyday functioning and learning. Brief language delays, temporary adjustment problems and short-term stammering (stuttering) are examples of transient difficulties. Dyslexia and hearing loss are examples where longer-term problems need treatment.

(2)   Diagnosis needs to avoid a few, simple tests and engage a wide diversity of measurement and observation devices (e.g. portfolios). Diagnosis needs to be extended over a longer time period and avoid an instant conclusion and instantaneous remedy. **Observing** the child in different contexts (and not just in the classroom) will provide a more valid profile of the child's language and other behavior. The family and educational history of the child need assembling. Parents and teachers need consulting, sometimes doctors, speech therapists and social workers as well. Samples of a child's natural communication need gathering, with the child in different roles and different situations.

(3)   The choice of **assessors** for the child will affect the assessment. Whether the assessors are perceived to be from the same language group as the child will affect the child's performance (and possibly the diagnosis). The perceived age, social class, powerfulness and gender of the assessor(s) will affect how the child responds and possibly the assessment outcomes. The assessment process is not neutral. Who assesses, using what devices, under what conditions, contributes to the judgment being made.

(4)   Ideally children need assessing as bilinguals – in both their languages. The tests and assessment devices applied, and the language of communication used in assessment, should ideally be in the child's stronger language. An assessment based on tests of (and in) the child's weaker language may lead to a misdiagnosis, a false impression of the abilities of the child and a very partial and biased picture.

(5)   Parents and educators need to make sure the **language used** in the test is **appropriate** to the child. For example, a translation of the test (e.g. from English to Spanish) may produce inappropriate, stilted language. Also, the variety of Spanish, for example, may not be the one that is used by the student. Chicano Spanish-speaking parents will want the tests in Chicano or at least Mexican Spanish rather than Cuban, Puerto Rican or Castilian Spanish. Once Spanish-speaking children have been in the United States for a time, their Spanish changes. English influences their way of speaking Spanish. So a test in 'standard' Spanish is inappropriate. A Spanish test may accept only one right answer, penalizing children for their bilingual-ism and their United States Spanish. A monolingual standard of Spanish is inappropriate to such bilingual children.

Since there are language problems with tests, it is important to distinguish between a child's language profile and **performance profile**. The performance profile is more important as it attempts to portray a child's underlying abilities rather than just language abilities. A performance profile seeks to understand the overall potential of the child, not just their language proficiency.

(6)   There are times when a test or assessment device cannot be given in the child's stronger language. For example, appropriate language minority professionals may not be available to join the assessment team, tests may not be available in the child's home language, and translations of tests may make those tests invalid and unreliable.

Interpreters (see Glossary) are sometimes necessary and valuable. If trained in the linguistic, professional and rapport-making competences needed, they can make assessment more fair and accurate. Interpreters can also bring a possible bias into the assessment (i.e. 'heightening' or 'lowering' the assessment results through the interpretation they provide).

(7)   There is a danger of focusing the assessment solely on the child. If the child is tested, the assumption is that the 'problem' lies within the child. At the same time, and sometimes instead, the **focus** needs to shift to **causes outside of the child**. Is the problem in the school? Is the school failing the child by denying abilities in the first language and focusing on failures in the school language? Is the school system denying a child's culture and ethnic character, thereby affecting the child's academic success and self-esteem? Is the curriculum delivered at a level that is beyond the child's comprehension or is culturally strange to the child? The remedy may be in a change to the school system and not to the child.

(8)   The danger of assessment is that it will lead to the disablement rather than the **empowerment** of bilingual children. If the assessment separates children from powerful, dominant, mainstream groups in society, the child may become disabled. The assessment may lead to categorization in an inferior group of society and marginalization. Instead, assessment should work in the best, long-term interests of the child. Best interests doesn't only mean short-term educational remedies, but also long-term employment and wealth-sharing opportunities. The assessment should initiate advocating for the child, and not against the child.

(9)   It is important to use the understanding of a child's **teachers** who have observed that child in a variety of learning environments over time. They see that child's class work on a daily basis and have an understanding of difficulties and progress. What do they think is the root problem? What solutions and interventions do they suggest? Have the child's teachers a plan of action? A team of teachers, meeting regularly to discuss children with problems, is a valuable first attempt to assess and treat the child. Such a team can also be the school decision-maker

for referral to other professionals (e.g. speech therapist, psychologist, counselor).

(10)   Norm-referenced **tests** are often used to assess the child. This means that the assessor can compare the child with 'normal' children. The test can indicate how different the child is from the average. Many such tests are built on scores from 'native' language majority children. Thus, comparisons can be unfair for language minority children.

Tests are often written by white, middle-class Anglo test producers. The test items often reflect their culture. For example, words such as 'tennis racquet', 'snowman' and 'credit cards' may be unfamiliar to some inmigrants who have never seen a snowman, played or watched tennis, or know about the culture of plastic money. Norm referenced tests are often 'pencil and paper' tests, sometimes involving multiple choice answers (one answer is chosen from a set of given answers). Such tests do not measure all the different aspects of language, of 'intelligence' or any curriculum subject. Spoken, conversational language and financial intelligence, for example, cannot be adequately measured by a simple pencil and paper test.

Some tests report the results in **percentiles** (especially in the United States). Percentiles refer to the percentage of children below (and above) the child being tested. For example, being in the 40th percentile means that 39% of children score lower than the child being tested. Sixty per cent of children of an age group score above the 40th percentile child. The child is in the 40th group from the bottom, all children being assumed to be divided into 100 equal size groups.

Norm-referenced tests essentially compare one person against others. Is this important? Isn't the more important measurement about what a bilingual child can and cannot do in each curriculum subject? To say a child is in the 40th percentile in English doesn't tell the parent or the teacher the nature of a child's strengths and weaknesses, or their capabilities and needs in English. **Curriculum-based assessment** is called criterion referenced testing (see Glossary), and seeks to establish the relative mastery of a child in a curriculum area. Such criterion referenced assessment of language minority students gives parents and teachers more usable and important information. It details what a child can do in a subject (e.g. Mathematics) and where development should move to next. Such assessment enables an individualized program (see Glossary) to be set for the child.

Are teachers trained to help bilingual children?

One problem in bilingual education is that there is little **teacher training** for working in bilingual schools and bilingual classrooms. In the majority of teacher training courses, even in bilingual countries, there are few courses that prepare teachers for educating bilingual children. With insufficient bilingual teachers, and with insufficient training for bilingual classrooms, much of the current expert knowledge about bilingual children and bilingual education is not filtering through to teachers.

Among those teachers who become headteachers, principals, advisers and educational administrators, there is sometimes a surprising **ignorance** about bilingual children and bilingual education. It is not surprising therefore, that some teachers have a prejudice against bilingual children, finding bilingualism a strange phenomenon, and do not know how to approach parents who have a keen interest in their children becoming bilingual and biliterate. Bilingual **parents** sometimes have more enthusiasm, erudition and educated knowledge of bilingualism.

The same situation tends to exist in **language minority schools**. Teachers may be trained to teach through the medium of the minority language – Welsh, Catalan, Basque and Irish. They are trained as monolingual teachers of a minority language. This is much to be applauded. However, such teachers understand little about bilingualism, bilingual classrooms and bilingual education. How to act as a bilingual teacher, encouraging the growth of two languages and cultural diversity is too often a foreign language to them.

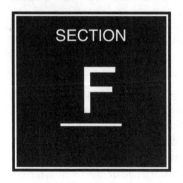

SECTION

F

Concluding
Questions

F1 **The economy and politics of the world is changing. Is there a future for bilingualism?**

As the global village develops, as the spread of information, the Internet, tele-communications, mass media break down national frontiers, major international languages, particularly English, grow in importance. As travel between conti-nents and countries becomes easier, cheaper and faster, minority languages tend to become less used and majority languages have more utility. As the European Community grows in strength, politically, economically, socially and culturally, as regions such as China and South America become stronger trading areas, and as the role of North America continues as important in world power and politics, the danger is that a few languages will have increasing use and value. At worst, other languages will be solely connected with sacred history and scattered homes.

Therefore, some commentators believe that there will be changes in the language economy. There may be an increasing movement towards international languages used for trade, information exchange and international relations. If such a view is believed, minority languages and bilingualism may be in danger. Some argue that bilingualism is merely a halfway house, a midway point in-between a flourishing minority language and a move to monolingualism in a majority language.

Michael Krauss of the Alaska Native Language Center has claimed that between 20 and 50% of the world's existing languages are likely to die or come perilously close to death in the next 100 years. In the long term he argues that it is a realistic possibility that 90% of mankind's languages will become extinct or doomed to extinction. Krauss argues that 50% of the world's languages are no longer being reproduced among children and will die unless there are urgent conservation measures. The IUCN Red List of Threatened Species (http://

www.redlist.org) lists 24% of mammals, 12% of birds and 3% of fish as 'critically endangered', 'endangered' or 'vulnerable'. There are consequently enthusiastic conservation measures for the preservation of the wonderful variety of flora and fauna. If 50 to 90% of the world's languages are threatened, similar conservation measures are urgently required to preserve the colorful diversity of human existence as expressed in its many languages and cultures.

A more positive and **optimistic** view is also possible. For centuries, many people who speak **two** or more **majority languages** have had status and prestige. The ability to speak French and English, German and French, German and Russian, Chinese and English, has always been a valuable asset, much in demand among traders, diplomats and travelers. The global village, the breaking down of trade and transport barriers has led to an increase in the value of those who can operate in two or more international languages. In Europe, there seems to be a growing demand and respect for those who can use two or more languages in the European Community and elsewhere in the world.

A different type of **optimism** may be possible with **minority languages**. As there is pressure to belong to the global village and be international, so there may also be a reactive need to go back to roots. As the world gets smaller and some differences start to fade, there may be an inner need to find who one is, from where one has come. An anchor is needed in a local identity as well as the larger identity.

Some **in-migrants** will assimilate into the majority language and culture. Others are keen to keep links with their past, and purchase some of the cultural wealth of the past. Family history, nostalgia for the heritage of one's ethnic group, an inner need to find rootedness and continuity with the 'glorious past' are powerful conscious and subconscious drives. For example, third and fourth generation in-migrants who have lost their heritage language sometimes become interested in their family and heritage culture in order to find their roots. Gaining access to the tradition of a minority culture may enable a security of self-identity, a sharing of the inheritance of the past, and giving some security and status within the 'small and known' rather than the 'large and unknown'.

Languages shift as politics, economics, culture, individual needs and personal motivations change. The long-term future of many minority languages is difficult to predict with any assurance. However, there has been a growing belief in the last decade that preserving the variety of languages in the world is both just and important. It maintains the diversity of the world, linguistically, culturally and spiritually.

Are monolinguals more common than bilinguals in the world?   F2

Many monolinguals tend to have the view that the state of monolingualism within an individual and within society is the most logical, acceptable and prevalent in the world. Yet, the reality is that **bilinguals are in the majority in the world**. Various estimates exist of what percentage of the world is bilingual. This is very difficult, because the definition of bilinguals may include or exclude those who have a little fluency in one language. Under the term 'bilinguals' go many different colors with many different shades and hues.*

* See page xvi ff

If Pidgins and Creoles (see Glossary) are included or excluded from the count, the estimate of the percentage of bilinguals in the world will change. When local dialects (see Glossary) are added into the confusion of producing an accurate figure, any percentage will be inaccurate. Estimates tend to vary **between 60 and 75%** of the world as bilingual. The conclusion is clear. Bilinguals are in the majority in the world, not monolinguals.

One problem for bilinguals is that monolinguals often have greater power and privilege, more status and prestige. For example, in England and the United States, Australia, New Zealand, France, parts of Germany and Canada, **monolinguals** tend to be over-represented in the ranks of **power elites**, among those with wealth and influence. In England and the United States for example, bilinguals tend to be regarded as an oddity, even a problem. English monolingual speakers in England are often amused to find people speaking Welsh or Scottish Gaelic – regarding it as rustic and picturesque, but also rude, disruptive and valueless. Therefore, the problem that some bilinguals face is that they are in the majority in the world, but have a minority of power.

F3

Why are many politicians against bilingualism and bilingual education?

Public and political discussion of bilingual education and languages in society often commences with the idea of language as causing complications and difficulties. This is well illustrated in discussions about the supposed **cognitive problems** of operating in two languages. **Personality and social problems** such as split-identity, cultural dislocation, a poor self-image and rootlessness are also sometimes attributed to bilinguals. Language is thus also viewed as a **political problem**. At a group rather than an individual level, bilingualism is sometimes connected with national or regional disunity and inter-group conflict.

Part of the 'language-as-problem' political orientation is that perpetuating language minorities and language diversity may cause less integration, less cohesiveness, more antagonism and more conflict in society. The perceived complication of minority languages is to be **solved by assimilation** (see Glossary) into the majority language. Such an argument holds that the majority language (e.g. English) unifies the diversity. The ability of every citizen to communicate with ease in the nation's majority language is regarded as the common leveler. A strong nation is regarded as a unified nation. Unity within a nation is seen as synonymous with uniformity and similarity. The opposing argument is that it is possible to have national unity without uniformity. Diversity of languages and national unity can coexist (e.g. as in Singapore, Luxembourg, Switzerland).

The coexistence of two or more languages is rarely a cause of tension, disunity, conflict or strife. The **history of war** suggests that economic, political and religious differences are prominent as causes. Language is seldom the cause of conflict. Religious crusades and jihads, rivalries between different religions, rivalries between different political parties and economic aggression tend to be the instigators of strife. Language, in and by itself, is rarely a cause of unrest. In a research study on causes of civil strife, the eminent United States academic, Joshua Fishman, found that language was not a cause. Rather, the causes of strife were found to be deprivation, authoritarian regimes and modernization.

A **minority language** is often connected with the **problems** of poverty, underachievement in school, minimal social and vocational mobility and with a lack of integration with the majority culture. In this perspective, the minority language is perceived as a partial cause of social, economic and educational problems. This 'language is an obstacle' attitude is summed up in the phrase, 'If only they would speak English, their problems would be solved'. The minority language is thus seen as a handicap to be overcome by the school system. One resolution of the problem is regarded as the increased teaching of a majority language (e.g. English) at the expense of the home language. The mainstreaming (see Glossary) of minority language children aims to develop their English language skills as quickly as possible so they are on a par with English first language speakers in the mainstream classroom.*

* See page 144

Bilingual education is sometimes perceived by politicians as **causing a language problem**. Such education, it is sometimes argued, will cause social unrest or disintegration in society. Fostering the minority language and ethnic differences might provoke group conflict and disharmony. The response is generally that bilingual education will lead to better integration, harmony and social peace.

Bilingual education should not be connected with causing language problems. Rather, the evidence suggests that developing bilingualism and biliteracy within bilingual education is educationally feasible and can lead to:

- higher achievement across the curriculum for minority language children;
- maintaining the home language and culture;
- fostering self-esteem, self-identity and a more positive attitude to schooling.

Such higher achievement may enable better usage of human resources in a country's economy and less wastage of talent. Higher self-esteem may also relate to increased social harmony and peace.

F4   Is bilingualism a natural right of any individual?

A different orientation to that of 'language as a problem' is thinking of language as a **basic, human right**. Just as there are individual rights in choice of religion, so there should be an individual right to choice of language. Just as there are attempts to eradicate discrimination based on color and creed, so language prejudice and discrimination need to be eradicated in a democratic society.

Language rights may be derived from **personal**, legal and constitutional rights. Personal language rights will draw on the right to freedom of individual expression. It may also be argued that there are certain natural language rights in **group**, rather than individual, terms. The rights of language groups may be expressed in terms of the importance of preservation of heritage language and culture communities. A further level of language rights may be **international**, derived from pronouncements from organizations such as the United Nations, UNESCO, the Council of Europe and the European Community. Each of these four organizations has declared that language groups have the right to maintain their language. For example, in the European Community, a directive (25th July 1977: 77/486/EEC) stated that Member States should promote the teaching of the mother tongue (see Glossary) and the culture of the country of origin in the education of migrant workers' children. However, individual countries have generally ignored such international declarations.

Language rights are not only expressed in legal confrontations (e.g. in the United States) with the chance of being established in law. Language rights are often expressed at the **grass-roots level** by protests and pressure groups, by local action and argument. For example, the *Kohanga Reo* (language nests) movement in New Zealand provides a grass-roots instituted, immersion pre-school experience for the Maori people. Beginning in 1982, these language nests offer a pre-school all-Maori language and cultural environment for children from birth to school age, aimed at fostering development and growth within a context where only the Maori language is spoken and heard.

Another example of a grass-roots expression of 'language as a right' is the recent Celtic (Ireland, Scotland and Wales) experience. In these countries, 'grass-roots' movements created pre-school playgroups, 'mother and toddler' groups and adult language learning classes, so that the heritage languages can be preserved in both adult social interaction and especially in the young. Strong language activism and insistent demands have led to the establishment of heritage language elementary schools, particularly in urban, mostly English-speaking areas. Not without struggle, opposition and antagonistic bureaucracy, parents have obtained the right for education in the indigenous tongue. Such pressure groups have contained parents who speak the indigenous language, and those who speak only English, yet wish their children to be taught in the heritage language of the area.

In North American and British society, no formal recognition is usually made in politics or the legal system of categories or groups of people based on their culture, language or race. Rather the focus is on **individual rights**. The accent is on individual equality of opportunity, individual rewards based on individual merit. Policies of non-discrimination, for example, tend to be based on individual rather than group rights. Language minority groups (see Glossary) will nevertheless argue for rewards and justice based on their existence as a definable group in society. Sometimes based on territorial rights, often based on ethnic identity (see Glossary), such groups may argue for rewards in proportion to their representation in society. **Group-based rights** are often regarded as a way of redressing injustices to language minorities. This may be a temporary step on the way to full individual rights. Alternatively, language minorities may claim the right to some independent power, some measure of decision making and some guarantee of self-determination.

Does my child have a right to bilingual education (e.g. in law, a natural right)?   `F5`

Where two high-status **majority languages** are used in the classroom (e.g. English, German), there tends to be political and public support for bilingual education. This represents **additive bilingualism** (see Glossary) – a second language and culture is added at no expense to the first language. Such bilingual education is seen by those in power as enriching, enhancing employment possibilities and as **civilizing**. 'Finishing Schools' in Europe – attended by the daughters of the affluent – are one example. The European Schools Movement is another example.* This support for bilingualism in two majority languages is not claimed as a right. It is granted willingly, and can be viewed as a privilege shared by the already advantaged.

* See page 139

Where **language minorities** exist, bilingual education is not usually granted as a group or individual right. If bilingual education exists, it has usually been fought for by protests, pressure, grass-roots assertiveness and constant campaigning. Parents and language minority activists have often combined to persuade administrators of the value of mother-tongue education. There is often a considerable **struggle** to win small concessions for bilingual education for language minorities. Growth in such bilingual education is usually slow, controversial, disputed by those in power and a source of continuing conflict. Yet paradoxically, in this struggle there is often added enthusiasm and extra commitment. Hearts and minds have to be won. In the fight, there is zeal and passion. The children benefit from the extra commitment and fervor that goes into the establishment of bilingual education. Bilingual education in such circumstances is granted more as a favor by those in power.

In many countries, education **law** is frequently about what is not permissible. 'Thou shall not' is joined by rules about central policy that must be followed by all. Therefore, there are often no expressed 'natural' rights or rights in law for parents to demand bilingual education. Since bilingual education is a minority pursuit, centralized policy sometimes sees bilingual education as an exception to the rule.

Not all countries fit this pattern. For example, in the United States, there are Constitutional **rights** that express personal freedoms, liberties and personal rights. Whereas language minority activists have been taken to court in Spain and Wales, in the United States, language minority activists have taken the government to court. The United States Constitution expresses the rights and freedoms of individuals, rather than the 'Thou shall not' approach.

Language minority activists have increasingly suggested that **empowerment** and **enablement** of language minorities is needed, and not just rights. Rather than purely being subservient, dependent, servile, lowly and subordinate, language minorities need education and encouragement to become independent, more self-reliant – particularly economically. Through creating employment in language minority areas, a language minority may attain more power over their own lives, enabling a rise in self-esteem and self-respect. Through ensuring literacy and biliteracy, children and adults are empowered and enabled. Literacy gives access to information. In information there is power.

'Rights' can give lawful, constitutional power to a language minority (e.g. to promote bilingual education). At the same time, language minorities often need to develop autonomy, freedom to promote their language and culture, to have power over their own lives and the destiny of their language community. Through education, employment and the economy, language minorities can strive to increase their power and their ability to control their own futures.

Language is an important part of our religion. Should my child learn a second language for this purpose?

For Moslems, Jews, Orthodox Christians and some Asian groups, there is a **religious language** that is important for their children to learn. To worship in the synagogue, Hebrew is often required, as is Arabic in the mosque. For the Greek or Russian Orthodox worshiper, Greek or Russian may be invaluable to penetrate the heart of the Orthodox tradition and its services. For those who worship in a temple, specific languages often need learning to participate, understand and engage in daily religious observances.

For many parents from such religious traditions, it is essential that children learn the appropriate religious language. To partake in **religious custom and worship**, to create a sense of continuity with the religious past, and sometimes to achieve greater holiness and heavenly prospects, religious language becomes crucial. It also gives the child pride, a sense of religious, ethnic and family identity, and provides a strong foundation in life's unpredictable journey.

One concern of some parents is the **level of language learning** that is achieved. For example, someone may learn enough Arabic to repeat prayers in the mosque, yet not understand Arabic in conversations. For the Orthodox Christian or the Jew, the language learned is sometimes specifically and purely for religious purposes. The vocabulary, and the feel for the language, does not exist outside prayers and the place of worship. Outside the Holy Book, the language for religion is not used.

This provides an interesting example of **language boundaries** and language compartmentalization. The child learns a different language, bounded in its function and place of use. This helps ensure languages do not become mixed but evolve in a separate fashion. Such language learning provides a potentiality to extend that language for other purposes. Jewish children often learn Hebrew for the synagogue. When visiting other friends or going to Israel they find that they can extend their Hebrew outside the synagogue. Those who use Arabic in the mosque and in reading the Koran may later extend that in greeting and meeting Arabic speakers. Providing a religious language provides a potentiality to extend that language.

I use a particular dialect/a Creole/a Pidgin language in the home. Is your advice about raising a bilingual child different or similar?

F7

It is often **difficult to define what is a language**. There are not sharp boundaries between different languages. Where a language stops and a dialect (see Glossary) starts can be a debated point. Some dialects have higher status, others lower status. The term 'language' is an arbitrary label attached to a politically recognized and socially accepted dialect. There is often amusing academic debate about whether English is a language. English is a concoction of Saxon, French, Latin and Greek. It hasn't the 'purity' of continuity that the Basque, Finnish, Welsh or Greek languages appear to have. No language stays the same or is completely standardized for all time. Language change is a sign of a lively, adapting language. A language that doesn't change has little future.

There is **constant change in language**. Reading Old English, Middle English, Chaucer, Shakespeare, Dickens in the English language reveals the speed of change. Read a textbook from the 1950s and see how quickly language (in terms of vocabulary, style and structure) has changed. As science, technology and computers have rapidly changed this century, so has vocabulary in English. Software programs, mobile phones, the World Wide Web, satellite dishes and hovercraft all provide part of modern vocabulary that our ancestors would not understand.

There are different Englishes in the world as the visitor to New York, Kuala Lumpur, Helsinki, Moscow, Johannesburg, Calcutta, Bombay, London, Trinidad, Kenya or Zaire will soon hear. There is considerable variation among apparent similarity. There are world Englishes rather than one English in the world.

Therefore, with Pidgin (see Glossary) languages and with Creoles (see Glossary), the **advice** of this book is no different. A Creole or a Pidgin often has unity within itself, some standardization of language although changing like any other language, and most important, is a living and thinking language for a group of people. Neither a Pidgin nor a Creole has barriers within it or constraints in a child learning to think, communicate or function orally in that language. A Creole or a Pidgin has an embedded experience, a vitality and a continuity of culture within it that is valuably transmitted as language grows.

Dialects can vary in their similarity and difference from each other and the 'standard' language. People can move inside England and the United States and understand other people speaking their dialect without much real difficulty. Variations in dialect are often a valued and important part of local identity. In this respect, it is often inappropriate to think of someone who has a local dialect and a more 'standard' production of that language as owning two different languages. There is so much overlap between the two that use of a dialect is not bilingualism.

However, there are other circumstances where dialects may be very different from each other (although part of a wider family) to the point at which two speakers of those dialects have difficulty in communicating with each other. In Africa and India for example this is sometimes the case. At what point two dialects are sufficiently apart to be regarded as two languages is going to require arbitrary and arguable judgment. The more there is mutual intelligibility, the less one can talk about two separate and different languages and hence bilingualism. However, there are some cases where two 'dialects' are sufficiently apart and mutually different for the advice about bilingualism in this book to hold.

I have a Deaf child. Is your advice about raising a bilingual child different or similar?

There is a growing merger between two hitherto distinct groups: those interested in bilingualism and those interested in Deaf children. There is a recognition that **much of what has been written about bilinguals applies to Deaf children**.

The '**medical' view** has historically been that Deaf children and many hearing-impaired children must be monolingual. To function in mainstream society, sign language (see Glossary) must be forgotten, and the vocal and written majority language must be learned. This is a deficit view of the Deaf person and of sign language. Although sign language comes naturally to the Deaf person, the 'medical' view has been that top priority is integration into mainstream society. Mainstream integration means avoiding Signing which purportedly restricts social and employment opportunities.

The '**bilingual' view** is that Deaf children and many hearing-impaired children should have sign language as their 'native', first language. For such children, Signing enables immediate, instinctively natural and full communication. Bilingualism is achieved by one (or both) of two routes. The second language can be a written majority (or minority) language, and/or the vocal form of that language. The vocal form of the language may be a deliberate combination of speech and sign, vocalization and gesture (e.g. 'Live English', 'Signed English', 'Sign Supported English').

There is **controversy** and passion around this area. The theme of this section is symbolized in the **spelling** of 'deaf' as preferred by Deaf groups. Just as it is accepted that we use a 'D' for Dutch and a 'F' for French, so a Deaf community, or someone who culturally identifies as a Deaf person, requires a 'D'. A lower case 'd' is reserved to refer to the audiological (non-hearing) condition. Also, rather than talking about 'the deaf', the use of 'Deaf people' is usually preferred. This moves from using an audiological condition solely to define the person, to accenting the humanity of Deaf people.

Some argue for indigenous signs for the Deaf child, some argue for signs that approximate, for example, English grammar, and others argue for the dominance of vocal speech. Complications arise because most (e.g. nine out of every ten) Deaf children have hearing parents, sign language users are not always a geographical community, and some Deaf people are against Signing.

As with hearing bilinguals, there is **transfer** from the first to the second language. The concepts, ideas, knowledge and skills learned through Signing transfer to the second language. A second language is learned through building on a child's existing linguistic and intellectual resources gained through Signing.

Sign Language (which is a language in itself) and a second language create **bilingual children**. Deaf children express themselves in a visual mode (Signing) which is a foundation for the development of a spoken and/or written form of language. A vocal/written language is acquired after sign language rather than simultaneously. Each language has different uses and functions with different people. There are language boundaries between each language, as with hearing bilinguals. A combination of Signing and vocal/written language is also a means of identifying with different groups of people.

Having a visual language (Signing) and a vocal/written language (e.g. English, French, German, Spanish) provides a wealth of different means of **expression**. Signing is very expressive, conveying vividly a whole range of feelings, with constant motion and color. Body language (and not just the hands) conveys a frame of mind, and emotions such as joy and jealousy, anxiety and anger. Poetry in motion.

Restricting Deaf children to sign language (e.g. American sign language, French sign language, Swedish sign language, British sign language) means they may not acquire their mother's tongue (if living with hearing parents). To expect Deaf children to remain monolingual (Signing only) is a 'deficit' view of Deaf children. **Wider communication**, access to different cultures, further 'worlds of experience' and wider employment opportunities are made possible by Deaf children (and adults) becoming bilingual. Similarly, forcing Deaf children to avoid Signing restricts their language development and denies them the chance of bilingualism.

With well-designed bilingual education and information to parents, Deaf children can acquire a second language as well as Signing. **Bilingual education** for Deaf children is growing, but slowly. Each language can be supported in the classroom. Bilingualism can help Deaf children become more integrated bilinguals into both hearing and Deaf societies.

Deaf children are particularly affected by **negative attitudes** to their bilingualism. They often do not have the supporting environment in the family or community that other language minority groups may experience. Deaf children born to hearing parents usually do not have an ethnic heritage, family traditions or cultural continuity to surround them. Participation, cultural identity and self-respect may be heightened when Deaf children are enabled to become bilingual.

Acquiring both a sign language and a second language needs **positive attitudes** among Deaf children, their parents, teachers and education administrators. Negative attitudes towards sign language and the subsequent enforced use of a vocal language (e.g. spoken English) in the classroom have led to the same type of underachievement that has marked language minorities who are forced to learn in their second language. There is a feeling among many Deaf people in Britain and the United States that they are held back educationally as a result of school pressure to learn English and through English. **Supporting bilingualism** among Deaf children is therefore supporting their first language (Signing) and bilingual education.

This brief consideration of Deaf children and bilingualism suggests that many issues discussed in this book are **relevant to such children**. Further information about bilingualism and Deaf people is available from Deaf Associations, Special Needs teams in school districts, and in publications.

Three books on Deaf children are recommended:

(1)   *The Care and Education of a Deaf Child: A Book for Parents* by Pam Knight and Ruth Swanwick (Clevedon: Multilingual Matters, 1999).

(2) *You and Your Deaf Child: A Self-Help Guide for Parents of Deaf and Hard of Hearing Children* by John W. Adams (Washington, DC: Gallaudet University, 1997, second edition).

(3) *Educating Deaf Children Bilingually* by Shawn Neal Mahshie (Washington, DC: Gallaudet University, 1995).

Finally, two addresses that will lead to up-to-date information. The first address is a UK book shop that specializes in all international publications on Deaf people. The second is the United States University that specializes in this area and often leads international developments in the education of Deaf people.

(1) The Forest Bookshop, 8 St John Street, Coleford, Gloucestershire, England, GL16 8AR. Their WWW address is: http://www.forestbooks.com/pages/.

(2) Gallaudet University, 800 Florida Avenue, NE Washington, DC 20002, US. Their Internet address is: http://www.gallaudet.edu/.

Books on child care and child development warn me against bilingualism. How should I react?

F9

Here are two **quotations** from popular best-seller books for parents on child care and child development. The first quotation comes from Drs Andrew and Penny Stanway's book *The Baby and Child Care Book: The Complete Guide to Your Child's First Five Years*:

> In general it has been found that one language tends to predominate in the child's mind and that most of these children take longer to become proficient in either language than their single-language contemporaries. Some children may appear to be backward in their language development because of this, whereas in fact they are simply confused.

> All children find it easier if they know at least some English words before starting school. In areas with high immigrant populations there are classes for teaching mothers English. They in turn can then teach their pre-school children.

From Hugh Jolly's book entitled *Book of Child Care: The Complete Guide for Today's Parents* comes the following quotation:

> Your child will be less confused if you always speak to him in the same language whether this is to be his 'first' or 'second' language ... But having a mother who tries to teach you two names for everything at once leads to confusion and rebellion.

While in both these books there are some positive comments about bilinguals, such books typically talk about mental and language confusion, of interference between languages and the paramount necessity of developing English language skills in the home. Such books are often written by doctors or child psychologists who know little or nothing about bilingualism, are not conversant with literature on bilingualism nor read the research on bilingual child development. This is simply not an area where medical writers usually have the expertise, or even the experience, to provide informed or expert comment.

React by thinking about the advice of this book and other similar books.* Find out **information** from sources where there is informed comment, expert understanding and greater experience and awareness of childhood bilingualism.

F10 · How do I contact other parents in a similar situation?

Raising a child bilingually will rarely be a smooth or easy process. Worries and problems are bound to arise along the journey. One valuable way through problems is to talk them out and discuss similar experiences with other parents who are raising bilingual children. Psychologists underline the importance of the 'social comparison process' where we compare ourselves with similar others to ensure that our behavior and attitudes are reasonable and rational. Through social comparison, we obtain catharsis for our anxieties by sharing problems. We gain the experience of others who have been along a similar journey.

How about placing an advert in a local newspaper or on the WWW? It doesn't always matter if bilingual parents who meet in a **local group** have different languages. The problems, anxieties and pleasures are often common. If there are enough local people who can meet as a language group, the exchange of books, cassette tapes, posters as well as experiences will be invaluable.

Another way of finding out about local and other language networks of parents with similar interests and worries is gained through the *Bilingual Family Newsletter*. For about two decades this quarterly publication has been found an invaluable asset for like-minded parents of bilingual children. All languages and situations, all kinds of problems are addressed in the newsletter. For more information and a free sample copy, write to Multilingual Matters.* There is also an online archive of over 20 years of copies of this newsletter that is available to subscribers: http://www.bilingualfamilynewsletter.com

F11 · Is the Internet going to affect my child's bilingualism?

A recent major impact on languages in the world has been the use of the Internet (World Wide Web). While there is much use of the Internet in English, other languages have grown in recent years. There is now information and exchange in many of the world's languages. How do such rapid changes in technology and communication affect children's bilingualism?

Cyberspace has been dominated by the English language, and a major anxiety of other majority languages as well as of minority languages is the extra emphasis, value and function given to English by the Internet. However, as more businesses begin to advertise using web pages, regional networks have developed using local languages on the Internet. It makes little sense advertising in English if the main customers speak another language. Also, as schools, colleges, universities, local government, libraries, record offices and local information agencies go online, their local pages are often in the regional language or are bilingual. Thus, whereas the World Wide Web was initially dominated by the English language, its use by other languages as a tool of communication has increased rapidly.

Non-English speakers have been the fastest growing group of new Internet users, many using the Internet bilingually or multilingually. Even where there are relatively high levels of English literacy, users typically indicate a preference for websites in their mother tongue.

When children use the Internet, language proficiency can be enhanced. Through the Internet, authentic language practice is possible via, for example, the use of electronic mail. There may be increased motivation to use a language via contact with children in other countries and which allows access to authentic language texts (see Glossary).

Electronic mail and electronic conferencing are already one of the major Internet activities, giving the feeling of the global village where barriers to communication (such as cost and the time of travel) are removed. Also, free translation has become possible on the WWW via various sites such as: http://babelfish.altavista.com/.

By its nature, the Internet brings people speaking both the same (and different) languages into closer contact. By exchanging information with children in other countries, children can build increasing independence in language use, vary their language according to audience, and use language for real purposes. Children can take part in conversations and conferences over the Internet with native speakers, using not only written text but increasingly phone, video and audio conferencing as well. Exchange visits can be reinforced with preparatory and follow-up Internet links, and there are possibilities of 'virtual exchanges' and 'telepresence'. The Internet promises increasing automatic online translation of messages and other text, and bilingual and trilingual children may be able to spot nuances of meaning by referring to both the original and translation.

The Internet provides teachers and learners with ready-to-use banks of mul-timedia resources: a wealth of video and audio recordings from all over the world, pictorial and written information, and activities generated by different language centers in different countries. Providers of information can use the Internet to publicize events, courses, materials, services and remote training, and information services.

A Potpourri of WWW Pages for Bilinguals

(1) iLoveLanguages
     http://www.ilovelanguages.com/
(2) The Bilingual/Bicultural Family Network
     www.biculturalfamily.org
(3) Ethnologue: Languages of the World
     http://www.sil.org/ethnologue/
(4) CILT (Centre for Information of Language Teaching and Research)
     http://www.cilt.org.uk/
(5) OISE, University of Toronto, Second Language Education on the
     Web (Canada)
     http://www.oise.utoronto.ca/~aweinrib/sle/
(6) Center for Applied Linguistics (US)
     http://www.cal.org/
(7) California Association for Bilingual Education (CABE)
     http://www.bilingualeducation.org/
(8) Teachers of English to Speakers of Other Languages (US)
     http://www.tesol.org/s_tesol/index.asp
(9) Bilingualism database
     http://www.edu.bham.ac.uk/bilingualism/database/dbase.htm
(10) The Office of English Language Acquisition, Language Enhance-
     ment, and Academic Achievement for Limited English Proficient
     Students (US)
     http://www.ed.gov/about/offices/list/oela/index.html
(11) National Clearinghouse for English Language Acquisition &
     Language Instruction Educational Programs (US)
     http://www.ncela.gwu.edu/
(12) Multilingual Matters
     http://www.multilingual-matters.com/
(13) Bilingual Families Web Page
     http://www.nethelp.no/cindy/biling-fam.html
(14) Multilingual Family in the UK
     http://www.multilingualfamily.co.uk/
(15) Bilingual Supplies for Children
     http://www.bilingual-supplies.co.uk
(16) Yahoo- Education- Bilingual
     http://dir.yahoo.com/Education/Bilingual/

How do I find out more information about bilingualism?

Parents are particularly encouraged to read the *Bilingual Family Newsletter*. This provides an up-to-date and most valuable source of information for parents. Using a combination of advice from experts, experiences of parents, information about networks of people, intercultural experiences, bilingual humor, Internet addresses and reviews of the latest publications, it has become recognized as a treasure of wisdom on bilingual children and their parents.

A free sample will be provided on request. Contact: Marjukka Grover, Multilingual Matters Limited, Frankfurt Lodge, Clevedon Hall, Victoria Road, Clevedon BS21 7HH, England.

There is a website for this *Newsletter*: http://www.bilingualfamilynewsletter. com. This website is the gateway for subscribers to access to the online 20 years archive of *Bilingual Family Newsletters*.

There are other books that provide extra depth and breadth to the discussions of this book. Some tend to be more academic in nature but are still aimed at thinking parents:

(1)   For those who want a comprehensive and reader-friendly introduction to this whole area, there is the *Encyclopedia of Bilingualism and Bilingual Education* (1998) by Colin Baker and Sylvia Prys Jones (Clevedon: Multilingual Matters: http://www.multilingual-matters.com/). The encyclopedia is lavishly illustrated with 340 pictures, mostly color, plus 117 main topics, 390 textboxes to illustrate the main topics, 228 profiles of languages in all countries of the world, plentiful maps and graphics, and is written in a comprehensible style for a lay audience.

Colin Baker's *Foundations of Bilingual Education and Bilingualism* (2006, 4th edition) (Clevedon: Multilingual Matters: http://www.multilingual-matters.com/) aims to provide a first academic introduction to the psychological, sociological, educational, political and cultural aspects that surround bilingualism. Written as a foundation-level textbook for students and teachers, the 19 chapters cover all the crucial issues and controversies about language minorities, language majorities and bilingual education.

A Spanish version of this *'Parents and Teachers'* book by Alma Flor Ada and Colin Baker was published in 2001 by Multilingual Matters and entitled *'Guia Para Padres Y Maestros De Ninos Bilingues'*. It is available from: http://www.multilingual-matters.com/).

(2)   When parents have different first languages, there is excellent discussion and advice in Suzanne Barron-Hauwaert's *Language Strategies for Bilingual Families: The One-Parent – One-Language Approach)* published by Multilingual Matters in 2004 (see:: http://www.multilingual-matters.com/).

(3)   *Growing Up With Two Language,* by Una Cunningham-Andersson and Staffan Anderson (Routledge, 2004) is illustrated by glimpses of life from

interviews with 50 families from all around the world. Edith Harding and Philip Riley's *The Bilingual Family: A Handbook for Parents* (Cambridge University Press, 2003) is for those families where there are **two majority languages**. The book is written by linguists with insights from that perspective.

(4)   An excellent Handbook for teachers and parents concerned with International Schools is by Coreen Sears, *Second Language Students in Mainstream Classrooms: A Handbook for Teachers in International Schools* (1998) and published by Multilingual Matters (http://www.multilingual-matters.com/). Written by an experienced International Schools teacher, the book covers areas such as the cultural adjustment of children, maintaining cultural identity, English as a second language at school, the curriculum of International Schools, and finishes with an extensive list of educational learning resources. This has more recently been joined by a thorough, expert and provocative book by Maurice Carder: *Bilingualism in International Schools* (2007) (Clevedon: Multilingual Matters).

(5)   For teachers and parents in multicultural and immigrant environments, a very readable and most valuable resource is Elizabeth Coelho's *Teaching and Learning in Multicultural Schools* (Clevedon: Multilingual Matters, 1998). The book provides extensive, expert and down-to-earth advice about children's cultural identities and the immigrant experience, as well as a detailed and comprehensive exploration of how to become a high quality and highly effective school with multicultural children.

(6)   An up-to-date list of information for parents will be found in the most recent Multilingual Matters catalog. This may be obtained free from: Multilingual Matters Ltd, Frankfurt Lodge, Clevedon Hall, Victoria Road, Clevedon, England BS21 7HH (Tel: +44 (0) 1275–876519; Fax: +44 (0) 1275–871673; e-mail: marjukka@multilingual-matters.com; Web page: http://www.multilingual-matters.com/.

(7)   'Growing up with English Plus' is an excellent 45-minute video created by Monash University's Language and Society Centre in 1999. It presents different ways of raising children bilingually, especially if one of the parents is a monolingual English speaker. It answers queries and dispels myths through the presentation of typical family situations. The families featured use Australian Sign Language, German, Italian, Mandarin/Chinese, Latvian, Serbian and Thai, as well as English. To purchase the video, link to: http://eshowcase.unimelb.edu.au/eshowcase/index.htm.

         Other queries about the video should be sent via email to: The Research Unit for Multilingualism and Cross-Cultural Communication at rumaccc-info@unimelb.edu.au.

(8)   The Bilingual/Bicultural Family Network is a WWW site with a wide variety of interesting and valuable content. It contains, for example, short

articles and extracts, tips and quotes, resources and products, WWW and blog links, and access to the *Multilingual Living Magazine*. Link to: www. biculturalfamily.org.

Glossary

The Glossary gives further information about some terms used in this book. It also includes terms not used in this but regularly found in other books for parents and teachers on bilingualism.

Accent: People's pronunciation which may reveal, for example, which region, country or social class they come from.

Acculturation: The process by which an individual or a group adapt to a new culture.

Active Vocabulary: This refers to the actual number of words that people use as opposed to a passive vocabulary which is words they understand. Native language speakers often have an active vocabulary of between 30,000 and 50,000 words. Their passive vocabulary may extend up to 100,000 words or more. In language learning, reasonable proficiency is said to be achieved when someone attains an active vocabulary of between 3000 and 5000 words with a passive vocabulary of up to 10,000 words.

Acquisition Planning: Part of formal language planning where interventions are made to encourage families to pass on their minority language, and schools to produce more minority language speakers.

Additive Bilingualism: A situation where a second language adds to, rather than replaces the first language. This is the opposite of subtractive bilingualism.

Affective Filter: Associated with Krashen's Monitor Model of second language learning, the affective filter is a metaphor which describes a learner's attitudes that affect the relative success of second language acquisition. Negative feelings such as a lack of motivation, lack of self-confidence and learning anxiety are like a filter which hinders and obstructs language learning.

Anomie: A feeling of disorientation and rootlessness, for example in in-migrant groups. A feeling of uncertainty or dissatisfaction in relationships between an individual learning a language and the language group with which they are trying to integrate.

Aphasia: Damage to the brain which causes a loss of ability to use and understand language. This may be partial or total and affect spoken and/or written language.

Artificial Language: (1) A language invented as a means of international communication (e.g. Esperanto, Ido). (2) A system of communication created for a specific purpose (e.g. computer language).

Assimilation: The process by which a person or language group lose their own language and culture which are replaced by a different language and culture. A political policy that seeks to absorb in-migrants into the dominant language and culture of the new country to attempt cultural and social unity.

Authentic Texts: Texts taken from newspapers, magazines, tapes of natural speech from radio and television. They are not created by the teacher but already exist in the world outside the classroom.

Autochthonous Languages: A term particularly used in Europe to describe indigenous languages or languages resident for a considerable length of time in a territory or region.

Back Translation: A translation is translated back into the original to assess the accuracy of the first translation.

Balanced Bilingualism: Approximately equal competence in two languages.

Basal Readers: Reading texts that use simplified vocabulary and grammar, carefully graded and structured.

BICS: Basic Interpersonal Communicative Skills. Everyday, straightforward communication skills that are helped by contextual supports.

Bicultural: Identifying with the culture of two different language groups. Being bilingual does not necessarily result in being bicultural.

Big Books: Used frequently in 'whole language classrooms'. They are teachers' books that are physically big so that students can read along with the teacher.

Biliteracy: Reading and writing in two languages.

Black English: The variety of English spoken by some black people in the United States, for example in cities such as New York and Chicago. Black English is regarded as a language variety in its own right with its own structure and system and not as a second-class variety of English.

Borrowing: A word or a phrase from one language that has become established in use in another language. When borrowing is a single word, it is often called a loan word.

CALP: Cognitive/Academic Language Proficiency. The level of language required to understand academically demanding subject matter in a classroom.

Such language is often abstract, without contextual supports such as gestures and the viewing of objects.

Caretaker Speech: A simplified language used by parents to children to ensure understanding, also called Motherese. Caretaker Speech usually has short sentences, is grammatically simple, has few difficult words, much repetition and with clear pronunciation.

Classroom Discourse: A special type of language used in the classroom. Such language is governed by the different roles that students and teachers assume and the kind of activities that occur in classrooms. The kind of 'open' (many different answers possible) or 'closed' questions (only one or a few correct answers possible) that teachers ask is one particular area of interest in Classroom Discourse.

Classroom Ethos: The atmosphere and feelings in the classroom that promote or detract from effective classroom learning.

Classroom Interaction: The interaction and relationships between teachers and students, and between students themselves both in terms of oral, written and non-verbal communication.

CLIL: (see Content and Language Integrated Learning).

Cloze Procedure: A technique for measuring students' reading comprehension. In a Cloze test, words are removed from a reading passage at specific intervals, and students have to fill in the blanks. The missing words are guessed from the context.

Code-switching: Moving from one language to another, inside a sentence or across sentences.

Codification: A systematic description of a variety of a language (e.g. vocabulary, grammar). This may occur when a language is being standardized, or when an oral language is being written down for the first time.

Cognition: The acquisition, storage, retrieval and use of knowledge. Mental processes of perception, memory, thinking, reasoning and language.

Cognitive/Academic Language Proficiency (CALP): The level of second language proficiency needed by students to perform the more abstract and cognitively demanding tasks of a classroom. Little support is offered in many classrooms from the context. CALP is distinguished from Basic Interpersonal Communication Skills (BICS), that are relatively undemanding cognitively and rely on the context to aid understanding.

Cognitive Style: The way in which different learners efficiently and effectively learn. Different students have different preferences, patterns and styles of learning.

Common Underlying Proficiency (CUP): Two languages working integratively in the thinking system. Each language serves one underlying, central thinking system.

Communal Lessons: Lessons in which students of different first languages are mixed for common activities, such as working on projects, doing art or physical education. The European Hours in the European Schools are Communal Lessons.

Communicative Approach: A second language teaching approach that accents the acquisition of a language by use in everyday communicative situations.

Communicative Competence: Proficiency in the use of a language in everyday conversations. This term accents being understood rather than being 'correct' in using a language. Not only knowing the grammar and vocabulary of a language, but also knowing the social and culturally appropriate uses of a language.

Community Language: A language used by a particular community or in a particular area, often referring to language minority groups. The term has been used in Britain to refer to the language of Asian and European groups which are resident in particular areas.

Community Language Learning: A second language teaching methodology based on Rogerian counseling techniques and responding to the needs of the learner 'community'.

Competence in Language: A person's ability to create and understand language. This goes further than an understanding of vocabulary and grammar, requiring the listener to understand sentences not heard before. Competence is often used to describe an idealized speaker/hearer with a complete knowledge of the whole language, and is distinguished from performance which is the actual use of the language by individuals.

Compound Bilingualism: One language is learnt at the same time as another, often in the same contexts.

Comprehensible Input: Language delivered at a level understood by a learner, often containing a few new elements.

Concept: The idea or meaning associated with a word or symbol in a person's thinking system. All languages can express the same concepts, although different languages construct concepts in different ways (e.g. languages tend to distinguish colors on the color spectrum in different ways).

Content and Language Integrated Learning (CLIL): An inclusive term, particularly used in Europe, for bilingual or multilingual education in which a second or later language is used for learning subject content, and where both language learning and content learning occur simultaneously with an emphasis on their integration.

Content-Based Instruction: A term particularly used in United States education programs. Such a program teaches students the language skills they will need in mainstream classrooms. The focus is on the language skills needed for content areas such as Mathematics, Geography, Social Studies and Science.

Context: The setting in which communication occurs, and which places possibilities and constraints on what is said, and how it is said. The context can refer to the physical setting or to the language context in which a word or utterance occurs.

Context-Embedded Language: Communication occurring in a context that offers help to comprehension (e.g. visual clues, gestures, expressions, specific location). Language where there are plenty of shared understandings and where meaning is relatively obvious due to help from the physical or social nature of the conversation.

Context-Reduced Language: Language where there are few clues as to the meaning of the communication apart from the words themselves. The language is likely to be abstract.

Contrastive Analysis: The comparison of the linguistic systems of two languages.

Core Language Class: Teaching the language as a subject. Used mostly to describe foreign language instruction.

Core Subject: A subject that is of prime importance in the Curriculum. In England, the three core subjects are Mathematics, English and Science. These are said to form the Core Curriculum.

Corpus Language Planning: Language planning which centers on linguistic aspects of language, vocabulary and grammar; for example, to try and ensure a normative or standardized system of language within an area (see also Language Planning).

Creole: A Pidgin language which has been adopted as the native language in a region. A Creole tends to be more complex in grammar with a wider range of vocabulary than a Pidgin language. There are, for example, English-based and French-based Creoles.

Creolization: The process by which a Pidgin becomes a Creole by the expansion of vocabulary and the development of a more complex linguistic structure.

Criterion-Referenced Testing: A form of educational assessment which compares students in terms of their mastery of a subject as opposed to a norm-referenced test where a student is compared with other students. A criterion-referenced test in language requires a clear specification of the structure of the language to be learnt.

Critical Period Hypothesis: A genetically determined period of child development when learning must take place, otherwise it will not be learned later. In language, this is a largely discredited theory that a child best learns a first or second language between birth and up to about 13 years of age.

Cultural Pluralism: The ownership of two or more sets of cultural beliefs, understandings, values and attitudes. Multicultural education is often designed to encourage cultural pluralism in children.

Culture: The set of meanings, beliefs, attitudes, customs, everyday behavior and social understandings of a particular group, community or society.

Culture Shock: Feelings of disorientation, anxiety or insecurity some people experience when entering a different culture. For example, when people move to a foreign country there may be a period of culture shock until they become more familiar with a new culture.

CUP: See Common Underlying Proficiency.

DBE: Developmental Bilingual Education: Also known as Two-Way Dual Language Programs and Two-Way Bilingual/Immersion Programs. Two languages are used for approximately equal time in the curriculum.

Decoding: In learning to read, decoding is the deciphering of the sounds and meanings of letters, combinations of letters, whole words and sentences of text. Sometimes decoding refers to being able to read a text without necessarily understanding the meaning of that text.

Deficit Model: The idea that some children have a deficiency in their language – in vocabulary, grammar or understanding, particularly in the classroom. The child has a perceived language 'deficit' that has to be compensated for by remedial schooling or compensatory education. The problem is seen to be located in the child rather than in the school system or society or in the ideology of the perceiver. The opposite is an enrichment model (see Enrichment Bilingual Education).

Developmental Bilingual Education: A US program that encourages bilingualism and biliteracy by including development of native language and literacy (e.g. Spanish). Such a program may last for five years and more.

Dialect: A language variety whose features identify the regional or social background of the user. The term is often used in relation to a standard variety of a language (e.g. a dialect of English).

Diglossia: Two languages or language varieties existing together in a society in a stable arrangement through different uses attached to each language.

Discourse: A term used to describe relatively large chunks of conversation or written text. Rather than highlighting vocabulary or grammar, discourse extends into understandings and meanings of conversation or written text.

Discourse Analysis: The study of spoken and written language particularly in terms of negotiated meanings between participants in speech, choice of linguistic forms, shared assumptions that underlie utterances, structures, strategies and symbolism in communicating, and the role relationships between participants.

Disembedded Thinking: Thinking that is not allied to a meaningful context but is treated as a separate, distinct task with little relevance in itself.

Distance Learning: Independent learning outside the classroom, by telephone, satellite, the World Wide Web, DVDs and distance learning packages, for example.

Divergent Thinking: Thinking that is original, imaginative and creative. A preference for open-ended, multiple answers to questions.

Domain: Particular contexts where a language is used. For example, there is the family domain where a minority language may be used. In the work domain, the majority language may be used.

Dominant Language: The language in which a person has greater proficiency or uses more often.

Double Immersion: Schooling where subject content is taught through a second and third language (e.g. Hebrew and French for first language English speakers).

Dual Language Program: see Two-Way Programs.

Dyslexia: Problems in learning to read; word blindness where students may have difficulty in, for example, distinguishing different letter shapes and words.

EAL: English as an Additional Language.

Early-Exit/Late-Exit Bilingual Education Programs: Early-exit programs move children from bilingual classes in the first or second year of schooling. Late-exit programs provide bilingual classes for three or more years of elementary schooling. Both programs are found in Transitional Bilingual Education.

EC: European Community. A grouping of most European countries for mutual economic, social and cultural benefit.

Eclectic Method: Using a variety of methods in language teaching.

EEC: European Economic Community. A grouping of European countries, accenting economic cooperation. This term has largely been superseded by EU (European Union).

EFL: English as a Foreign Language.

ELL: English Language Learners. This is sometimes preferred to LEP (Limited English Proficiency) as it focuses on development rather than deficit.

ELT: English language teaching.

Empowerment: The means by which those of low status, low influence and low power are given the means to increase their chances of prosperity, power and prestige. Literacy and biliteracy are major means of empowering such individuals and groups.

English-Only: An umbrella term for federal and state legislation and organizations that aim to make English the official language of the US. This includes two national organizations: US English and English First.

English Plus: A US movement promoting the belief that all US residents should have the opportunity to become proficient in a language other than English.

Enrichment Bilingual Education: A form of bilingual education that seeks to develop additive bilingualism, thus enriching a person's cultural, social and personal education. Two languages and cultures are developed through education.

ERASMUS: A European program for students to take part of their higher education at one or more European universities or colleges as well as their 'home' university or college.

ESL: English as a Second Language. An ESL program (e.g. in the US) usually involves little or no use of the first language, and occurs for part of the school timetable.

ESOL: English for Speakers of Other Languages.

ESP: English for Special Purposes. For example, English may be taught for its use in the science and technology curriculum, or English for business, specific vocational needs and professions.

Ethnic Identity: Those aspects of an individual's thinking, feelings, perceptions and behavior that are due to ethnic group membership, as well as a sense of belonging and pride in the ethnic group.

Ethnic Mosaic: In-migrants of different geographical origins coexisting in a country (e.g. Canada, United States) and retaining constituents of their ethnicity.

Ethnocentrism: Discriminatory beliefs and behaviours based on ethnic differences. Evaluating other ethnic groups by criteria specific to one's own group.

Ethnographic Pedagogy: Teaching practices and learning strategies that are derived from ethnography (see below) and conducted in the classroom. An ethnographic researcher becomes involved in a classroom, observing, participating and helping transform teaching practices. Ethnographic pedagogy includes learning to read by harnessing students' prior cultural knowledge and experience, and encouraging peer interaction.

Ethnography: Research that describes and analyzes groups (e.g. ethnic, cultural) and is qualitative rather than quantitative in approach (e.g. engages in fieldwork, interviews and observation). Such research is often intensive and highly detailed.

Ethnography of Communication: The study of the place of language in different groups and communities. Language is particularly studied for its social and cultural purposes.

Ethnolinguistic: A set of cultural, ethnic and linguistic features shared by a cultural, ethnic, or sub-cultural social group.

EU: European Union. A term to describe the grouping of European countries for mutual benefit.

FEP: Fluent English Proficient.

First Language: This term is used in different, overlapping ways, and can mean (a) the first language learnt, (b) the stronger language, (c) the 'mother tongue' (d) the language most used.

Foreign Language: A language taught in school which is not normally used as a means of instruction in schools or as a language of communication within the country, in the community or in bureaucracy.

Foreigner Talk: The kind of speech used by native speakers when talking to foreigners who are not proficient in their language. Foreigner talk is often slower, with clear pronunciation, simplified vocabulary and grammar with some degree of repetition. This makes the speech easier for foreigners to understand.

Funds of Knowledge: Knowledge that exists in communities and individuals outside of school that is valuable to share. Such knowledge particularly derives from language and cultural minorities and is not transmitted in a majority language school curriculum.

Gastarbeiter: (German term) An in-migrant or guest worker.

Gemeinschaft: A society based on close community bonds, kinship, close family ties; an emphasis on tradition and heritage. Sometimes portrayed stereo-typically as village life.

Geolinguistics: The study of language or dialects as spoken in different geo-graphical areas and regions. Sometimes referred to as Areal Linguistics.

Gesellschaft: A society with less emphasis on tradition and more on rational goals; duty to organizations with many secondary relationships. Sometimes portrayed stereotypically as one type of urban existence.

Graded Objectives: Objectives in a language curriculum which describe levels of attainment at different stages. These provide short-term, immediate goals for learners who are required to gain mastery of these goals before moving on to higher objectives.

Graded Reader: A simplified book or set of children's books, carefully graded in terms of increasingly difficult vocabulary and complexity of grammar. Such books are written for first language learners, adult second language learners and students learning a second language. In order to control the linguistic features precisely, authenticity may be sacrificed.

Grammar: The structure of a language; the way in which elements are combined to make words and the way in which words and phrases are combined to produce sentences.

Graphology: The study of systems of writing and the way a language is written.

Guest Workers: People who are recruited to work in another society. Also known as Gastarbeiter.

Hegemony: Domination; the ascendance of one group over another. The dominant group expects compliance and subservience from the subordinate group.

Heritage Language: The language a person regards as their native, home, ancestral language. This covers indigenous languages (e.g. Welsh in Wales) and in-migrant languages (e.g. Spanish in the United States).

Heterogeneous Grouping: The use of mixed ability and/or mixed language groups or classes. The opposite is 'homogeneous grouping' or tracking (see below).

Hispanics: Spanish speakers in the United States. The term is, for example, officially used in the United States Census.

Immersion Bilingual Education: Schooling where some or most subject content is taught through a second language. Pupils in immersion are usually native speakers of a majority language, and the teaching is carefully structured to their needs.

Incipient Bilingualism: The early stages of bilingualism where one language is not strongly developed. Beginning to acquire a second language.

Indigenous Language: A language relatively native to an area, contrasted with an in-migrant language.

Individualized Instruction: A curriculum which is carefully structured to allow for the different needs and pace of learning of different students. Individualized instruction tries to give learners more control over what is learned, the style of learning and the rate of progress.

In-migrants: Encompasses immigrants, migrants, guest workers and refugees. The term in-migrant can be used to avoid the negative connotations of the term 'immigrant' and to avoid the imprecise and loaded distinctions between migrant workers, guest workers, short-stay, long-stay and relatively permanent in-migrants.

Input: A distinction is often made in second language learning between input and intake. Input is what the learner hears but which may not always be understood. In contrast, intake is that which is assimilated by the learner.

Input Hypothesis: The idea that language in the second language classroom should contain elements that are slightly beyond the learner's present level of understanding. Using contextual clues to understand, the learner will gradually increase in language competence.

Institutionalized Racism: Processes, attitudes and behavior in an organization that are discriminatory through unthinking prejudice, ignorance, thoughtlessness and racist stereotyping which disadvantage minority ethnic individuals and groups.

Instrumental Motivation: Wanting to learn a language for utilitarian reasons (e.g. to get a better job).

Integrated Approach: The integration of listening, speaking, reading and writing in language teaching and language assessment.

Integrative Motivation: Wanting to learn a language to belong to a social group (e.g. make friends).

Interactionism: A position which argues that language cannot be understood without reference to the social context in which language occurs.

Interference: Interference (or transfer) in second language learning is said to occur when vocabulary or syntax patterns transfer from a learner's first language to the second language, causing errors in second language performance. The term interference has been decreasingly used because of its negative and derogatory connotations. See Language Transfer.

Interlanguage: An intermediate form of language used by second language learners in the process of learning a language. Interlanguage contains some transfers or borrowing from the first language, and is an approximate system with regard to grammar and communicating meaning.

Interlocutors: Those who are actively engaged in a conversation as opposed to those who are silent participants.

Interpreting: The process of oral translation from one language to another. Consecutive interpreting occurs when an interpreter orally translates while a speaker pauses. Simultaneous translation occurs when the interpreter orally translates while the speaker continues to speak.

Intranational Language: A high prestige language used as a medium of general communication between different language groups within a country (e.g. English in India).

Involuntary Minorities: Also known as 'caste-like minorities'. They differ from immigrants and 'voluntary minorities' in that they have not willingly migrated to the country.

Koine: The spoken language of a region that has become a standard language or lingua franca.

L1/L2: First Language/Second Language.

Language Ability: An 'umbrella' term and therefore used ambiguously.

Language ability is a general, latent disposition, a determinant of eventual language success. Language ability is also used to describe the outcome of language learning, in a similar but less specific way than language skills, providing an indication of current language level. Language ability measures what a person can currently do, as different from what they may be able to do in the future.

Language Achievement: Normally seen as the outcome of formal language instruction. Proficiency in a language due to what has been taught or learnt in a language classroom.

Language Acquisition: The process of acquiring a first or second language. Some linguists distinguish between language acquisition and 'language learning' of a second language, using the former to describe the informal development of a person's second language, and the latter to describe the process of formal study of a second language. Other linguists maintain that no clear distinction can be made between informal acquisition and formal learning.

Language Across the Curriculum: A curriculum approach to language learning that accents language development across all subjects of the curriculum. Language should be developed in all content areas of the curriculum and not just as a subject in its own right. Similar approaches are taken in writing across the curriculum and reading across the curriculum.

Language Approach: A term usually used in a broad sense to describe the theories and philosophies about the nature of language and how languages are learned (e.g. aural/oral approach, communicative approach). The term 'method' is used to describe how languages are taught in the classroom (e.g. audiolingual method), and the term 'techniques' is used to describe the activities involved (e.g. role playing, drill).

Language Aptitude: A particular ability to learn a language as separate from intelligence, motivation.

Language Arts: Those parts of the curriculum which focus on the development of language: reading, writing, spelling as well as oral communication.

Language Attitudes: The beliefs and values expressed by people towards different languages in terms of favorability.

Language Attrition: The loss of a language within a person or a language group, gradually over time.

Language Awareness: A comprehensive term used to describe knowledge about and appreciation of the attributes of a language, the way a language works and is used in society.

Language Change: Change in a language over time. All living languages are in a process of gradual change (e.g. in pronunciation, grammar, vocabulary).

Language Code: A neutral term used instead of language or speech or dialect.

Language Competence: A broad and general term, used particularly to describe an inner, mental representation of language, something latent rather than overt. Such competence refers usually to an underlying system inferred from language performance.

Language Contact: Contact between speakers of different languages, particularly when they are in the same region or in adjoining communities.

Language Death: Language death is said to occur when a declining language loses its last remaining speakers through their death or their shift to using another language. This language no longer exists as a medium of communication in any language domains.

Language Demographics: The distribution of the use of a language in a defined geographical area. Also called Geolinguistics.

Language Dominance: One language being the stronger or preferred language of an individual, or the more prestigious language within a particular region.

Language Family: A group of languages historically derived from a common ancestor.

Language Isolate: A language that has no apparent relationship to any other known language.

Language Laboratory: A room with individual booths for language learning. Students listen to recordings and practice speaking exercises which can be monitored by teachers. The room may have individual multimedia computer equipment for language learning.

Language Learning: The process by which a first or second language is internalized. Some authors restrict the use of the term to formal learning (e.g. in the classroom). Others include informal learning (e.g. acquisition in the home). See also Language Acquisition.

Language Loss: The process of losing the ability or use of a language within an individual or within a group. Language loss is particularly studied among in-migrants to a country where their mother tongue has little or no status, little economic value or use in education, and where language loss subsequently occurs.

Language Loyalty: The purposeful maintenance and retention of a language, when that language is viewed as being under threat. This is often a concern of language minorities in a region where another language is the dominant language.

Language Maintenance: The continued use of a language, particularly among language minorities (e.g. through bilingual education). The term is often used with reference to policies that protect and promote minority languages.

Language Minority: A language community (or person) whose first language is different from the dominant language of the country. A group who speaks a language of low prestige, or low in power, or with low numbers in a society.

Language of Wider Communication: A language used for communication within a region or country by different language groups.

Language Performance: A person's production of language particularly within a classroom or test situation. The outward evidence of language competence, but which is not necessarily an accurate measure of language competence.

Language Planning: The development of a deliberate policy to engineer the use of language. Language planning often involves Corpus Planning (the selection, codification and expansion of norms of language), Status Planning (the choice of language varieties for different functions and purposes) and Acquisition Planning (acquiring the language in the family and/or at school).

Language Proficiency: An 'umbrella' term, sometimes used synonymously with language competence; at other times as a specific, measurable outcome from language testing. Language proficiency is viewed as the product of a variety of mechanisms: formal learning, informal uncontrived language acquisition (e.g. on the street) and of individual characteristics such as 'intelligence'.

Language Revitalization: The process of restoring language vitality by promoting the use of a language and its range of functions within the community.

Language Shift: A change from the use of one language to another language within an individual or a language community. This often involves a shift from the minority language to the dominant language of the country. Usually the term means 'downward' shift (i.e. loss of a language).

Language Skills: Language skills are usually said to comprise: listening, speaking, reading and writing. Each of these can be divided into sub-skills. Language skills refer to specific, observable and clearly definable components such as writing.

Language Transfer: The effect of one language on the learning of another. There may be negative transfer, sometimes called interference, and much more often positive transfer, particularly in understandings and meanings of concepts.

Language Variety: A regionally or socially distinctive variety of language. A term used instead of 'dialect' because of the negative connotations of that term, and because 'dialect' is often used to indicate a hierarchical relationship with a standard form of a language.

Language Vitality: The extent to which a language minority vigorously maintains and extends its everyday use and range of functions. Language vitality is said to be enhanced by factors such as language status, institutional support, economic value and the size and distribution of its speakers.

Latinos: Spanish speakers of Latin American extraction. This Spanish term is now used in English, especially by US Spanish speakers themselves. Often preferred by such speakers to 'Hispanics'.

Learning Journal: Students record in a note book or log book their personal experiences in and out of school, and often record their responses and reactions to their reading and other curriculum activity. Such journals may be shared with the teacher who responds with a non-judgmental written reply. Journals aim to encourage students through personalization, increased motivation and enjoyable dialogue.

LEP: Limited English Proficient (US term). Used to refer to students in the United States who are not native speakers of English and who have yet to reach 'desired' levels of competence in understanding, speaking, reading or writing English. Such students are deemed to have insufficient English to cope in English-only classrooms.

Lexical Competence: Competence in vocabulary.

Lexis/Lexicon: The vocabulary or word stock of a language, their sounds, spelling and meaning.

LINGUA: A European program to increase majority language learning across Europe. The program funds scholarships, student exchanges and teaching materials to improve language learning and teaching in the European (EU) countries.

Lingua Franca: A language used for communication between different language groups. A lingua franca may be a local, regional, national or international language. It may be the first language of one language group. Lingua francas are especially common in multilingual regions.

Linguicism: The use of ideologies, structures and practices to legitimize and reproduce unequal divisions of power and resources between language groups.

Linguistic Purism: A deliberate attempt to rid a language of perceived undesirable elements (e.g. dialect forms, slang, foreign loan words).

Literacy: The ability to read and write in a language.

LM: Language Minority.

LMS: Language Minority Students.

Loan Word: An item of vocabulary borrowed by one language from another. A loan blend occurs when the meaning is borrowed but only part of the form is borrowed; loan shift when the form is nativized; and loan translation when the components of a word are translated (e.g. 'skyscraper' into *'gratte ciel'* in French).

Machine Translation: Translation from one language to another by computer.

Mainstreaming: Putting a student who has previously been in a special educational program into ordinary classes. Language mainstreaming occurs when children are no longer given special support (e.g. English as Second Language classes) and take their subjects through the majority language.

Maintenance Bilingual Education: A program that uses both languages of students to teach curriculum content.

Majority Language: A high-status language usually (but not always) spoken by a majority of the population of a country. 'Majority' refers to status and power rather than the numerical size of a language group.

Marked Language: A minority language spoken by a minority of the population in a country (as distinct from a majority language), and therefore often lowly valued in society.

Meaningful Learning: Learning which becomes accommodated within a person's conceptual system. This has been distinguished from rote learning which is not necessarily integrated into existing conceptual understandings and may exist for a short, temporary period of time.

Medium of Education: The language used to teach content. Also medium of instruction.

Medium of Instruction: The language used to transmit instructional material.

Melting Pot: Used mainly in the US to describe how a variety of in-migrant ethnic groups have blended together to create modern US society.

Message: The meaning of a communication which may be conveyed in verbal form but also by non-verbal communication such as eye contact, gestures and posture. A distinction is often made between the form of message and message content. The form refers to how communication occurs and the content as to the meaning conveyed.

Metacognition: Becoming aware of one's own mental processes.

Metalinguistic: Using language to describe language. Thinking about one's language.

Metalinguistic Knowledge: An understanding of the form and structure of language arrived at through reflection and analyzing one's own communication.

Minority Language: A language of low prestige and low in power. Also used by some to mean a language spoken by a minority of the population in a country.

Miscue Analysis: Analysis of errors and incorrect responses readers make in reading.

Monitor Hypothesis: A theory of second language developed by Krashen. According to this theory, language can only be acquired in a natural, subconscious manner. The consciously learned rules of language have the function of monitoring or editing communication. This involves monitoring one's own speech or writing, to ensure accuracy of form and meaning, making corrections where necessary.

Monogenesis: A theory that all the languages in the world derive historically from a single ancestor.

Monoglot: See Monolingual.

Monolingual: A person who knows and/or uses one language.

Morphology: The internal structure of words (a morpheme is the smallest unit of meaning).

Mother Tongue: The term is used ambiguously. It variously means (a) the language learnt from the mother, (b) the first language learnt, irrespective of 'from whom', (c) the stronger language at any time of life, (d) the 'mother tongue' of the area or country (e.g. Irish in Ireland), (e) the language most used by a person, (f) the language to which a person has the more positive attitude and affection.

Motherese: A simplified language used by parents to children to ensure understanding. See Caretaker Speech.

Multilingual: A person who knows and/or uses three languages or more.

National Language: On the surface, this refers to a prestigious, authorized language of the nation, but the term has varying and debated meanings. Sometimes it is used interchangeably with 'official language'. However, in multilingual countries, an official language (or languages) may coexist with one or more national languages. Such national languages are not so widely used in public and official use throughout the country, but carry symbolic status and prestige. Also, a national language may be formally recognized as such, or may be informally attributed as a national language.

Native Language: The language which a person acquires first in life, or identifies with as a member of an ethnic group.

Negotiation: Negotiation occurs in a conversation so that successful and smooth communication occurs. The use of feedback, corrections, exemplification, repetition, elaboration and simplification may aid negotiation.

NEP: Non-English Proficient.

Network: A group of people within a community who are regularly in communication with each other and whose manner of communication is relatively stable and enduring. Analysis of a language network examines different status relationships within the network.

Non-Native Variety: A language variety not indigenous to a region, but imported by in-migrants.

Non-Verbal Communication: Communication without words, for example, via gestures, eye contact, position and posture when talking, body movements and contact, tone of voice.

Official Language: The language used in a region or country for public, formal and official purposes (e.g. government, administration, education, media).

Orthography: Correct spelling.

Paired Reading: Where parents share reading at home with their children, often with direction from the school, and sometimes using a reading scheme.

Parallel Teaching: Where bilingual children are taught by two teachers working together as a team, each using a different language. For example, a second language teacher and the class teacher planning together but teaching independently.

Passive Bilingualism: Being able to understand (and sometimes read) in a second language without speaking or writing in that second language.

Personality Principle: The right to use a language based on the history and character of the language, rather than a right to use that language based on territorial rights. See Territorial Principle.

Phoneme: The smallest part of spoken language that creates the meaning of a word. Most words have more than one phoneme: The word 'of' has two phonemes: 'o' and 'f'. 'Chip' has three phonemes: 'ch', 'i' and 'p'. A phoneme can be represented by more than one letter.

Phonemic awareness: The ability to identify and use individual sounds, called phonemes (see Glossary), in *spoken* words.

Phonetics: The study of speech sounds.

Phonics: A method of teaching reading based on recognizing the relationship between phonemes (the sounds of *spoken* language) and graphemes (the letters and spellings that represent those sounds in *written* language).

Phonology: The sound system of a language.

Pidgin: A language that develops as a means of communication when different language groups are in regular contact with one another. A Pidgin usually has a small vocabulary and a simplified grammatical structure. Pidgins do not usually have native speakers although there are expanded Pidgins (e.g. in Papua New Guinea) where a Pidgin is the primary language of the community. If a Pidgin language expands to become the native language of a group of speakers, with a larger vocabulary and a more complex structure, it is often called a Creole.

Pidginization: (1) The evolution of a Pidgin language. (2) In second and foreign language learning, the development of a simplified form of the target language (also called interlanguage). This intermediate stage is usually temporary, but according to the pidginization hypothesis, it may become permanent when learners remain socially apart from native speakers, or when the target language is infrequently used.

Plurilingual: Someone competent in two or more languages.

Polyglot: Someone competent in two or more languages.

Pragmatics: The study of the use of language in communication, with a particular emphasis on the contexts in which language is used.

Preferred Language: A self-assessment of the more proficient or favored language of an individual.

Primary Bilingualism: Where two languages have been learnt 'naturally' (not via school teaching, for example).

Primary Language: The language in which bilingual/multilingual speakers are most fluent, or which they prefer to use. This is not necessarily the language learnt first in life.

Process Approach in Language Teaching: This is particularly used in teaching children to write where planning, drafting and revising are used to improve writing competence. The process rather than the product is regarded as the important learning experience.

Process Instruction: An emphasis on the 'activity' of a classroom rather than creating a product. A focus on procedures and techniques rather than on learning outcomes, learning 'how to' through inquiry rather than learning through the transmission and memorization of knowledge.

Productive Bilingualism: Speaking and writing in the first and second language (as well as listening and reading).

Productive Language: Speaking and writing.

Project Work: Independent work by an individual student or a group of students often on an interdisciplinary theme. The process of planning, execution, discussion and dialogue, reviewing and reflecting, evaluating and monitoring is an important part of the process. Project work accents cooperative group work and authentic language situations.

Prosody: The study of the melody, loudness, speed and rhythm of spoken language; apart from intonation, it includes the transmission of meaning that can be understood from different emphases.

Psychometric Tests: Tests to measure an individual's characteristics. The best known psychological tests are IQ tests. Other dispositions are also measured (e.g. attitudes, creativity, skills, dyslexia, personality, needs and motives).

Pull-Out Program: Minority language students are taken out of regular, mainstream classrooms for special instruction in the majority language. Special language classes are provided to try to raise a child's level of language in the dominant language of the classroom or of the school.

Racism: A system of privilege and penalty based on race. It is based on a belief in the inherent superiority of one race over others, and the maintenance or promotion of economic, social, political and educational differences based on such supposed superiority.

Readability: The level of difficulty in a written passage. Readability depends on factors such as length of words, length of sentences, grammatical complexity and word frequency.

Reception Classes/Centers: For newly arrived students in a country, to teach the language of the new country, and sometimes the culture.

Receptive Bilingualism: Understanding and reading a second language without speaking or writing in that language.

Receptive Language: Listening/understanding and reading.

Register: (1) A variety of a language closely associated with different contexts in which the language is used (e.g. courtroom, classroom, church) and hence with different people (e.g. police, professor, priest). (2) A variety of a language used by an individual in a certain context.

Remedial Bilingual Education: Also known as Compensatory Bilingual Education. Uses the mother tongue only to 'correct' the student's presumed 'deficiency' in the majority language.

SAIP: Special Alternative Instructional Programs (US).

Scaffolding: Building on a student's existing repertoire of knowledge and understanding. As the student progresses and becomes more of an independent learner, the help given by teachers can be gradually removed.

Second Language: This term is used in different, overlapping ways, and can mean: (1) the second language learnt (chronologically); (2) the weaker language; (3) a language that is not the 'mother tongue'; (4) the less used language. The term is sometimes used to cover third and further languages. The term can also be used to describe a language widely spoken in the country of the learner (as opposed to a foreign language).

Self-fulfilling Prophecy: A student is labeled (e.g. by a teacher as having 'limited English'). The label is internalized by the student who behaves in a way that serves to confirm the label. Other people's expectations becoming internalized by a student, for example, and then becoming part of their regular behavior.

Semantics: The study of the meaning of language.

Semilingual: A controversial term used to describe people whose two languages are both at a low level of development.

Separate Underlying Proficiency: The largely discredited idea that two languages exist separately and work independently in the thinking system.

Sequential Bilingualism: Bilingualism achieved via learning a second language later than the first language. This is distinct from Simultaneous Bilingualism where two languages are acquired concurrently. When a second language is learnt after the age of three, sequential bilingualism is said to occur.

Sheltered English: Content (subject) classes that also include English language development. The curriculum is taught in English in the United States at a comprehensible level to minority language students. The goal of sheltered English is to help minority language students acquire proficiency in English while at the same time achieving well in content areas of the curriculum.

Sight Vocabulary: Words which a child can recognize in reading that require no decoding of letters or blends of letters. The instant recognition of basic words.

Sign Language: Languages used by many Deaf people and by those people who communicate with Deaf people that make use of non-verbal communication to communicate meaning. Sign languages are complete languages with their own grammatical systems. Various sign languages have developed in different parts of the world (e.g. American sign language; British sign language; French sign language).

Silent Way: A method of second language learning emphasizing independent student learning by means of discovery and problem solving.

Simultaneous Bilingualism: Bilingualism achieved via acquiring a first and a second language concurrently. This is distinct from Sequential Bilingualism where the two languages are acquired at different ages. When a second language is learnt before the age of three, simultaneous bilingualism is said to occur.

Skills-based Literacy: Where the emphasis is on the acquisition of phonics and other language forms, rather than on ways of using those forms.

Sociolinguistics: The study of language in relation to social groups, social class, ethnicity and other interpersonal factors in communication.

Speech Variety: A neutral term sometimes used instead of 'dialect' or 'language' where a distinction is difficult.

Standard Language: A prestigious variety of a language that has official, formal use (e.g. in government and schooling). A standard language usually has norms for spelling, grammar and vocabulary. The standard variety is often used in literature and other forms of media (e.g. radio, television), in school textbooks, in centralized policies of the curriculum.

Standardization: The attempt to establish a single standard form of a language particularly in its written form, for official purposes, literature, school curriculum, etc.

Standard Variety: See Standard Language.

Status Language Planning: Language planning which centers on language use and prestige within a region and within particular language domains. See Language Planning.

Stereotyping: Classifying members of a group (e.g. a language minority) as if they were all the same. Treating individuals of that group as if no other characteristics of that group were important or existed. Where one characteristic of a group is seen as always associated with other (often negative) characteristics.

Streaming: The use of homogeneous groups in teaching (also called tracking, setting, banding, ability grouping).

Structured Immersion: The curriculum is taught in English in such programs in the United States at a comprehensible level to minority language students. The goal is to help minority language students acquire proficiency in English while at the same time achieving well in content areas of the curriculum.

Submersion: The teaching of minority language pupils solely through the medium of a majority language, often alongside native speakers of the majority language. Minority language pupils are left to sink or swim in the mainstream curriculum. Also called Mainstreaming.

Subtractive Bilingualism: A situation in which a second language is learnt at the expense of the first language, and gradually replaces the first language (e.g. immigrants to a country or minority language pupils in submersion education).

SUP: see Separate Underlying Proficiency.

Syntax: The study of how words combine into sentences. Rules governing the ways words are combined and organized.

Target Language: A second or foreign language being learned or taught.

TBE: Transitional Bilingual Education. Temporary use of the child's home language in the classroom, leading to only the majority language being allowed in classroom instruction. (See Early-Exit/Late-Exit Bilingual Education Programs).

Teacher Talk: A variety of communication used by teachers in classrooms. Teacher talk is specific to the needs of instruction and classroom management, sometimes simplified as in foreigner talk.

TEFL: Teaching English as a Foreign Language.

Territorial Principle: A claim to the right to a language within a territory. The right to use a language within a geographical area.

TESFL: Teaching English as a Second and a Foreign Language.

TESL: Teaching English as a Second Language.

TESOL: (1) Teachers of English to Speakers of Other Languages. (2) Teaching English as a Second or Other Language.

Threshold Level: (1) A level of language competence a person has to reach to gain cognitive benefits from owning two languages. (2) The Threshold Level is used by the Council of Europe to define a minimal level of language proficiency needed to function in a foreign language. Various contexts are specified where languages are used and students are expected to reach specific objectives to attain the threshold level.

Total Communication: A method of teaching Deaf and hearing-impaired children based on the use of both sign language and spoken language.

Tracking: The use of homogeneous ability groups in teaching (also called setting, streaming, banding, ability grouping).

Trade Language: A language that is adopted or evolves as a medium of communication in business or commerce between different language groups. Many pidgins evolved as trade languages in ports or centers of commerce.

Transfer: See Language Transfer.

Transitional Bilingual Education (TBE): The primary purpose of these US programs is to facilitate a student's transition to an all-English instructional environment while initially using the native language in the classroom. Transitional bilingual education programs vary in the amount of native language instruction provided and the duration of the program.

Two-Way Programs: Also known as Developmental Bilingual Education, Two-Way Dual Language Programs and Two-Way Bilingual/Immersion Programs. Two languages are used for approximately equal time in the curriculum. Classrooms have a mixture of native speakers of each language.

Unmarked Language: A majority language distinct from a minority language, and usually highly valued in society.

US English: An organization committed to making English the official language of the United States.

Vernacular: An indigenous or heritage language of an individual or community. A vernacular language is used to define a native language as opposed to (1) a classical language such as Latin and Greek, (2) an internationally used language such as English and French, (3) the official or national language of a country.

Whole Language Approach: An amorphous cluster of ideas about language development in the classroom. The approach is against basal readers and phonics in learning to read. Generally the approach supports a holistic and integrated learning of reading, writing, spelling and oracy. The language used must have relevance and meaning to the child. Language development engages cooperative sharing and cultivates empowerment. The use of language for communication is stressed; the function rather than the form of language.

Withdrawal Classes: Also known as 'pull-out' classes. Children are taken out of an ordinary class for special instruction.

Writing Conference: The teacher and the student discuss the writing the student is to complete, the process of composing. The teacher plans regular discussions with individual students about their writing to promote personal awareness of their style, content, confidence and communication of ideas.

Zone of Proximal Development: New areas of learning within a student's reach. Vygotsky saw the zone of proximal development as the distance between a student's level of development as revealed when problem solving without adult help, and the level of potential development as determined by a student problem solving in collaboration with peers or teachers. The zone of proximal development is where new understandings are possible through collaborative interaction and inquiry.

Acknowledgement

The author wishes to thank Professor Ofelia García and Dr Sylvia Prys Jones for their contributions to this Glossary. This Glossary originates from *Policy and Practice in Bilingual Education: A Reader Extending the Foundations*, by O. García and C. Baker (Clevedon: Multilingual Matters, 1995) and *The Encyclopedia of Bilingualism and Bilingual Education*, by Colin Baker and Sylvia Prys Jones (Clevedon: Multilingual Matters, 1998).

Index